THE PORTLAND SEA DOGS

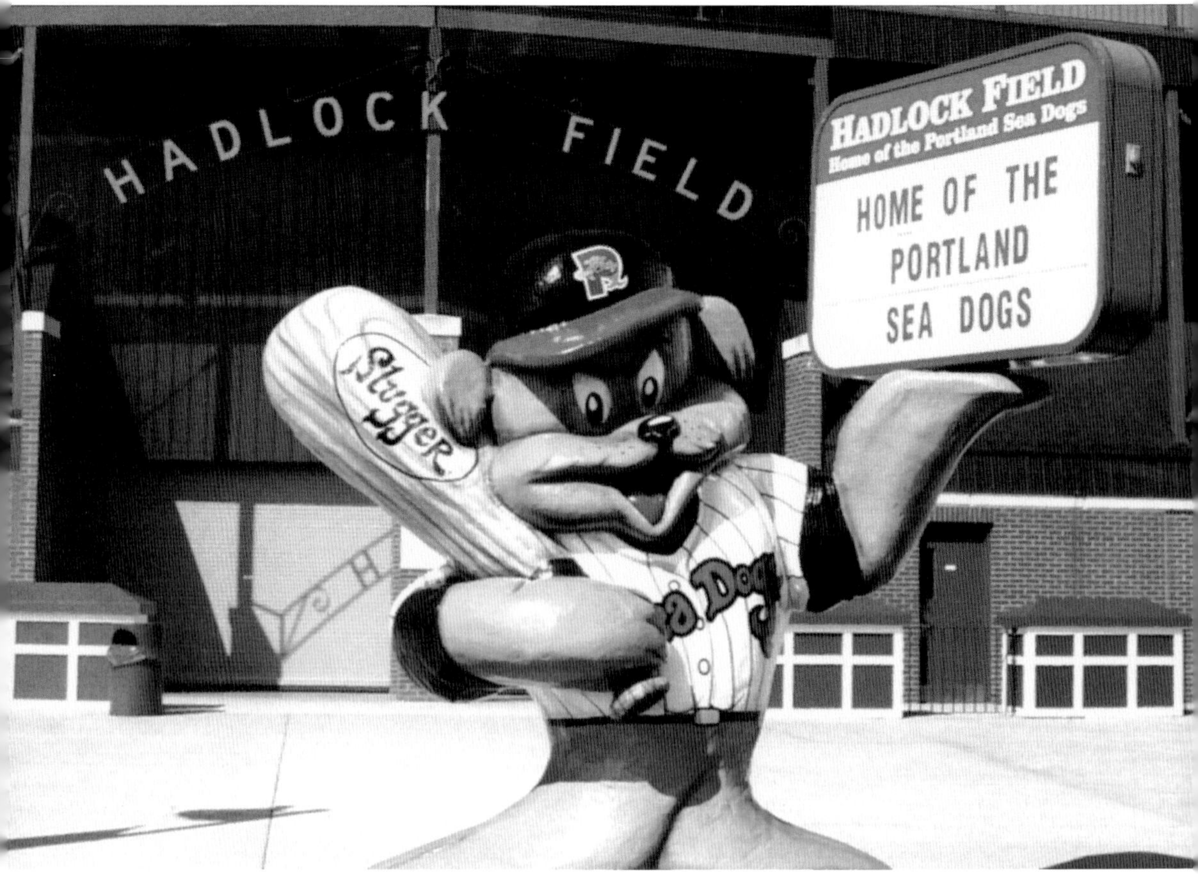

One of the more popular tourist picture spots in Portland, Maine, is the Slugger statue, which stands outside the main entrance to Hadlock Field. Hadlock Field is the minor-league home of the Eastern League Portland Sea Dogs. The Sea Dogs, originally affiliated with the Florida Marlins, became the Boston Red Sox affiliate in the fall of 2002. The Slugger statue underwent renovation before the 2003 season, including a new paint job in Red Sox colors. (Courtesy of the Sea Dogs.)

On the front cover: Please see page 38. (Photograph by Stewart Smith.)

On the back cover: Please see page 119. (Courtesy of the Sea Dogs.)

Cover background: Please see page 14. (Courtesy of the Sea Dogs.)

THE PORTLAND SEA DOGS

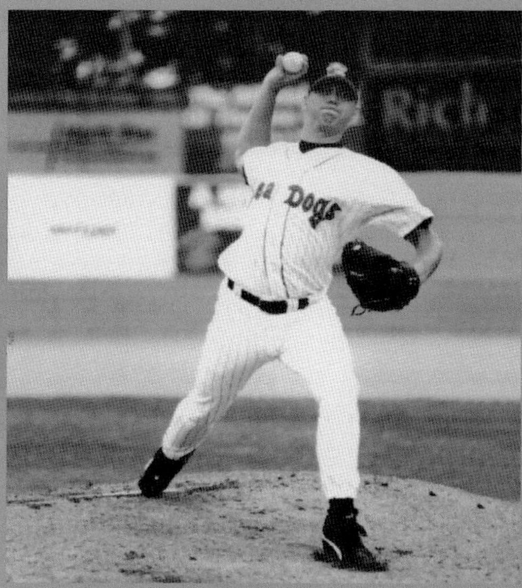

Wendy Sotos

ARCADIA
PUBLISHING

ISBN 978-0-7385-5712-0

Published by Arcadia Publishing
Charleston SC, Chicago IL, Portsmouth NH, San Francisco CA

Printed in the United States of America

Library of Congress Catalog Card Number: 2007940134

For all general information contact Arcadia Publishing at:
Telephone 843-853-2070
Fax 843-853-0044
E-mail sales@arcadiapublishing.com
For customer service and orders:
Toll-Free 1-888-313-2665

Visit us on the Internet at www.arcadiapublishing.com

To my parents, for your love, support, and belief in me. And to Andy Young, former storyteller of the Portland Sea Dogs. Your encouragement and belief in my writing helped bring a latent talent to life. I value our friendship.

CONTENTS

ACKNOWLEDGMENTS

This book would not have been possible without the support and backing of the Portland Sea Dogs. Thank you for allowing me to share the Portland Sea Dogs story. I would especially like to thank John Kameisha and Chris Cameron. John, thanks for your help. Chris, thanks for your friendship and assistance throughout every phase of this book; I could not have done it without you.

Additionally, a book such as this one relies on photographs, for without any, it would not exist. An enormous thanks to the Boston Red Sox photograph department, with a very special thank-you to Julie Cordiero. Thanks to Stewart Smith for his photographs of Sea Dogs favorites from the past. A special thanks to Joel Marsden and Matt and Melanie Aber, loyal fans of the Sea Dogs who went through their photo albums to send me some of their favorites. Unless otherwise noted, all images are courtesy of the author's collection.

Thank you to Tiffany Howe and Arcadia Publishing, who believed in this book and my storytelling. Thank you, Tiffany, for your support; you are the book's backbone.

To the front office, my souvenir store staff, and the fans of the Portland Sea Dogs, who adopted me as one of their own when I was an intern. Your friendships are all very dear to me and what inspired me to write this book.

INTRODUCTION

Some men see things as they are, and say why, I dream of things that never were and say why not?
—Robert F. Kennedy

Since their arrival in 1994, the Portland Sea Dogs have quickly captured the hearts and loyalty of the citizens of Portland, Maine. For the citizens of Portland, it was a long time coming.

Professional baseball and Portland share a fickle relationship. Since 1907 and Portland's first entry into the National Association of Professional Baseball Leagues, the Duffs, Eskimos, Mariners, Hustlers, Gulls, Pilots, and Sea Dogs have all called Portland home. Maine residents last bid adieu to baseball after the Portland Pilots folded following the 1949 season. For Portland, professional baseball's homecoming to Maine in 1984 was bittersweet.

In 1983, Bangor attorney Jordan Kobritz petitioned Portland City Council to bring minor-league baseball back to the city. The council rejected the petition, and Kobritz moved his club, the Maine Guides, to Old Orchard Beach. Before a sellout crowd, baseball returned to Maine in April 1984. In September 1988, the hometown Phillies won the final game of professional baseball played in the state for another five years.

In June 1991, baseball commissioner Fay Vincent announced Major League Baseball's first expansion since 1977. Miami and Denver were selected over Buffalo, Washington, D.C., St. Petersburg–Tampa, and Orlando.

A year later, 1 of 13 applicants vying for one of the two new Double-A teams that resulted from the National League's expansion was Dan Burke. Burke, then president and chief executive officer for Capital Cities/ABC, filed an application with the Eastern League to establish a minor-league franchise in Portland.

In September 1992, the expansion committee announced Portland was a finalist, and members of the committee descended upon the city. Impressed with the city and its support for a team, Portland, along with New Haven, Connecticut, was awarded a team.

Burke contacted Charlie Eshbach, then president of the Eastern League. Burke hired Eshbach as president and general manager of the newly established Portland franchise. The team was named the Sea Dogs, and in May 1993, the team signed an affiliation agreement with the Florida Marlins. Groundbreaking ceremonies were held at Hadlock Field later that month.

On April 7, 1994, the Sea Dogs took the field for the first time versus the Reading Phillies. An extra-inning affair, future major leaguer Charles Johnson broke a 1-1 deadlock. Johnson's homer in the 14th inning led the Sea Dogs to a 2-1 victory. On April 18, baseball officially returned to Portland. Before a sellout crowd, the Sea Dogs lost to the Albany-Colonie Yankees 7-6. Despite the loss, the team was a hit. By season's end, 375,197 fans came out to Hadlock Field, establishing a new all-time Eastern League attendance record.

Hadlock Field quickly became the training grounds for blossoming talent and young, emerging major-league stars of the future. Good scouting and recruiting by the Marlins helped the Sea Dogs establish themselves as the Eastern League's Northern Division team to beat.

In 1995, teenage prodigy Edgar Renteria was turning heads in the stands and press boxes. Livan Hernandez, a talented young Cuban, made his pitching debut for the Sea Dogs in 1996. In 1997, the Sea Dogs made minor-league baseball history. For the first time, five teammates hit 20 or more home runs. The elite quintet included future major leaguers Josh Booty, Ryan Jackson, Mark Kotsay, Kevin Millar, and John Roskos.

Under new manager Fredi Gonzalez, the Sea Dogs were Northern Division winners for a third consecutive season in 1997 and made their third playoff appearance in four years. In a repeat of the 1996 Eastern League Championship Series, the Sea Dogs lost to the Harrisburg Senators.

During this time, the Sea Dogs continued to break attendance records. Only in their third season, the Sea Dogs welcomed their one-millionth fan through the turnstiles in 1996.

Players at the minor-league level are much like a revolving door: in with the hopefuls, out with the talent. With so many promising young players, chances are good that by next season (if not before), most will have moved up the next rung of the organizational ladder. Keeping a championship team intact at the minor-league level for more than a season is hard. That was what made the Sea Dogs' feat of three straight playoff runs so impressive.

Despite three division titles and two Eastern League championship runs, the next eight seasons the Sea Dogs finished no higher than third, including a dismal fifth in 2002. However, these seasons still provided fans several opportunities to stand and cheer.

On August 8, 1999, after a three-and-a-half-hour rain delay, Brad Penny made his Sea Dogs debut. Penny, along with Luis Arroyo, combined to toss the first no-hitter in Sea Dogs history.

In June 2000, the Sea Dogs defeated the Florida Marlins in an exhibition game at Hadlock Field. The game brought many former Sea Dogs favorites and alumni back to Portland.

In 2001, top pitching prospect Josh Beckett made his Double-A debut in front of a sellout crowd. Eight out of the first nine batters faced were strikeout victims. A month later, Beckett, Brandon Bowe, and Aaron Scheffer combined to pitch the second no-hitter in franchise history.

In September 2002, the Sea Dogs terminated their nine-year affiliation with the Marlins and signed an agreement with the Boston Red Sox. In spite of mediocre play, the fans' loyalty never wavered, and they continued to come out in record numbers. The two-millionth (1998), three-millionth (2001), and four-millionth (2004) fans attended games during this time.

Glory days returned to Portland in 2005 under new skipper Todd Claus.

As a testament to the Sea Dogs organization and its fans, the Eastern League selected Hadlock Field and Portland as hosts of the 2005 Eastern League All-Star Game. On July 13, 2005, the Eastern League stars, with a record seven Sea Dogs, shined in Portland.

In September, the Sea Dogs reclaimed first place and the Northern Division crown. In the Eastern League Championship Series, the Akron Aeros defeated the Sea Dogs three games to one.

On September 17, 2006, the Sea Dogs captured their first Eastern League crown over the Aeros. It was Maine's first professional baseball championship in 91 years. The Sea Dogs also welcomed their five-millionth fan.

The citizens of Portland and fans of the Sea Dogs have exemplified "if you build it, they will come." For the fans and players, Hadlock Field has become their own field of dreams and a place where dreams come true.

1

If You Build It (1992–1994)

If you build it, he will come.

—The Voice, *Field of Dreams*

On April 18, 1994, it all came to an end. Because of Major League Baseball's first expansion in over a dozen years, two new Double-A teams became available. Including Dan Burke, 13 filed an application with the Eastern League. Burke's goal was simple: bring professional baseball back to Portland. Burke presented his plan to Portland City Council, and by an eight-to-one margin, the council voted to support Burke and his efforts to bring baseball back to the city. Portland city manager Robert (Bob) Ganley became Burke's biggest supporter and ally.

The diligence and determination of Burke and Ganley paid off when the expansion committee awarded Maine's biggest city a franchise in October 1992.

Ganley's support and "successful bid to bring the Sea Dogs to Portland was just the beginning." His "leadership, vision, and determination lead to the renovation of Hadlock Field."

A year and half after the expansion committee's announcement, baseball returned home to Portland. On April 18, 1994, the Sea Dogs took the field for the first time at Hadlock Field. The Sea Dogs lost their home opener but won something much more valuable—the hearts and loyalty of the city.

Some Sea Dogs firsts in this year included the first hit, Jesus Tavarez; first run, Terry Jorgensen; and first home run, Charles Johnson. Marc Valdes and Vic Darensbourg were also among the first Sea Dogs to earn Eastern League Pitcher of the Week honors.

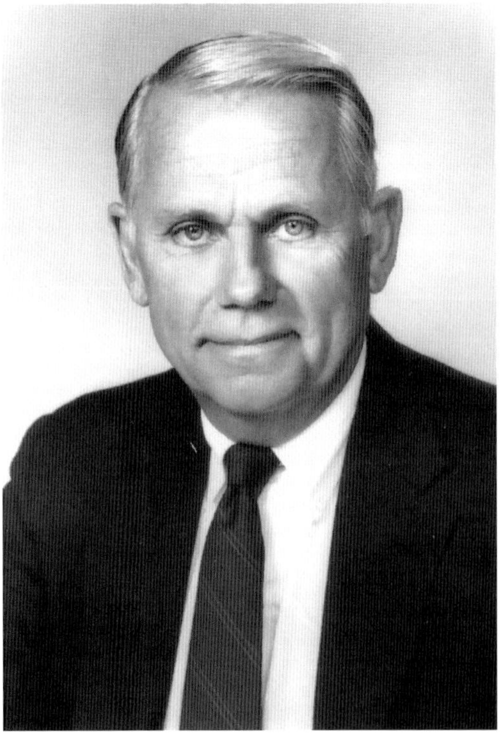

In June 1992, Dan Burke (left), then president and chief executive officer of Capital Cities/ABC, applied for one of the two expansion teams available because of Major League Baseball's first expansion since 1977. Burke's hope was to return professional baseball to Portland. Portland had been without a team since 1949, after the Pilots folded at the completion of the season. Burke gained an ally after presenting his plan to Portland City Council. Former city manager Bob Ganley (below) enthusiastically jumped on Burke's bandwagon, and the two men worked tirelessly to bring baseball back to Maine's largest city. The Eastern League awarded its diligence in October 1992. The expansion committee, impressed with both the city and its support of a team, awarded Portland, along with New Haven, Connecticut, a team. (Courtesy of the Sea Dogs.)

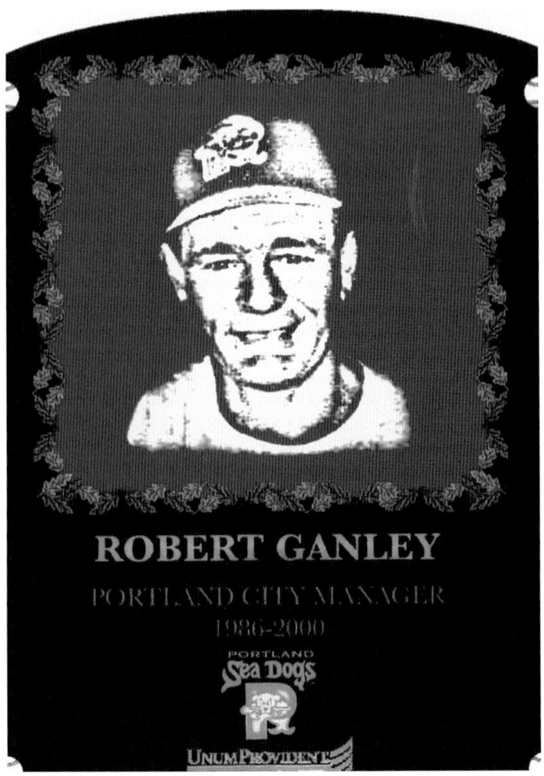

Burke contacted Charlie Eshbach, president of the Eastern League, and offered Eshbach the position of president and general manager of his new franchise. Eshbach is no stranger to baseball. His résumé includes a stint as interim president of minor-league baseball in 1988. Eshbach accepted Burke's offer. The Eastern League named Eshbach as its Executive of the Year in 1994 and 2002. (Courtesy of the Sea Dogs.)

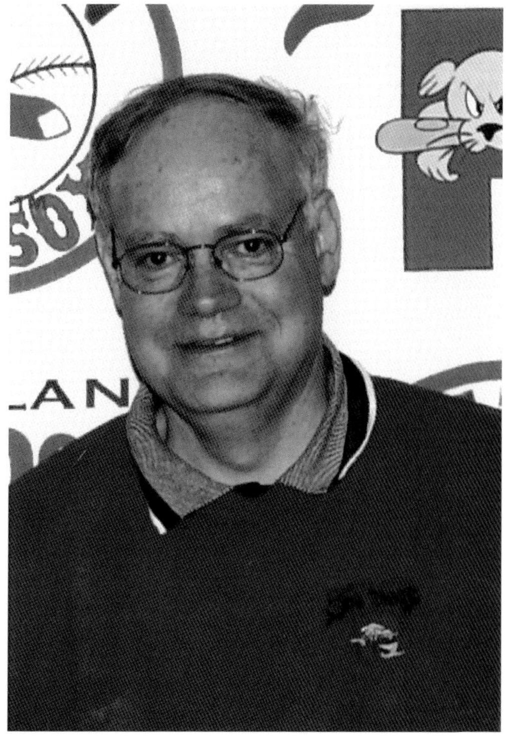

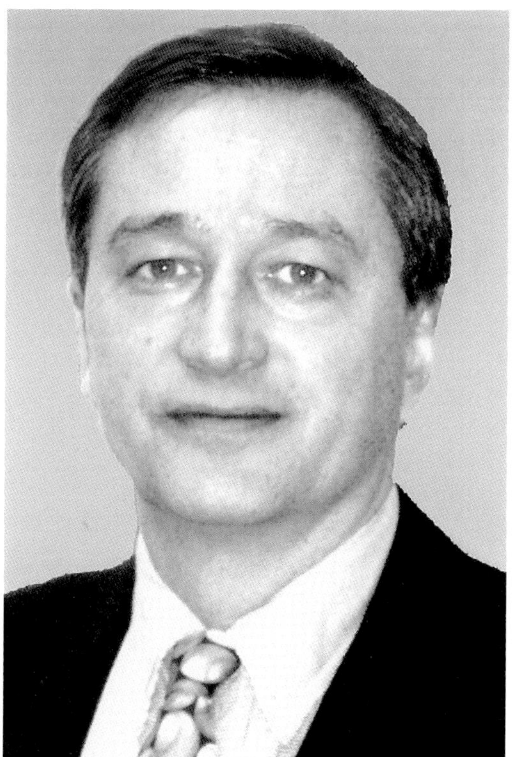

Eshbach contacted John Kameisha, who had spent the past six seasons with the New Britain Red Sox. Kameisha joined the Sea Dogs staff in their inaugural season as assistant general manager. Kameisha currently serves as executive vice president of the Sea Dogs. (Courtesy of the Sea Dogs.)

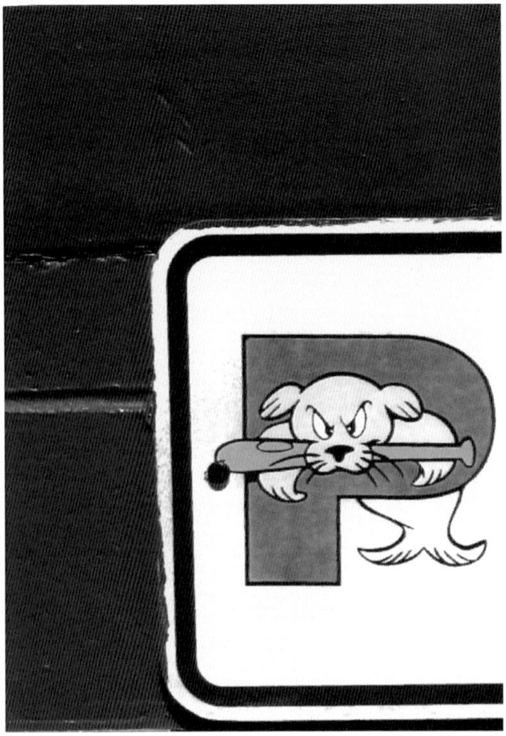

In March 1993, the new Portland franchise conducted a name-the-team contest. The name *Sea Dogs* was chosen from more than 600 entries. Designed by Connecticut native Guy Gilchrist, the logo depicts a seal with a baseball bat clenched firmly in his mouth and sticking his head out from the letter *P*. The logo is one of the most popular and best selling in minor-league baseball.

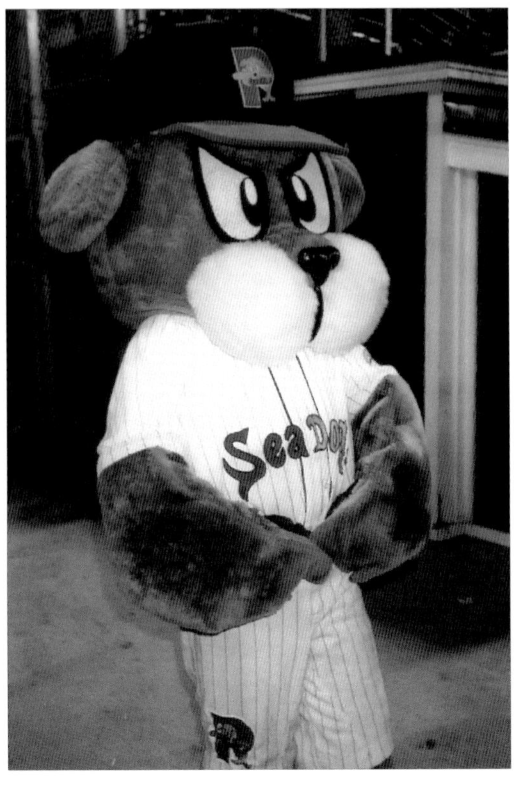

After finding someone who could "train" him "properly," on May 7, 1994, Slugger the Sea Dog made his debut at a Portland Sea Dogs game. Slugger instantly became a fan favorite and quickly became one of the most sought out members of the Portland Sea Dogs family. Slugger is not only a fixture at home games but in the Portland community as well. (Courtesy of the Sea Dogs.)

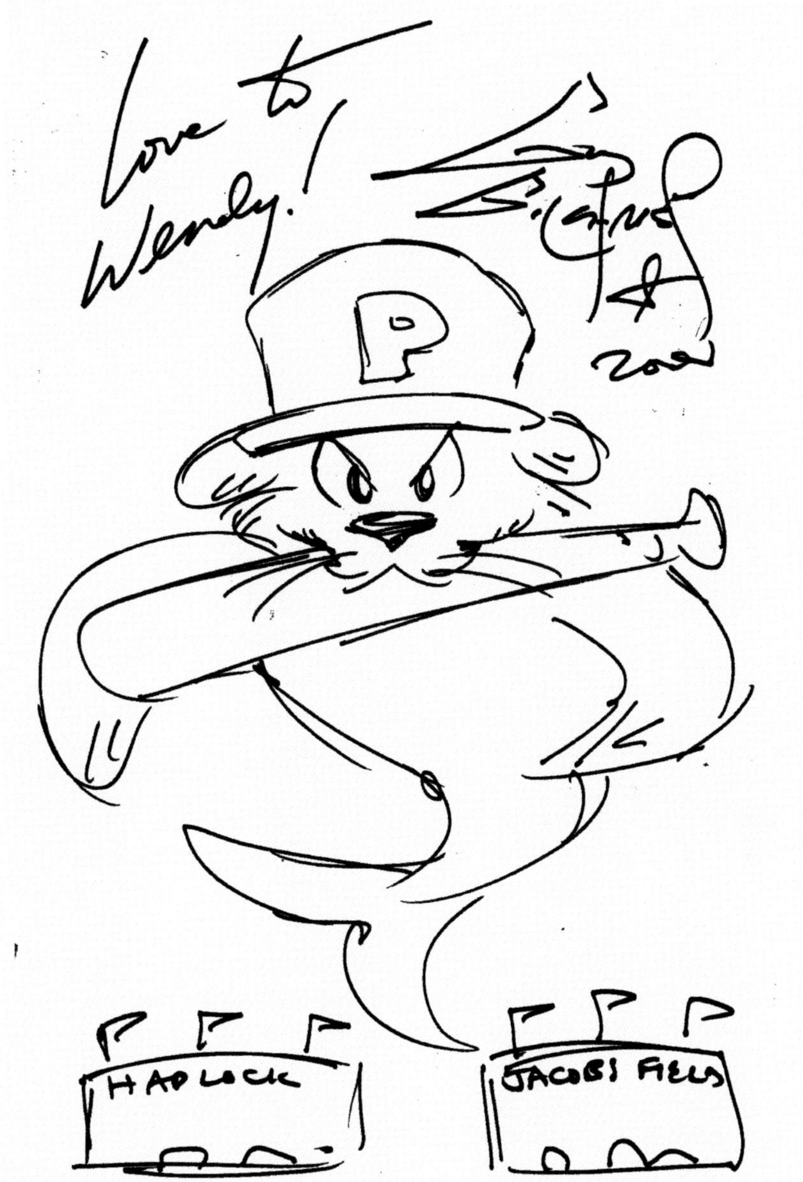

Guy Gilchrist, former Muppeteer for the late Jim Hensen, designed several logos for minor-league baseball's Eastern League. In addition to the Sea Dogs logo, the New England native designed the logos for the Norwich Navigators, the Binghamton Mets, and the New Britain Rock Cats. Gilchrist, a well-known cartoonist and illustrator, was recipient of the National Cartoonist Society's Magazine and Book Illustration Award in 1997 and 1998. His comic strip *Mudpie* tells about the adventures and misadventures of a young cat and the cat's family. Gilchrist wrote a series of strips that depicted Mudpie and the family's visit to Portland and attending a Sea Dogs game. A Reuben Award nominee, Gilchrist's work is permanently enshrined and on display at the Smithsonian Institute in Washington, D.C., and a sketch of his appears above.

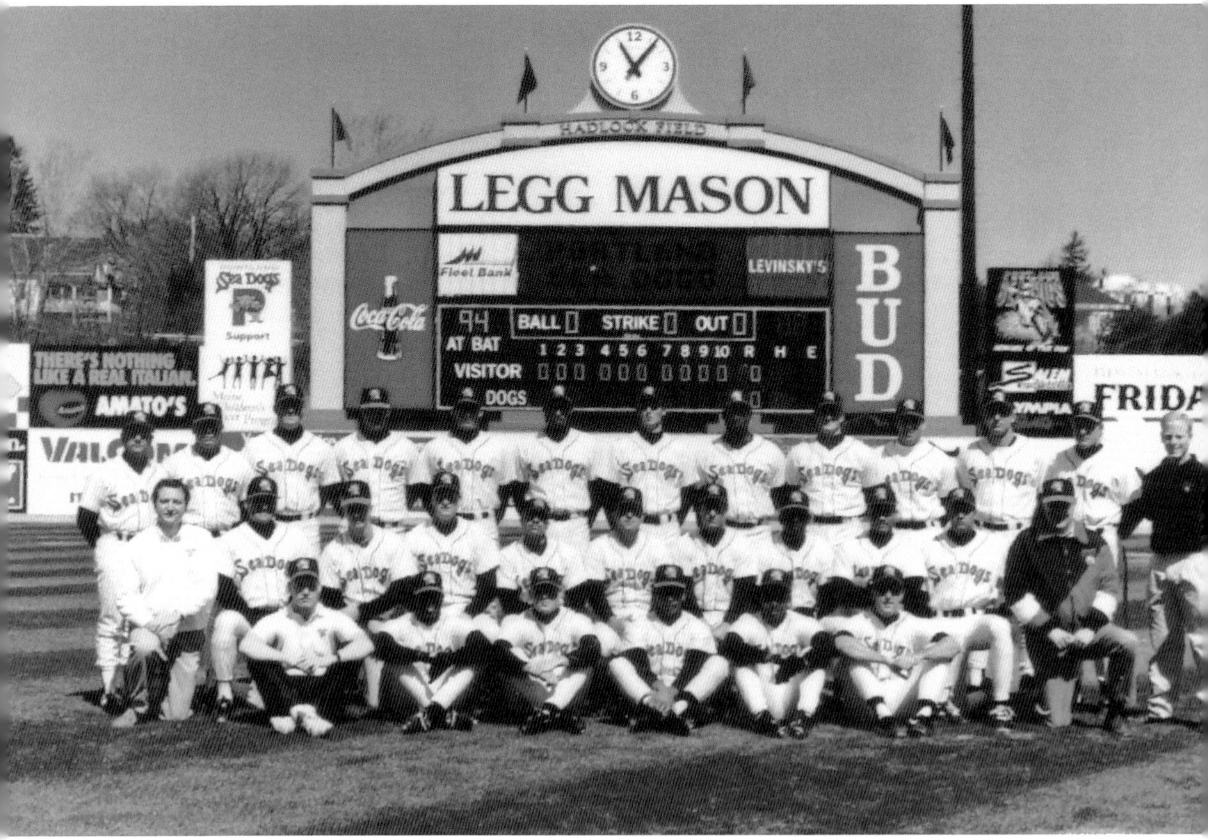

On April 7, 1994, the Florida Marlins' new Double-A affiliate, the Portland Sea Dogs, took the field for the very first time against the Reading Phillies in Pennsylvania. The first batter up for Sea Dogs manager Carlos Tosca was center fielder Jesus Tavarez. Tavarez got the first hit in Portland Sea Dogs history, with a single. In the third inning, Terry Jorgensen headed home to score the first Sea Dogs run. After nine innings of play, the score was 1-1, and the game went into extra innings. Future major-league catcher Charles Johnson blasted a 14th-inning, game-winning home run to send everyone home and give the Sea Dogs a dramatic 2-1 victory. Relief pitcher Don Perigny earned the first Sea Dogs win, and future major leaguer Vic Darensbourg collected the first Sea Dogs save. (Courtesy of the Sea Dogs.)

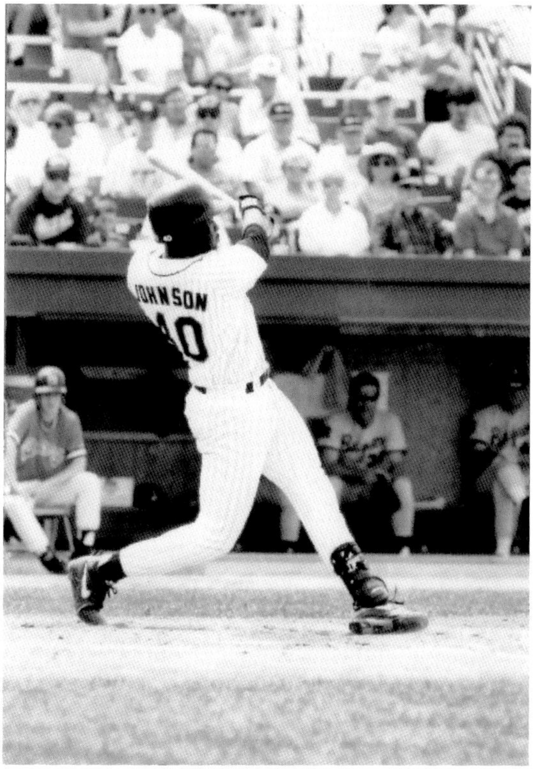

With a panache for the dramatic, future major-league catcher Charles Johnson's debut with the Sea Dogs was memorable. In Portland's first game versus the Reading Phillies, Johnson's legendary extra-inning home run gave the Sea Dogs a 2-1 victory. Days later, in the Sea Dogs' home opener, Johnson brought the fans to their feet when he hit two homers late in the game. (Courtesy of the Sea Dogs.)

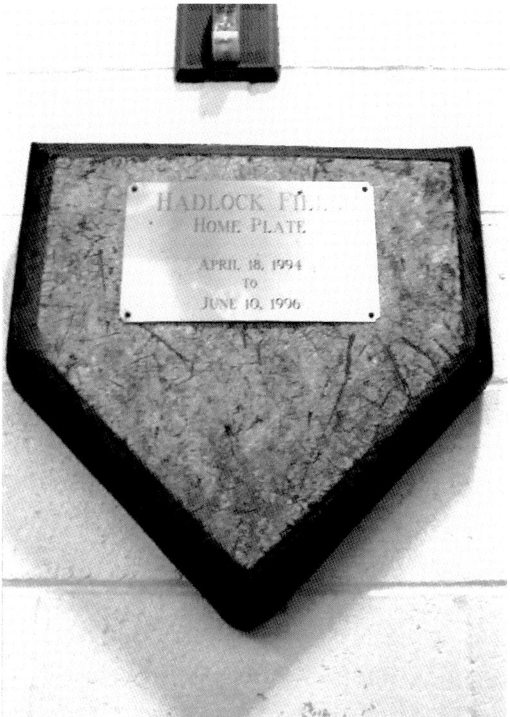

On April 18, 1994, before a sellout crowd, the Portland Sea Dogs took the field for the first time at Hadlock Field. When they did, professional baseball, absent in the city since 1949, returned. The first Portland Sea Dog to cross home plate at Hadlock Field was infielder Ramon Martinez, in the first inning against the Albany-Colonie Yankees. The Sea Dogs lost their home opener 7-6.

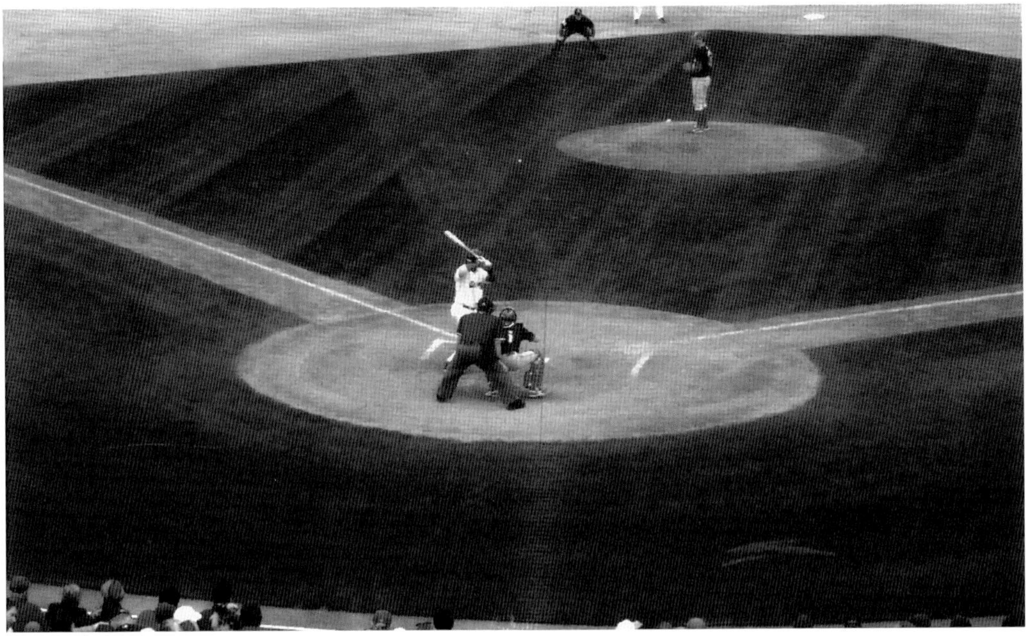

On May 6, 1994, in a special on-field, pregame ceremony, the Portland Sea Dogs formally dedicated their new home, Hadlock Field. Recognized by the Sea Dogs were those who assisted in bringing professional baseball back to the city of Portland and to the state of Maine. The City of Portland received a plaque recognizing its contributions to the construction of Hadlock Field. "The city of Portland, acting as general contractor, was responsible for management, design, and engineering all aspects of this project." The plaque hangs in the main concourse of Hadlock Field. (Courtesy of the Sea Dogs.)

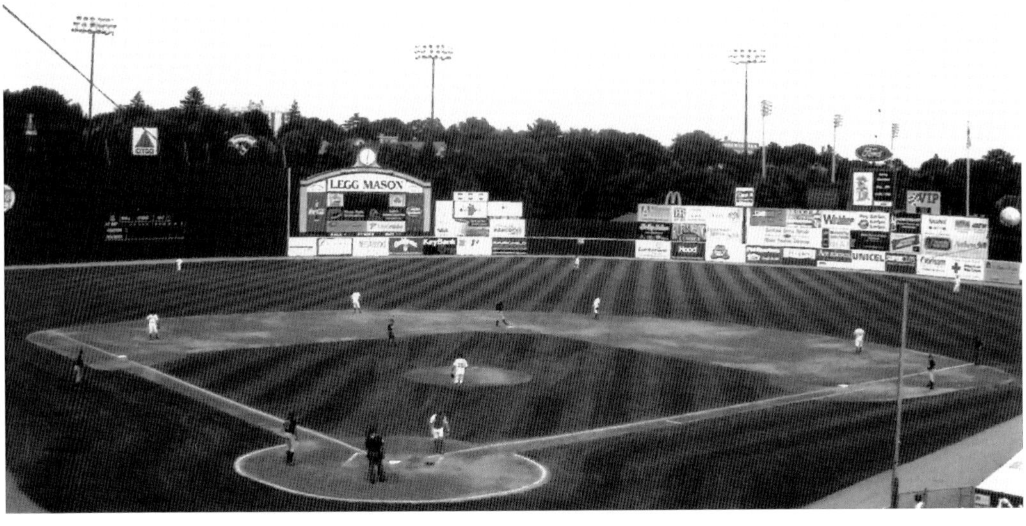

2

Go the Distance (1995–1997)

Go the distance.

—The Voice, *Field of Dreams*

With the pomp and circumstance of their inaugural season behind them, the Portland Sea Dogs quickly established themselves as the Eastern League's Northern Division team to beat. The next three seasons, the Sea Dogs finished in first place and made it to the playoffs each year.

Hadlock Field became the training ground for emerging major-league stars of the not-too-distant future. A few of the big-league stars of tomorrow included Luis Castillo, Todd Dunwoody, Alex Gonzalez, Livan Hernandez, Mark Kotsay, Kevin Millar, Edgar Renteria, and Tony Saunders.

The fans continued to come and in record numbers. Only halfway through their third season, the Sea Dogs welcomed their one-millionth fan in franchise history on June 29, 1996.

Eastern League Players of the Week from this time period included Billy McMillon, Edgar Renteria, Kevin Millar, Glenn Reeves, and John Roskos. Eastern League Pitchers of the Week included Rey Mendoza, Marc Valdes, William Cunnane, Tony Saunders, Gregg Press, and Brian Meadows. Other Sea Dogs to earn honors during this period were John Roskos (Eastern League Player of the Month), Kevin Millar (Eastern League MVP), Mark Kotsay (Eastern League Rookie of the Year), Todd Dunwoody (Eastern League All-Star Game MVP), Carlos Tosca (the Eastern League's and *Baseball America*'s Manager of the Year), and Livan Hernandez (Major League Baseball World Series MVP).

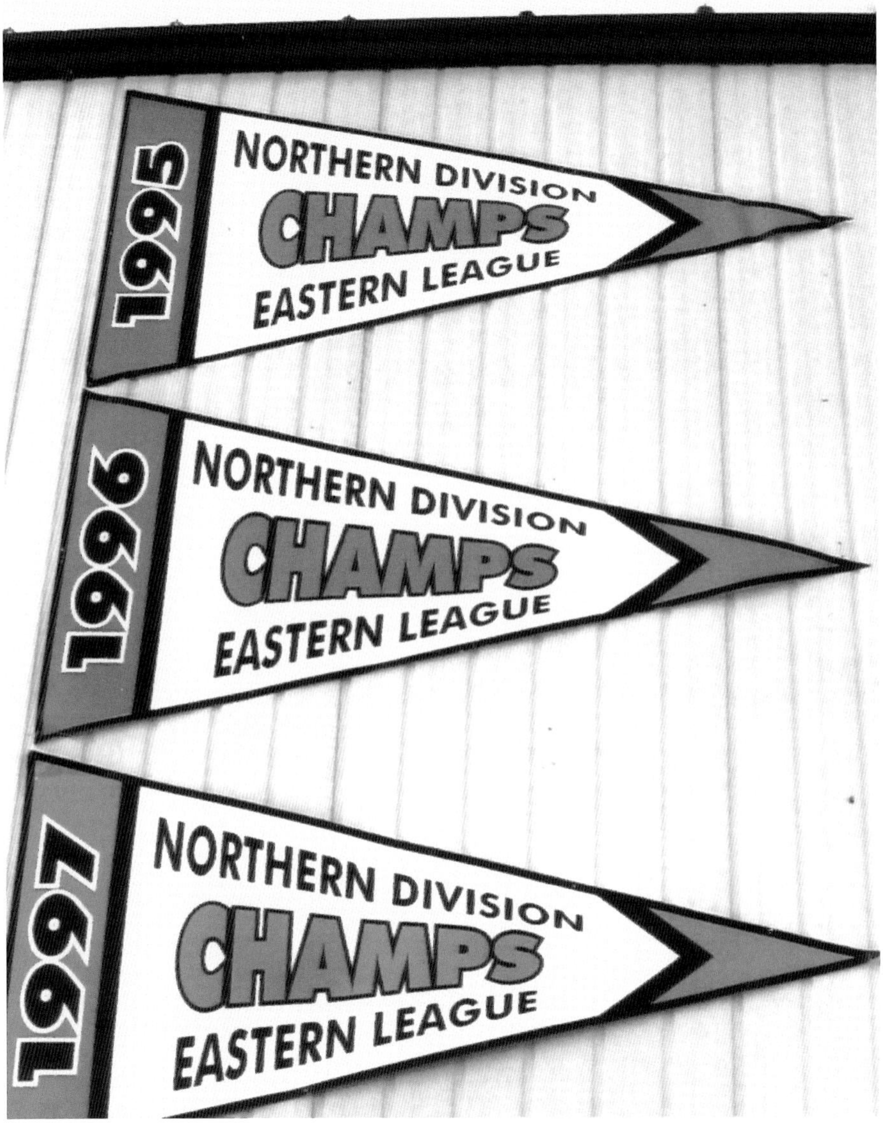

The 1995 Sea Dogs finished the season with an 86-56 record. The Sea Dogs and the New Haven Ravens, both of whom entered the Eastern League the year before, advanced to the playoffs. The Ravens defeat the Sea Dogs in the first round of playoffs, three games to one. The 1996 Sea Dogs finished the season with an 83-58 record. Portland defeated the Binghamton Mets in the first round to advance to the Eastern League Championship Series for the first time in franchise history. The Sea Dogs lost the deciding game of the Eastern League Championship Series to the Harrisburg Senators at Hadlock Field. The Sea Dogs finished the 1997 season with a 79-63 record. Portland won its third Northern Division title in four years and advanced to the Eastern League playoffs for the third consecutive year. Portland defeated the Norwich Navigators three games to two and again faced the Senators for the Eastern League title. The Sea Dogs lost the series and failed to bring the trophy home to the city of Portland.

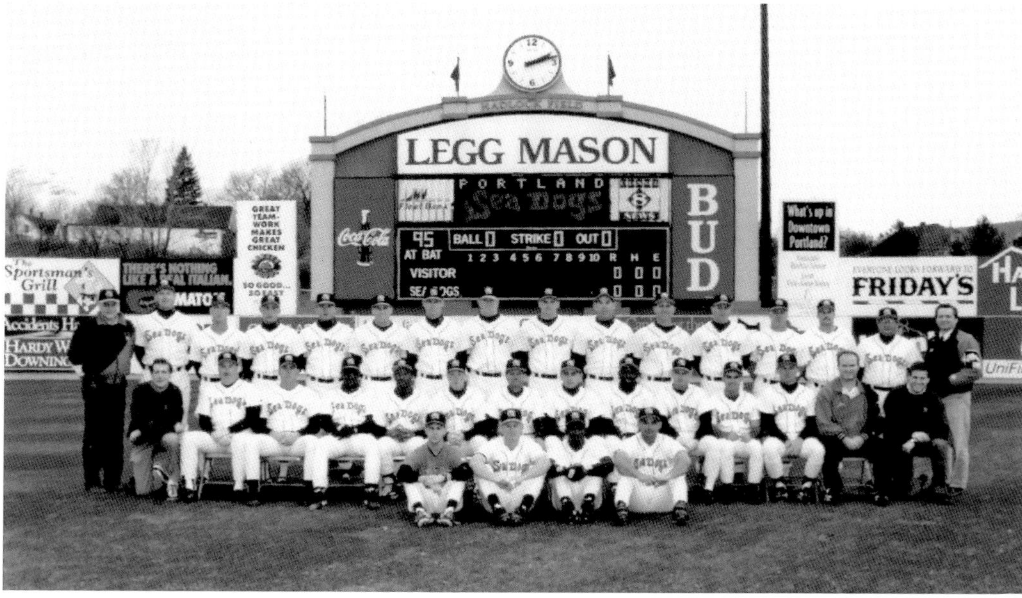

The Florida Marlins became the fastest expansion team to play in and win a World Series when they defeated the Cleveland Indians in 1997. Close to one-third of the Florida Marlins World Series roster made a stop in Portland between 1994 and 1997. The 1995 Portland Sea Dogs team included 1997 World Series stars such as Charles Johnson, Edgar Renteria, Antonio Alfonseca, and Jay Powell. (Photograph by Stewart Smith.)

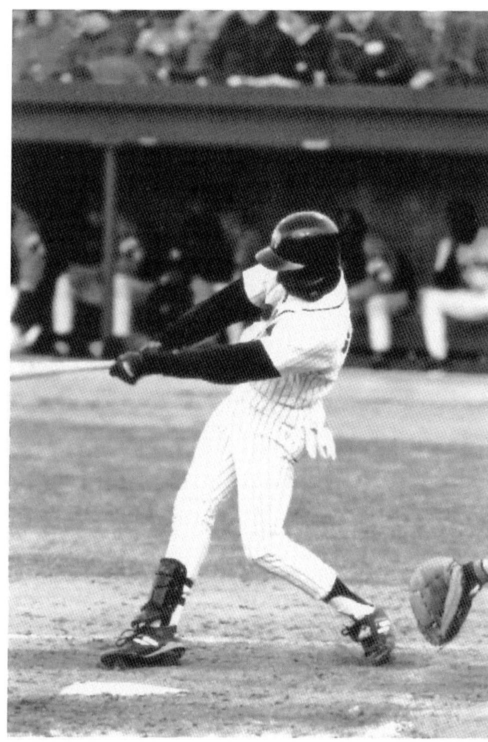

One of the more potent bats in the Sea Dogs lineup in 1995 belonged to left fielder Billy McMillon. McMillon led the offensive assault in five offensive categories. He led the team in average (.315), home runs (14), RBIs (93), hits (162), and on-base percentage (.423). McMillon was the first Sea Dog to win Eastern League Player of the Week honors. (Photograph by Stewart Smith.)

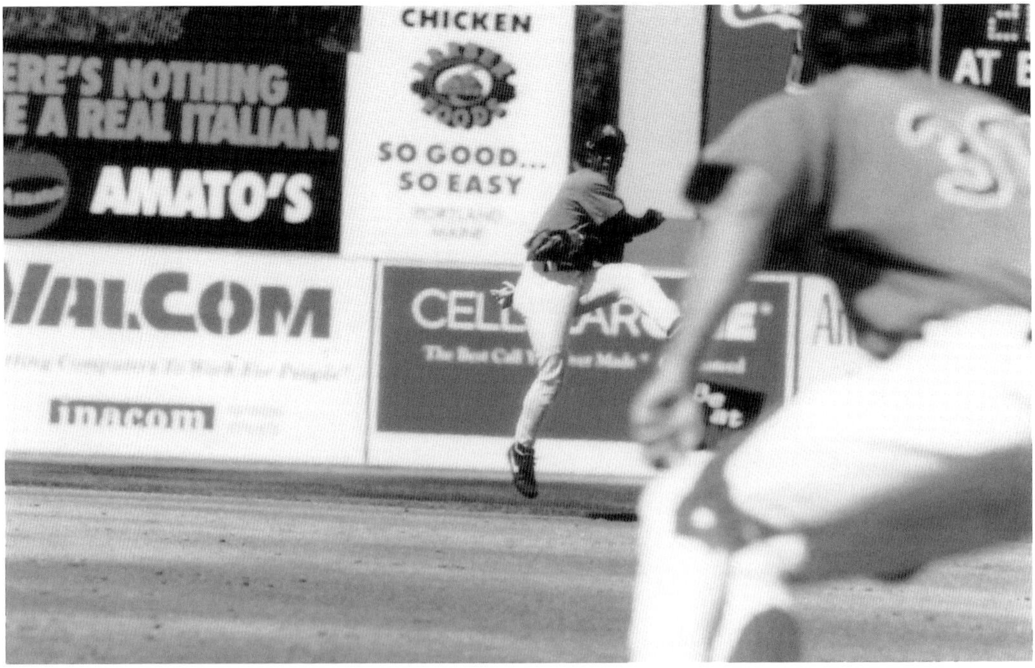

Two seasons before his game-winning hit in Game 7 of the 1997 World Series, Edgar Renteria turned heads in Portland. Renteria was only a "kid" when he played ball for the Sea Dogs in 1995. Howe Sportsdata selected the 19-year-old Colombian shortstop and future World Series hero for its all-teenage team at the conclusion of the 1995 season. (Photograph by Stewart Smith.)

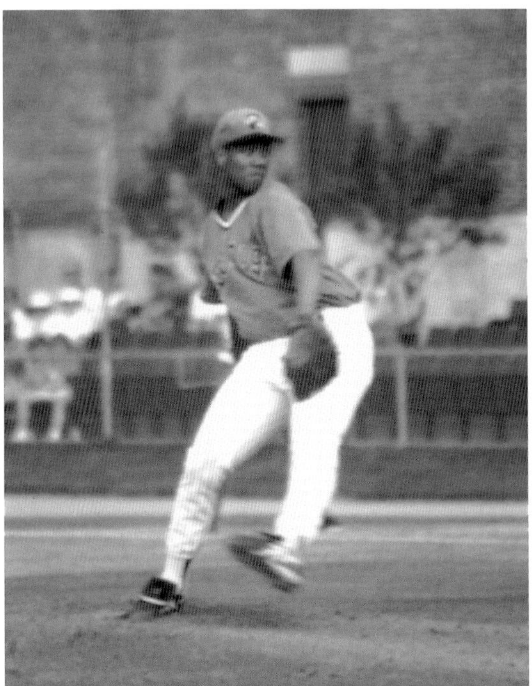

Leaving his mother and family behind to chase his dreams, Eisler Livan Hernandez Carrera, along with half brother Orlando, defected from his homeland Cuba to the United States in 1995. A year later, Hernandez made his first appearance at Hadlock Field and for the Sea Dogs in June 1996. Major League Baseball would name him MVP for the 1997 World Series 16 months later. (Photograph by Stewart Smith.)

Luis Castillo let his legs do the talking and left opposing players behind, eating his dust in 1996. *Baseball America* named the speedy Sea Dogs second baseman as the "Best and Fastest Base Runner" in the Eastern League in 1996. Castillo's 51 stolen bases topped the Eastern League in 1996 and established a Portland Sea Dogs record for the most stolen bases in a single season. (Photograph by Stewart Smith.)

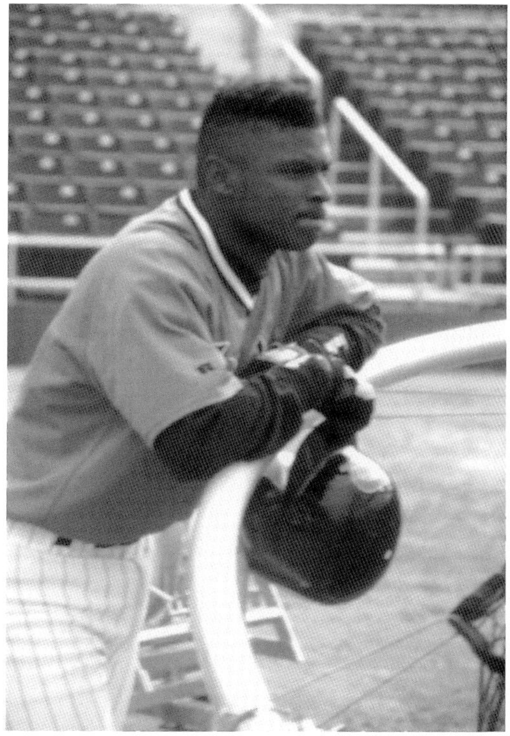

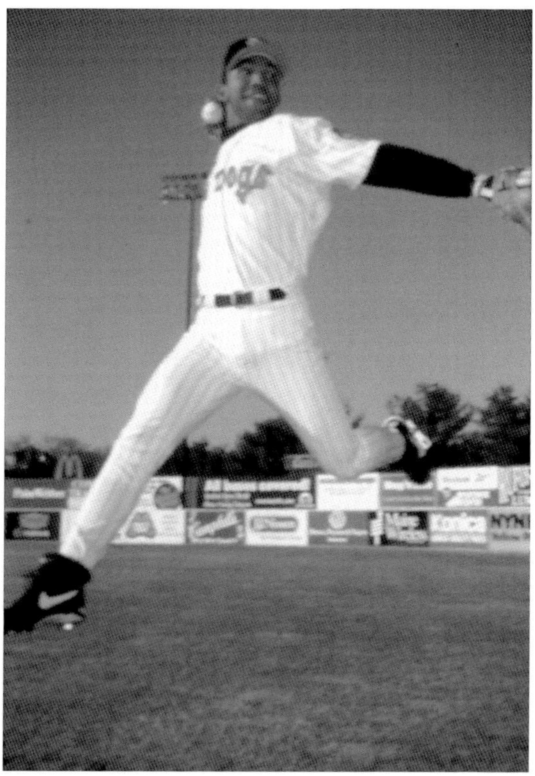

On the field or at the plate, Alex "Gonzo" Gonzalez utilized all his tools of the trade for Portland in 1997. His jaw-dropping defensive plays at shortstop drew comparisons to fellow Venezuelan shortstop Omar Vizquel. In May, Gonzalez became the first Sea Dog to hit three home runs in one game. *Baseball America* named Gonzalez Best Defensive Shortstop and a top Eastern League prospect in 1997. (Photograph by Stewart Smith.)

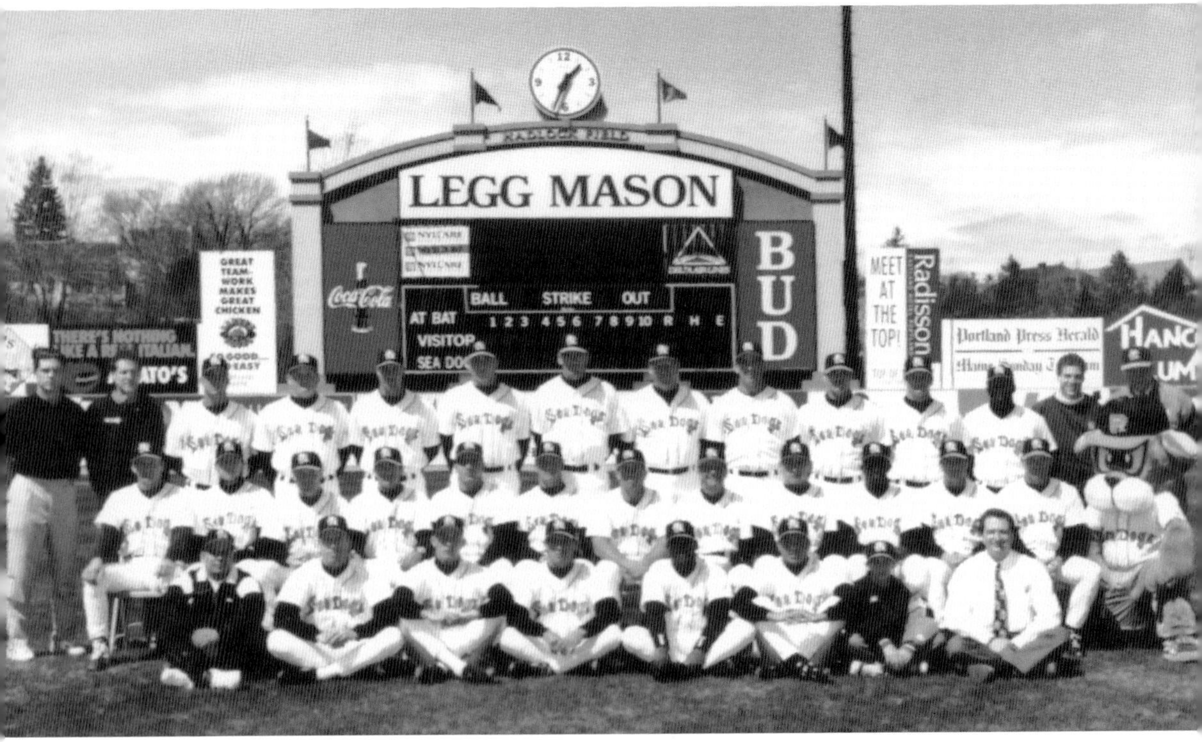

The 1996 season was the final one for skipper Carlos Tosca, manager of the Sea Dogs since their inception in 1994. During his three-year tenure with Portland, the team made its first playoff appearance (1995) and appeared in its first Eastern League Championship Series (1996). *Baseball America* and the Eastern League both named Tosca Minor League Manager of the Year in 1996. The team continued to develop major-league-caliber players in 1996. At the plate, Stars of Stars award winner and Eastern League All-Star Game MVP Todd Dunwoody led the Sea Dogs in four offensive categories. On the mound, Tony Saunders led the pitching staff and Eastern League with a 2.63 ERA and 156 strikeouts. Closer Bill Hurst recorded 30 saves, most in the Eastern League and most all-time for a Sea Dog. A young Cuban by the name of Livan Hernandez, defecting to the United States only a year before, made his Portland debut. His story became the subplot to the 1997 World Series 16 months later. (Photograph by Stewart Smith.)

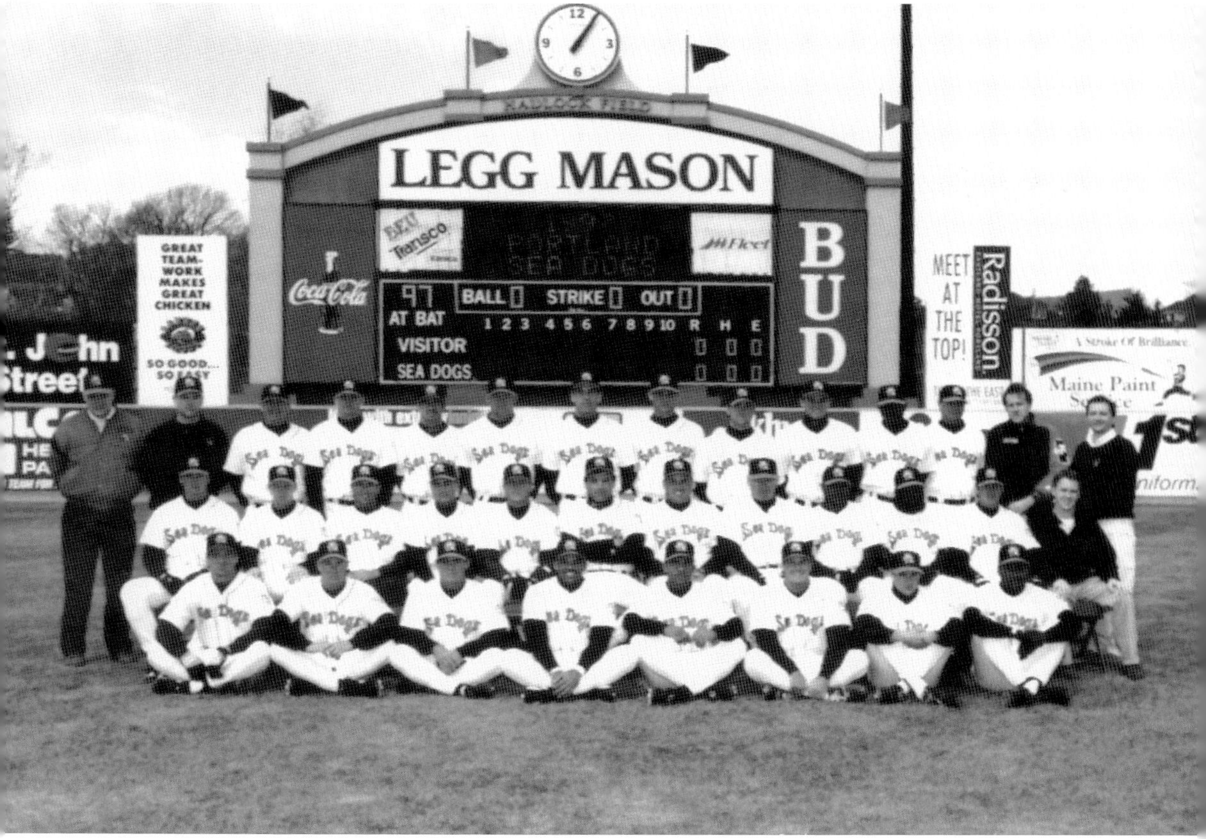

Prior to the start of the 1997 season, Fredi Gonzalez replaced Carlos Tosca as manager of the Portland Sea Dogs. Several players emerged as major-league stars after having minor-league "career years" in 1997. On the mound, starting pitcher Hector Mercado overpowered opposing batters and led the Sea Dogs staff in wins (11), ERA (3.96), and strikeouts (125). Randy Winn led the way with 35 stolen bases and six triples. The class of 1997 also included fan favorite Kevin Millar and Eastern League Rookie of the Year Mark Kotsay. Millar and Kotsay, along with three other teammates, made minor-league baseball history. For the first time, five teammates hit 20 or more home runs in the same season. The elite quintet included future major leaguers Millar, Kotsay, Josh Booty, Ryan Jackson, and John Roskos. (Photograph by Stewart Smith.)

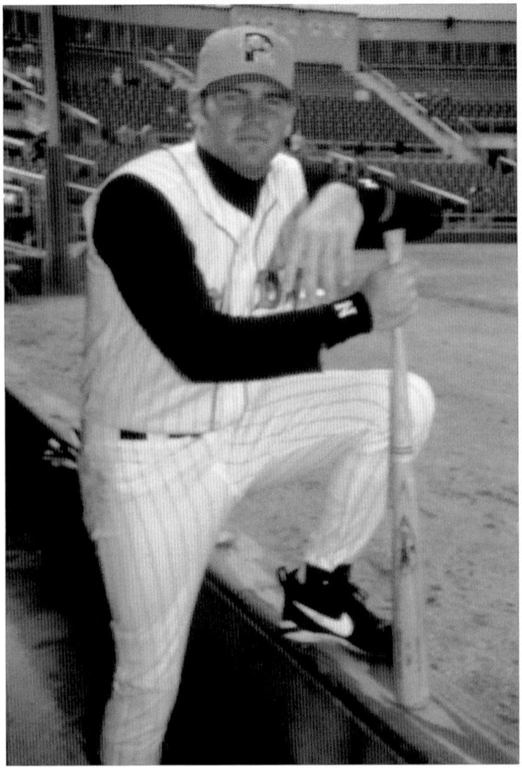

Two members of the elite home-run quintet include Ryan Jackson (left) and John Roskos (below). Perhaps overshadowed by Kevin Millar and Mark Kotsay during the season of the long ball, Jackson and Roskos both had impressive seasons of their own in 1997. Jackson smashed 26 homers, drove in 98 runs, and slapped out 153 hits, with a .544 slugging percentage. In June, Roskos became the first Sea Dog to win Eastern League Player of the Month honors, after winning Player of the Week honors in the same month. In 1997, the Sea Dogs hit three grand slams, two by Roskos and one by Jackson. (Photographs by Stewart Smith.)

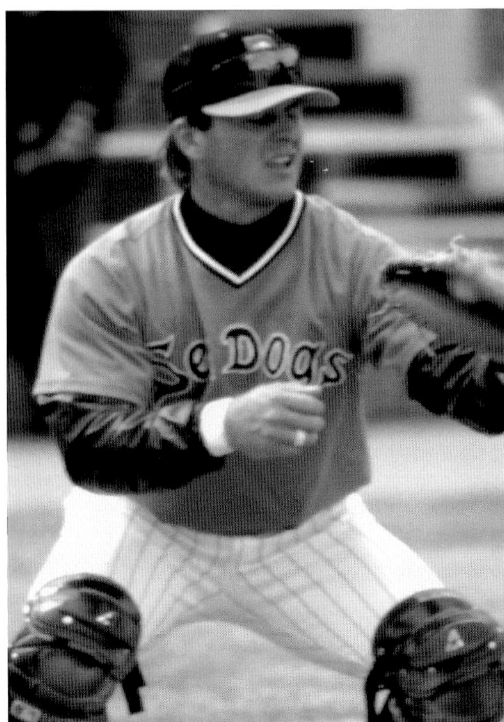

Former silver medalist Josh Booty (right) appeared in only 13 major-league games before he became the 172nd pick in the 2001 NFL draft. The Seattle Seahawks selected the former Sea Dog in the sixth round. He was the 10th quarterback taken overall. The Seahawks traded Booty to Cleveland, where he was the Browns' third-string quarterback until they cut him in 2003. In 2007, Booty was waived by the Oakland Raiders. Booty's ex-teammate Mark Kotsay (below) currently plays for Oakland's hometown baseball team, the Athletics. Appearing in 114 games with the Sea Dogs in 1997, Kotsay, the former *Baseball America* No. 1 prospect, hit .306 with 20 homers and 77 RBIs. The 1997 Eastern League Rookie of the Year scored a league-high 103 runs. (Photographs by Stewart Smith.)

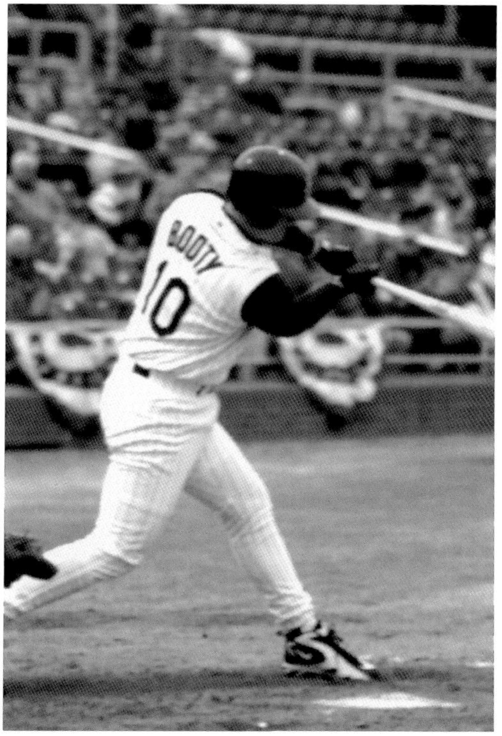

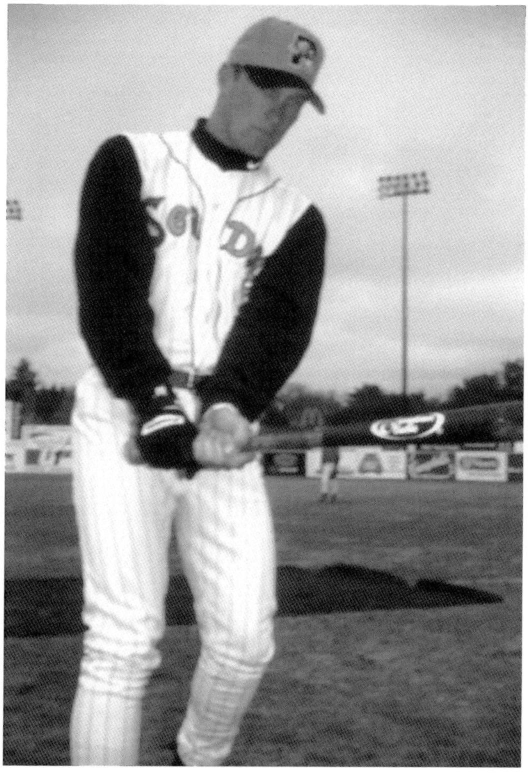

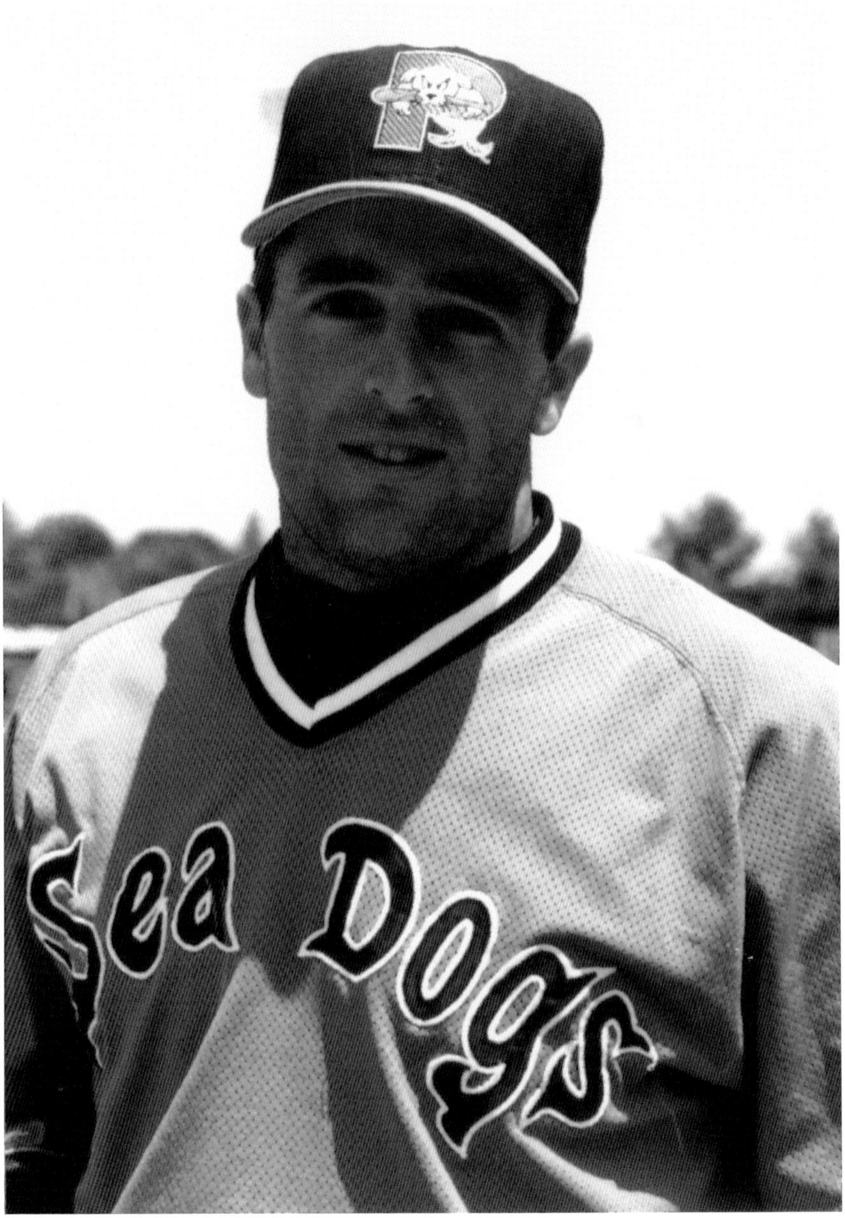

Kevin Millar's professional baseball career began in 1993, when he played for the St. Paul Saints, an independent team in the Northern League. At the end of the season, the Florida Marlins purchased his contract. Millar enjoyed a minor-league career year with Portland in 1997. The Marlins' Organizational Hitter of the Year batted .342, hit 32 homers, and knocked in 131 runs for the Sea Dogs. At the end of the season, the Eastern League selected Millar as the league's Player of the Year. Over a decade later, Millar is still the Sea Dogs' franchise leader in four, and runner-up in three, offensive categories. He is the franchise leader in batting average (.328), RBIs (220), hits (326), and runs scored (164). Millar is second in franchise history in home runs (51), doubles (66), and slugging percentage (.552). (Photograph by Stewart Smith.)

3

Ease Their Pain (1998–1999)

Ease his pain.

—The Voice, *Field of Dreams*

Spoiled by their hometown heroes' rapid success, the heartache of almost winning it all was difficult for the fans of the Sea Dogs and left them aching for more. Portland slipped and took a disappointing step back in 1998 and 1999 and finished both seasons in third place.

Players at the minor-league level are much like a revolving door: in with the hopefuls, out with the talent. Keeping a championship-caliber team at the minor-league level intact for more than a season, much alone a whole season, is difficult, if not impossible.

Easing the fans' pain and bringing fans to their feet was Chris Norton's home run chase, Nate Rolison's two-season dominance at the plate, and Michael Tejera's authority on the mound. In 1999, a lucky "penny" emerged after a three-and-a-half-hour rain delay.

In the stands, fan number two million in Sea Dogs history was welcomed to Hadlock Field on September 6, 1998.

Off the field, the renowned baseball publication *Baseball America* awarded the Portland Sea Dogs organization the Bob Freitas Award at the conclusion of the 1999 season.

Eastern League Players of the Week of this period included Nate Rolison, Mike Gulan, Joe Funaro, and Chris Norton. Eastern League Pitchers of the Week included Michael Tejera and Gary Knotts. Tejera also earned Eastern League Pitcher of the Year honors.

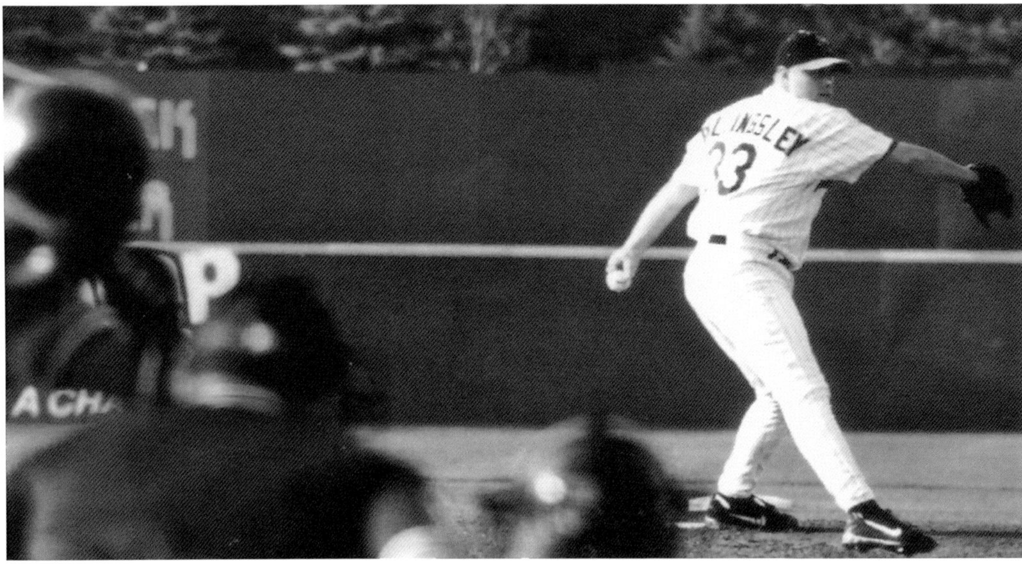

Whenever Brent Billingsley took the mound, opposing hitters only had a whiff of a chance of making contact with the ball. Billingsley set a Sea Dogs single-season record, striking out 183 batters in 171 innings. His 183 strikeouts were also tops in the Eastern League for 1998. (Photograph by Stewart Smith.)

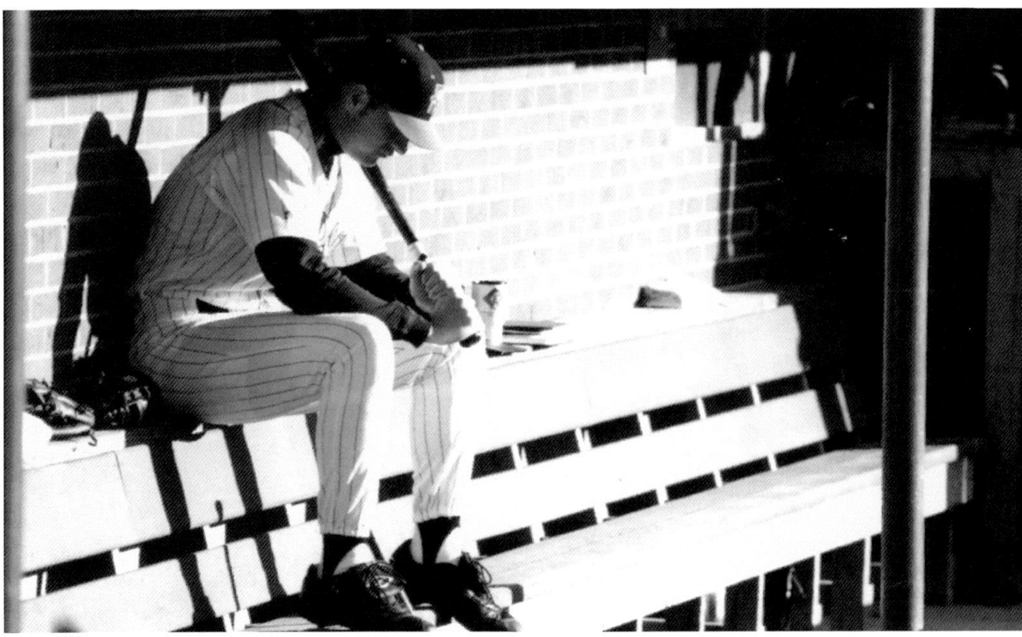

Following on the heels of Kevin Millar's minor-league career year, Sea Dogs first baseman Nate Rolison enjoyed one of his own in 1998. Rolison was the Sea Dogs leader in homers (16), RBIs (83), doubles (35), and runs scored (80). He also led the team in on-base percentage in 1998 (.365) and 1999 (.399). Rolison batted .299, tops for the Sea Dogs for 1999. (Photograph by Stewart Smith.)

Future major-league pitcher Nate Bump debuted with the Sea Dogs in 1999. His 21 wins tied him for third place, and his 375 innings pitched and 253 strikeouts place him third and fourth, respectively, in franchise history. During the 2000 season, Bump pitched a complete game, one-hitter against the Binghamton Mets. It was the best pitching performance (at the time) in franchise history. (Photograph by Stewart Smith.)

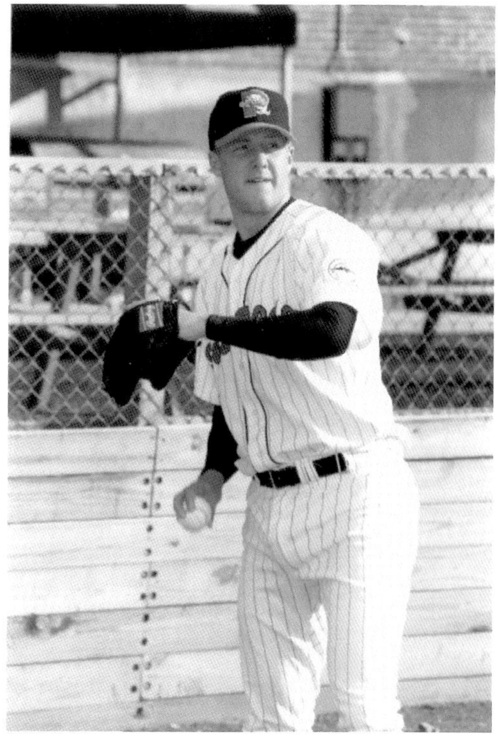

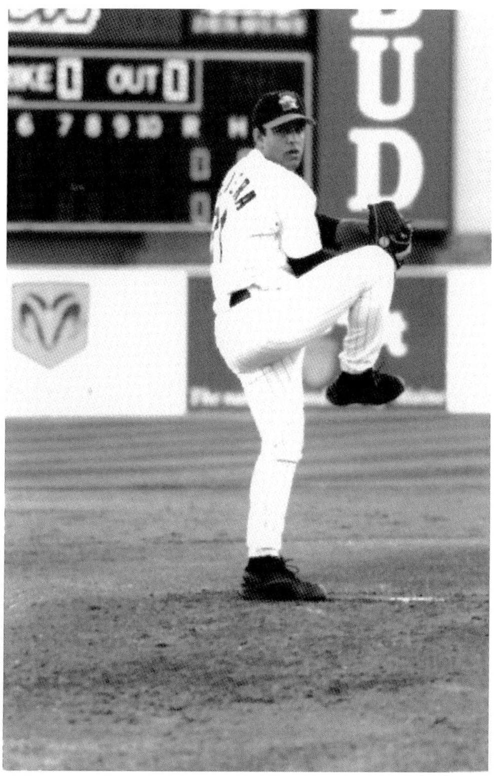

Michael Tejera dominated and overpowered opposing batters in 1999. His season-high 13 victories tied him with Tony Saunders for most in a season. By a mere fraction, Tejera broke Saunders's single-season ERA with an impressive 2.62, second best in franchise history. Tejera led the pitching staff with 152 strikeouts. Tejera is the Sea Dogs' franchise leader with 31 wins, 380 strikeouts, and 403 innings pitched. (Photograph by Stewart Smith.)

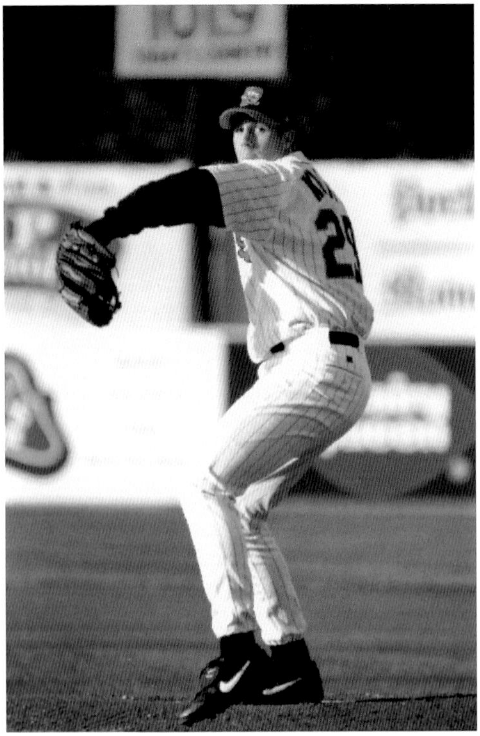

Right-handed pitcher Gary Knotts appeared in his first game with the Sea Dogs in 1999. In 12 appearances, Knotts went 6-3 with one complete game. In his first full season with Portland in 2000, Knotts led the staff with 113 strikeouts. Knotts defeated former teammate A. J. Burnett when Burnett and the Florida Marlins played a special exhibition game at Hadlock Field during the 2000 season. (Photograph by Stewart Smith.)

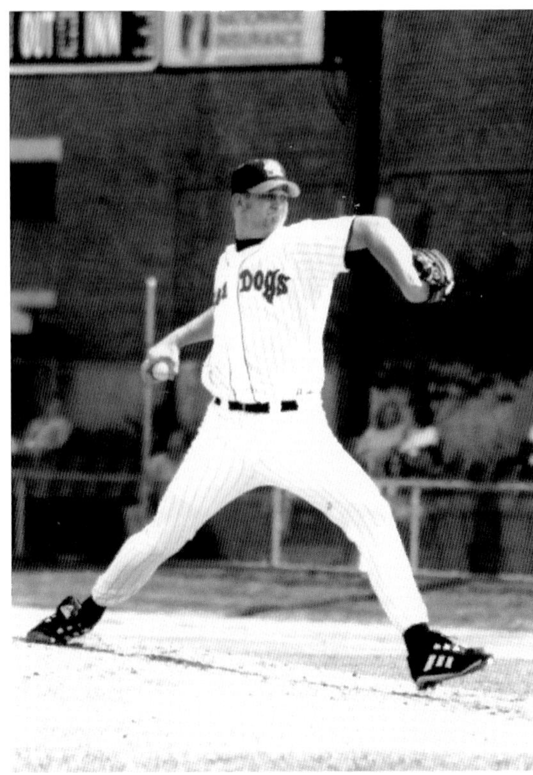

Originally part of the Arizona Diamondbacks organization, Brad Penny was traded by the Diamondbacks to the Florida Marlins for reliever Matt Mantei. Penny made his organizational debut with the Sea Dogs on a rainy Sunday afternoon in early August. After a lengthy rain delay, Penny (six innings) and teammate Luis Arroyo (three innings) combined to pitch the first no-hitter in franchise history in 1999. (Photograph by Stewart Smith.)

Julio Ramirez left the opposition behind while etching his name into the Sea Dogs record book in 1999. Ramirez stole 64 bases, best in the Eastern League. Ramirez established a new single-season high, surpassing the record set by Luis Castillo (51 stolen bases) in 1996. Currently second in franchise history, Ramirez is two behind Pablo Ozuna (66) for the most stolen bases by a Sea Dog. (Photograph by Stewart Smith.)

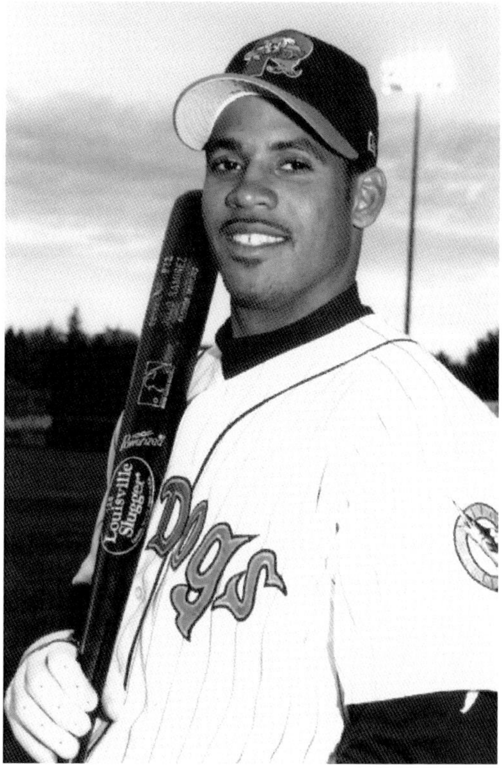

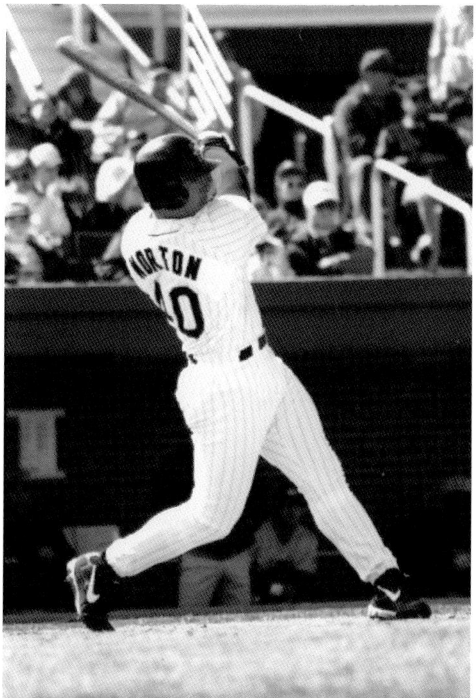

Power hitter Chris Norton constantly brought Portland Sea Dogs fans to their feet in 1999. Fans eagerly followed every long fly ball hit, hopefully into the stands. Norton belted out a team record and a league-high 38 homers in 1999. His 38 homers are 3 short of the all-time Eastern League record of 41, held by Ken Strong (1930) and Rick Lancellotti (1979). (Photograph by Stewart Smith.)

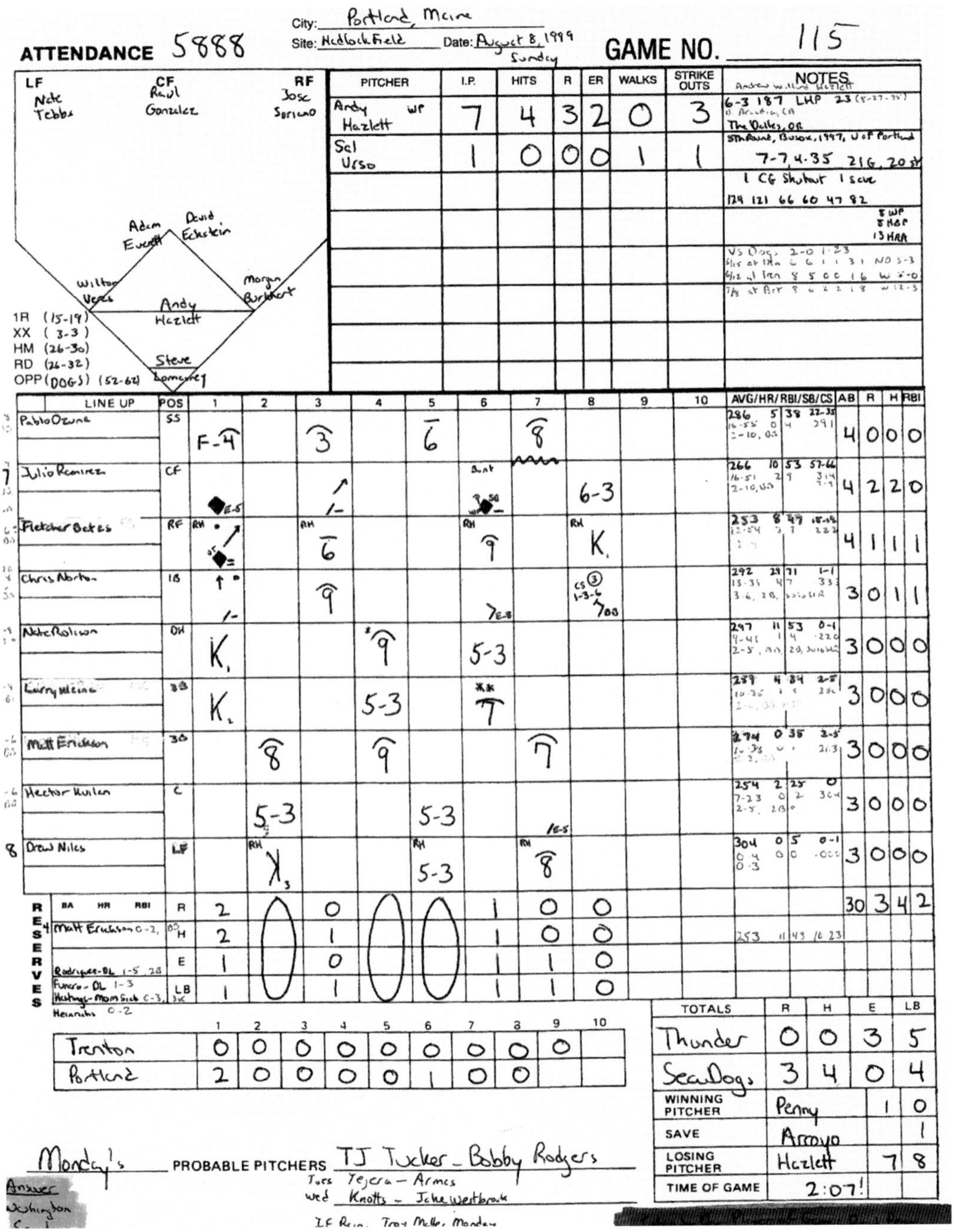

Sunday, August 8, 1999, was a rainy day in Portland. Over at Hadlock Field, newly acquired pitcher Brad Penny waited for the heavy rains to stop so he could make his organizational debut.

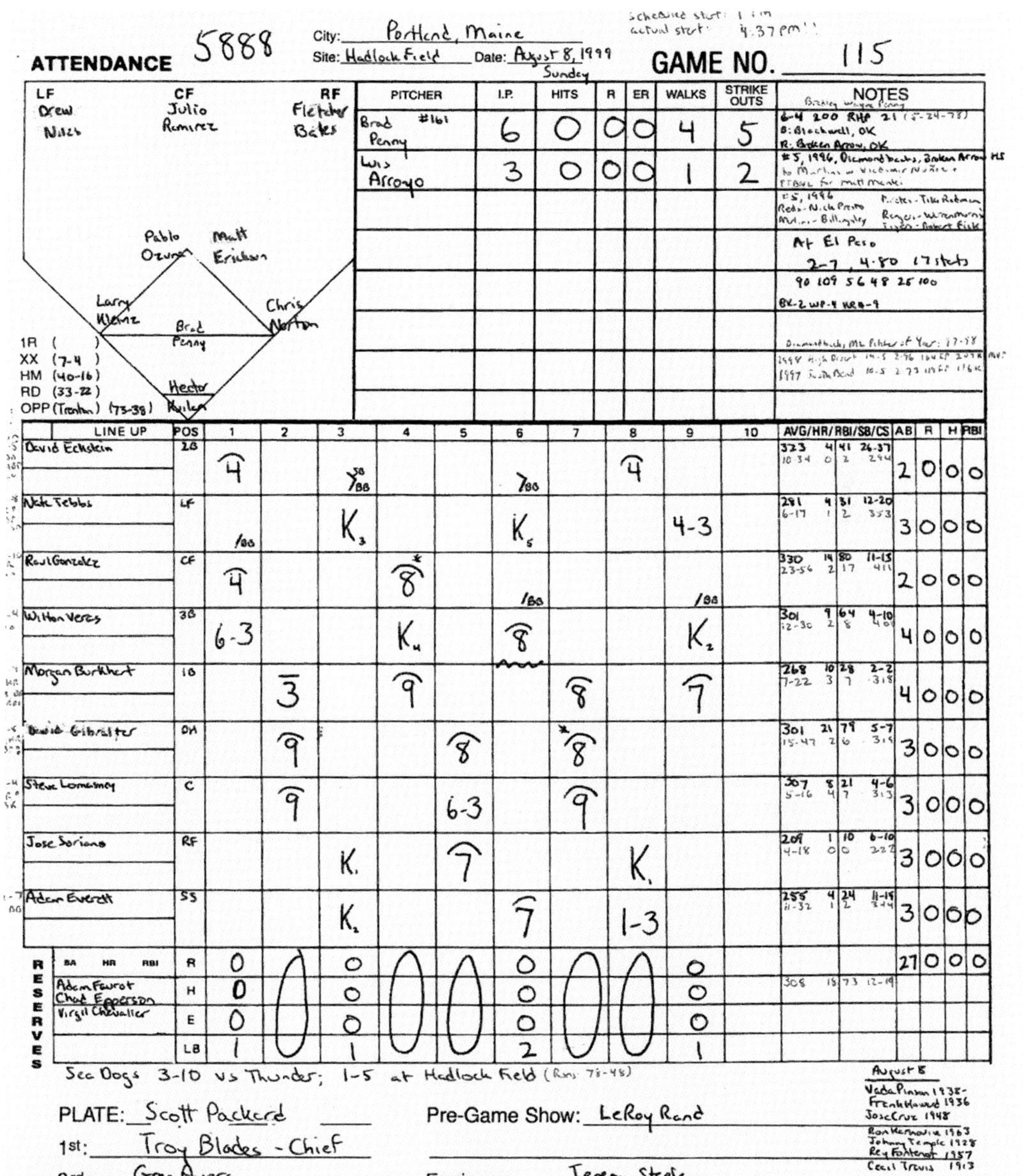

ATTENDANCE 5888

City: Portland, Maine

Site: Hadlock Field Date: August 8, 1999 Sunday

GAME NO. 115

PITCHER	I.P.	HITS	R	ER	WALKS	STRIKE OUTS
Brad Penny #161	6	0	0	0	4	5
Luis Arroyo	3	0	0	0	1	2

LINE UP	POS	1	2	3	4	5	6	7	8	9	10	AB	R	H	RBI
David Eckstein	2B	4		BB			BB		4			2	0	0	0
Nate Tebbs	LF	BB		K			K			4-3		3	0	0	0
Raul Gonzalez	CF	4			8		BB			BB		2	0	0	0
Wilton Veras	3B	6-3			K		8			K		4	0	0	0
Morgan Burkhart	1B		3		9			8		7		4	0	0	0
David Gibralter	DH		9			8		8				3	0	0	0
Steve Lomasney	C		9			6-3		9				3	0	0	0
Jose Soriano	RF			K		7			K			3	0	0	0
Adam Everett	SS			K			7		1-3			3	0	0	0
R		0		0			0			0		27	0	0	0
H		0		0			0			0					
E		0		0			0			0					
LB		1		1			2			1					

Sea Dogs 3-10 vs Thunder; 1-5 at Hadlock Field

PLATE: Scott Packard

1st: Troy Blades - Chief

3rd: Greg Ayers

Pre-Game Show: LeRoy Rand

Engineer: Jeremy Steele

TRIVIA Which major league team hired Ted Williams to be their manager in 1969?

After a delay of 3 hours and 37 minutes, the rains departed and, unfortunately, so did many fans. Those fans could only shake their heads and say "no-no" the next morning while reading their *Portland Press Herald*. After the heavy rains had come and gone, Penny and reliever Luis Arroyo combined to pitch the first no-hitter in franchise history. (Courtesy of Andy Young.)

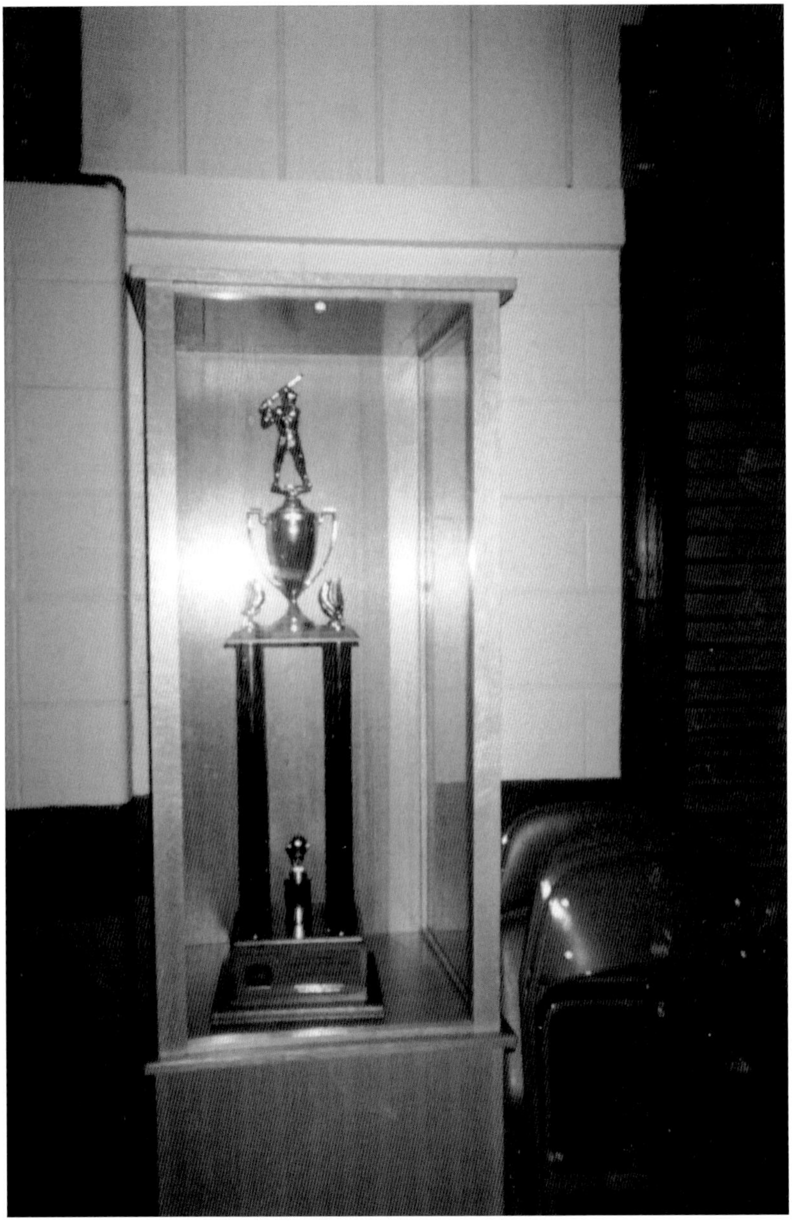

At the annual Baseball Winter Meetings, the renowned baseball magazine *Baseball America* selected the Portland Sea Dogs as the 1999 winner of the Bob Freitas Award at the Double-A level. Bestowed annually since 1989, the Bob Freitas Award recognizes minor-league organizations that maintain excellence in all aspects of their baseball operations, both on and off the field. In their first season, the Sea Dogs set a new all-time Eastern League attendance record. In their first four seasons, the Sea Dogs won three Northern Division titles and advanced to the Eastern League Championship Series twice. An organization cannot be considered for the honors until after five seasons of operation. The Sea Dogs, who entered the Eastern League in 1994, won the award after their sixth season.

4

A New Century of Baseball (2000–2002)

The one constant through all the years, Ray, has been baseball. America has rolled by like an army of steamrollers. It has been erased like a blackboard, rebuilt and erased again. But baseball has marked the time. This field, this game: it's a part of our past. It reminds us of all that once was good and it could be again.

—Terrence Mann, *Field of Dreams*

The Sea Dogs began a new century of baseball with high hopes and expectations. With winning streaks of 11 and 10 games in April and August, respectively, and a losing streak of 7 games in July, the 2000 season was a streaky one for Portland. Before the season began, the Florida Marlins hired former player Rick Renteria to manage the team. On June 29, the Sea Dogs entertained the Florida Marlins in a special exhibition game held at Hadlock Field. The game, which brought many former Sea Dogs favorites and alumni back to Portland, highlighted the 2000 season.

During the off-season, the Sea Dogs lost a member of the family. Bob Ganley, instrumental in professional baseball's return to Portland, passed away.

Future major-league pitching sensation Josh Beckett made his Double-A debut in 2001. By the end of the 2001 season, more than three million fans had taken in a game at Hadlock Field since 1994.

In 2002, the Sea Dogs, playing under new skipper Eric Fox, tied the Trenton Thunder for last place.

However, the winds of change were about to sweep through Portland.

Eastern League Players of the Week in this era included Cesar Crespo, Wynter Phoenix, Quincy Foster, and Jesus Medrano. Eastern League Pitchers of the Week included Claudio Vargas, Kevin Olsen, Josh Beckett, Hansel Izquierdo, and Justin Wayne. Eastern League Players of the Month included Cesar Crespo and Josh Beckett. Beckett also earned Topps Minor League Player of the Month honors. The John H. Johnson Award went to the Portland Sea Dogs.

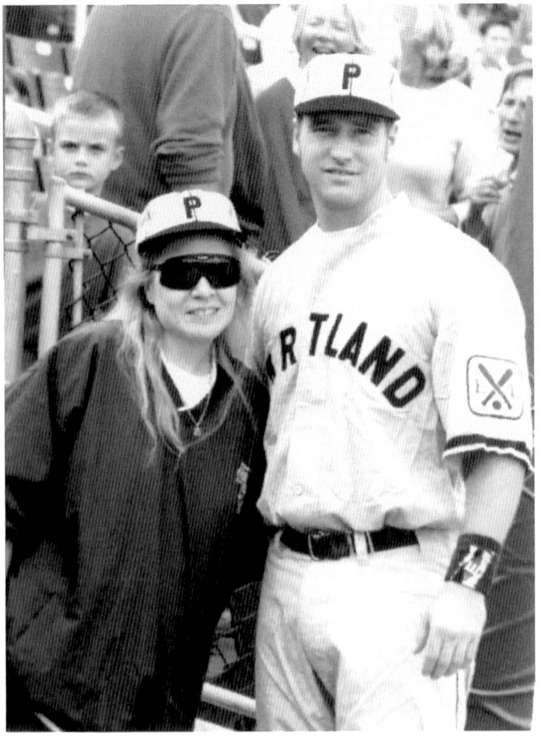

For Todd Betts, his journey to Portland was a long (and scenic) one. After spring training concluded in Melbourne, Florida, the Marlins sent Betts to Calgary, the Marlins' Triple-A affiliate in Canada. After one game, the Marlins sent Betts down again—to Portland. Betts drove 4,000 miles from Alberta to Maine. In his first game, Betts hit a dramatic extra-inning, game-winning home run over Trenton.

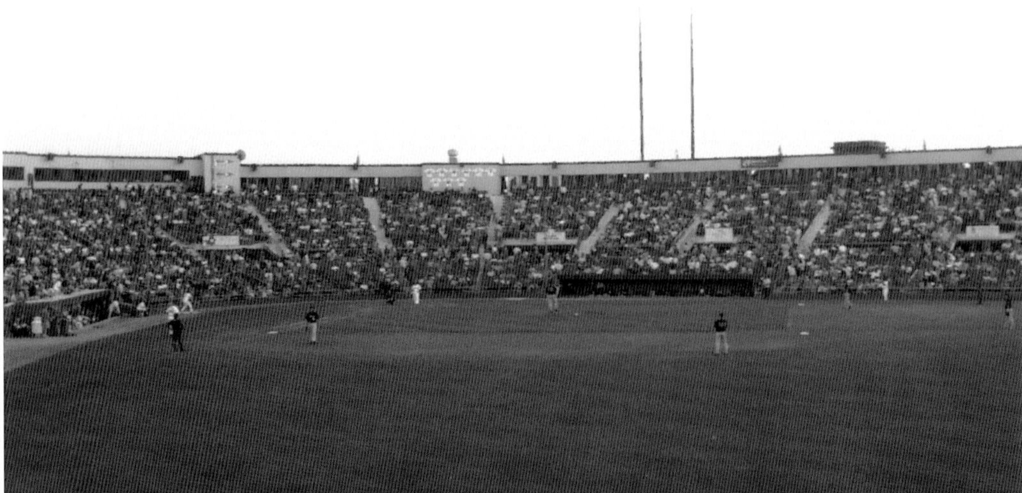

The Portland Sea Dogs received the John H. Johnson Award, minor-league baseball's top honor, in 2000. The award recognizes minor-league baseball's most "complete franchise." Selection factors include stability, contributions to the league and to baseball in the community, and promotion of the baseball industry. (Courtesy of the Sea Dogs.)

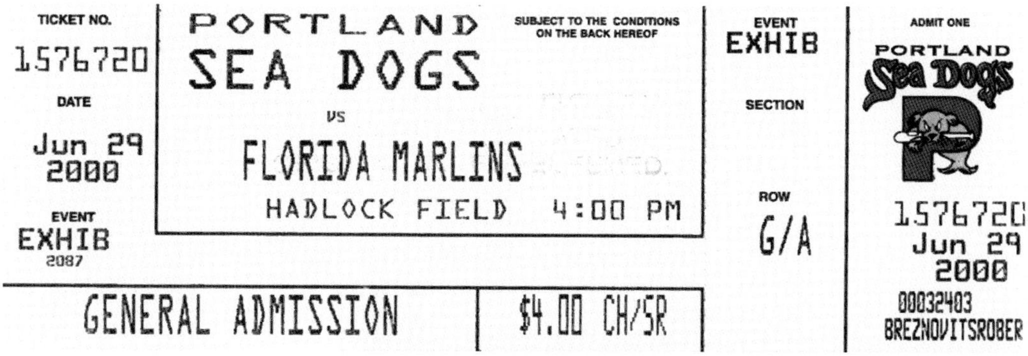

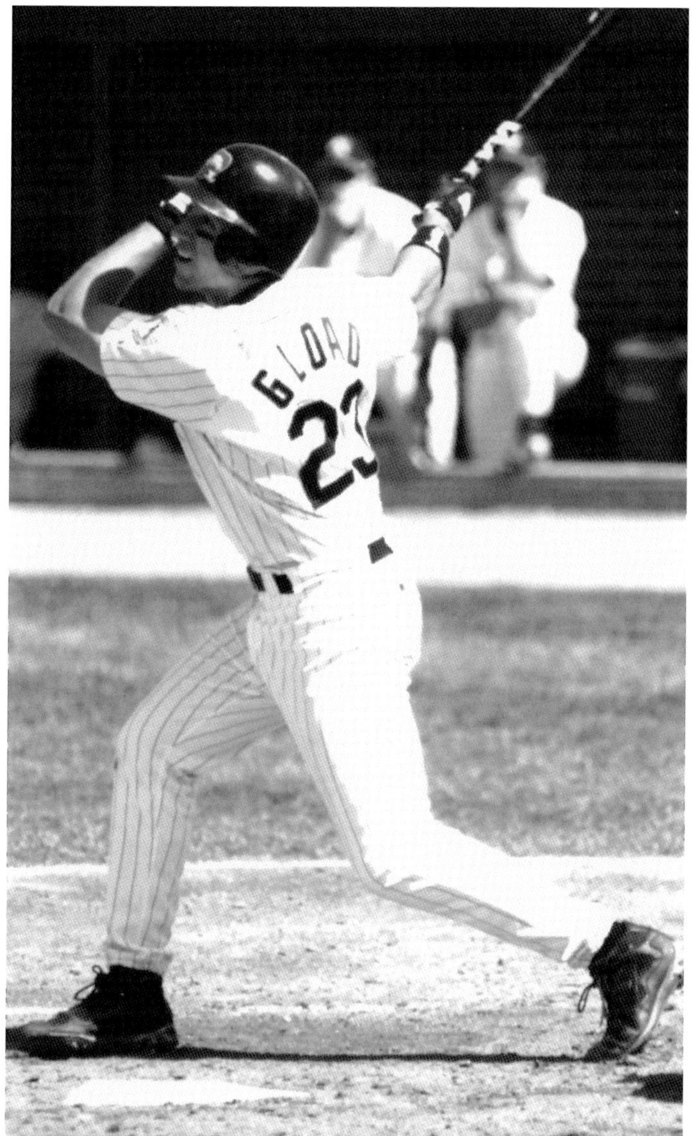

On June 29, 2000, the Sea Dogs hosted a special exhibition game against their major-league affiliate, the Florida Marlins, at Hadlock Field. In front of 6,910 fans, the Sea Dogs defeated the Marlins 9-2. Gary Knotts beat former teammate A. J. Burnett. Ross Gload (right) hit for the cycle and won Player of the Game honors. Part of the pregame festivities included a home run derby. The Marlins' lineup included Cliff Floyd, Preston Wilson, hall of famer Tony Perez, 1987 National League home run king Andre Dawson, and fan favorite Kevin Millar. The Sea Dogs countered with Heath Honeycutt, Ross Gload, Chris Norton, hitting coach Jose Castro, and skipper Rick Renteria. Renteria, known for hitting in the clutch during his playing days, hit five home runs in the Sea Dogs' final at bat, lifting the Sea Dogs to victory 17-16. (Photograph by Stewart Smith.)

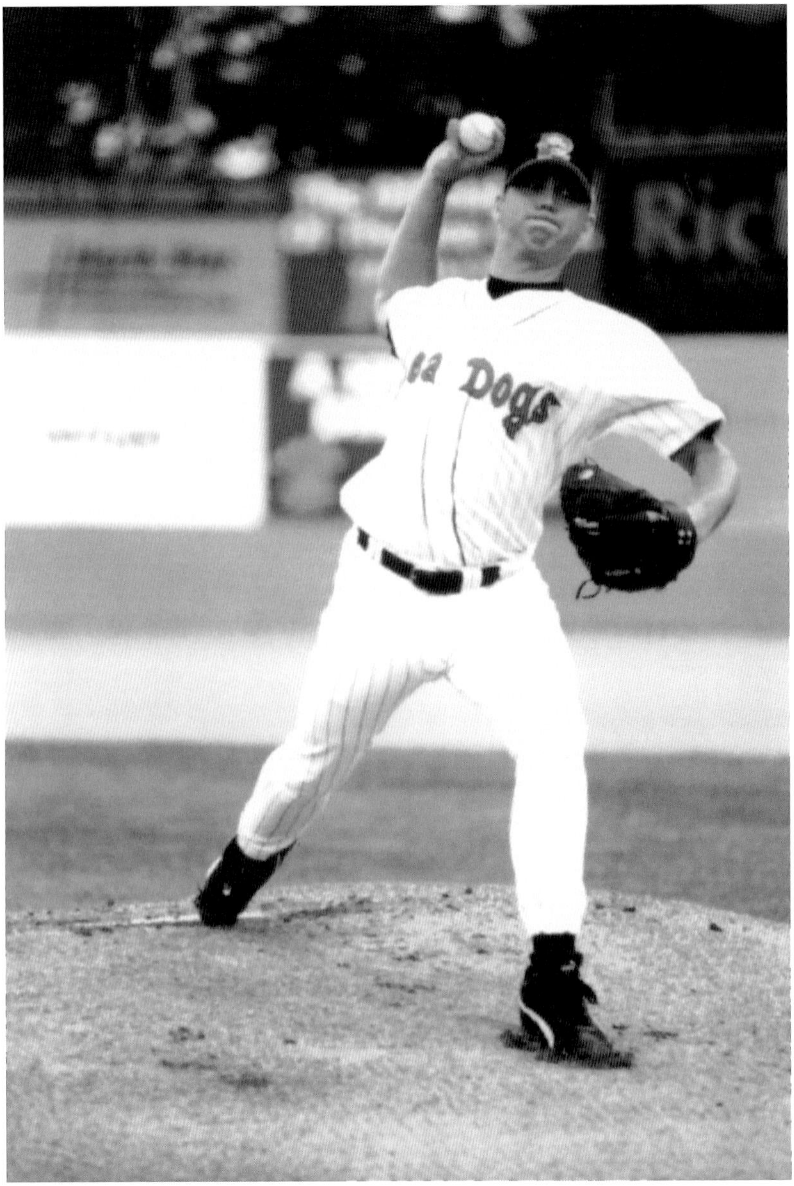

In June 2001, right-handed pitcher Josh Beckett made his Double-A debut with the Portland Sea Dogs. In front of a capacity crowd, which included Florida Marlins owner John Henry, Beckett overpowered the first nine batters he faced, striking out eight. Two months later, on August 13, Beckett (seven innings) and Brandon Bowe and Aaron Scheffer (one inning each) combined to toss the second no-hitter in franchise history, defeating the Binghamton Mets. A future World Series MVP, Beckett was the recipient of many awards and honors during and after the season. These awards and honors included Eastern League Pitcher of the Week and Month, Topps Minor League Player of the Month, and Sportsticker Minor League Pitcher of the Year. *Baseball America*, *USA Today*, the *Sporting News*, and Topps all named Beckett as their Minor League Player of the Year. (Photograph by Stewart Smith.)

5

Slugger Changes His Sox (2003–2004)

The Voice is back.
Oh, Lord. You're supposed to build a football field now?
—Ray and Annie Kinsella, *Field of Dreams*

After one of the worst seasons in Sea Dogs history concluded, the front office conducted a press conference to make a major announcement. Together since both their inceptions, the Portland Sea Dogs and Florida Marlins were parting ways. The 2002 season had been the Sea Dogs' final one affiliated with the Marlins. Despite losing their parent organization, the Sea Dogs would not stay orphans for long.

In Boston, the Red Sox announced they had severed ties with their Double-A affiliate, the Trenton Thunder. Portland and Boston held a press conference and ended months of speculation. They inked a new affiliation agreement with each other.

Over the next few months, a flurry of excitement and activity fell over Portland and Hadlock Field. At Hadlock Field, major renovations were underway in anticipation of opening day. The Slugger statue also underwent renovation, which included a new paint job in Red Sox colors.

Becoming Boston's affiliate was huge for the Sea Dogs organization and the Portland economy. With three Red Sox affiliates now in New England (Triple A in Pawtucket, Rhode Island; Double A in Portland; and Single A in Lowell, Massachusetts), fans could have the ultimate Red Sox summer vacation.

Portland established a new attendance record as 434,684 fans came out to see the Sea Dogs play ball in 2004, including the four-millionth fan in April. Despite a roster of new players, the Sea Dogs finished the next two seasons in third (2003) and fourth (2004) place.

Eastern League Players of the Week in this era included Jeremy Owens and John Hattig. Eastern League Pitchers of the Week included Chris Smith and Kason Gabbard. The Major League Baseball World Series MVP in 2003 was Josh Beckett.

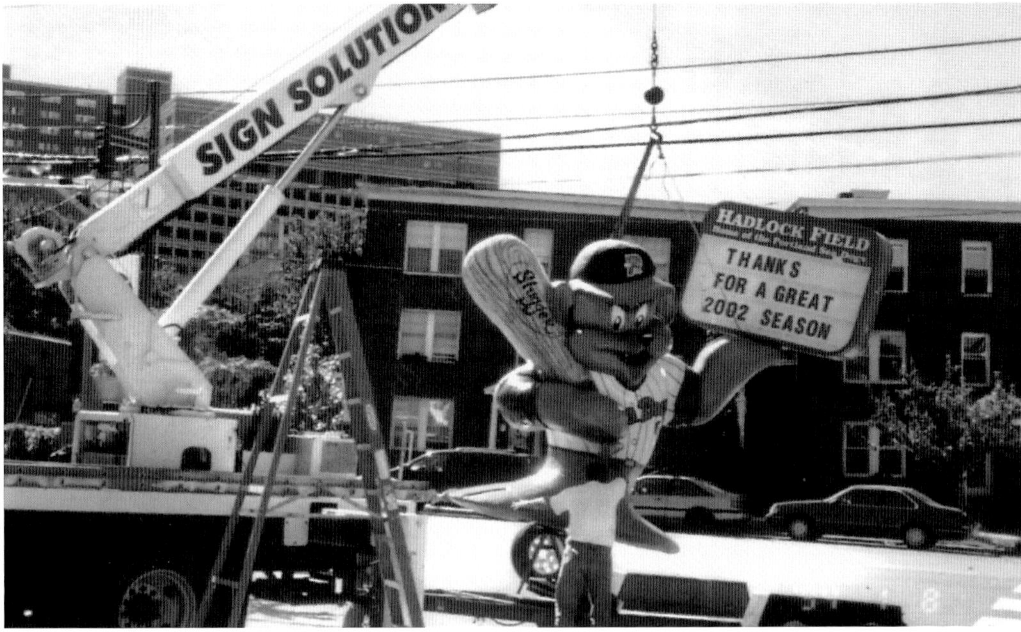

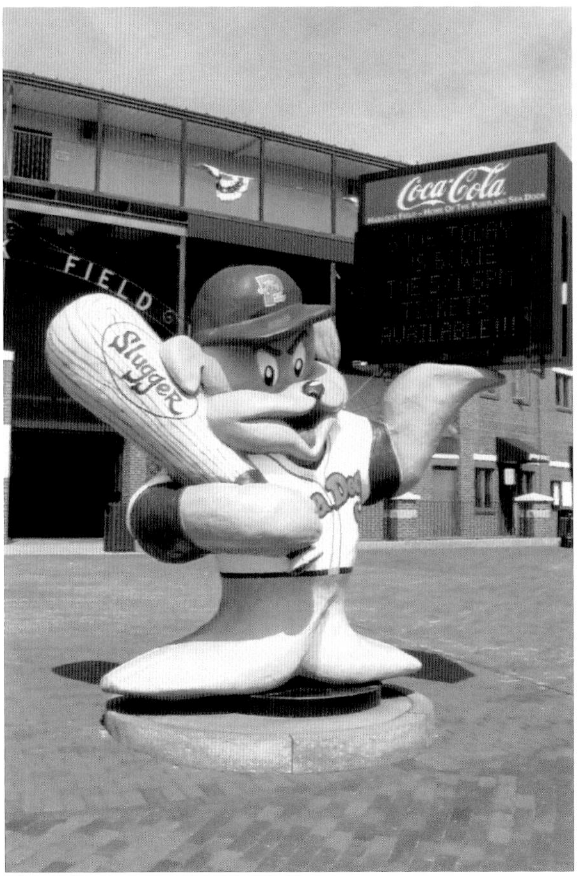

The Portland Sea Dogs announced at the end of the 2002 season that the Sea Dogs and the Florida Marlins, together since both their inceptions, were parting ways. After nine seasons, the Sea Dogs inked a new affiliation agreement with the Boston Red Sox. To celebrate the event, team colors switched from teal and black to Red Sox blue and red. The change in team colors was just the beginning. Over the next few months, a flurry of excitement and activity fell over Hadlock Field. Major renovations were underway in anticipation of opening day. The organization renamed all its skyboxes after Boston Red Sox greats. Former players who had boxes named after them included Dwight Evans, Carlton Fisk, Carl Yastrzemski, and Ted Williams. The Slugger statue also underwent renovation, including a new paint job in Red Sox colors. (Above, courtesy of the Sea Dogs.)

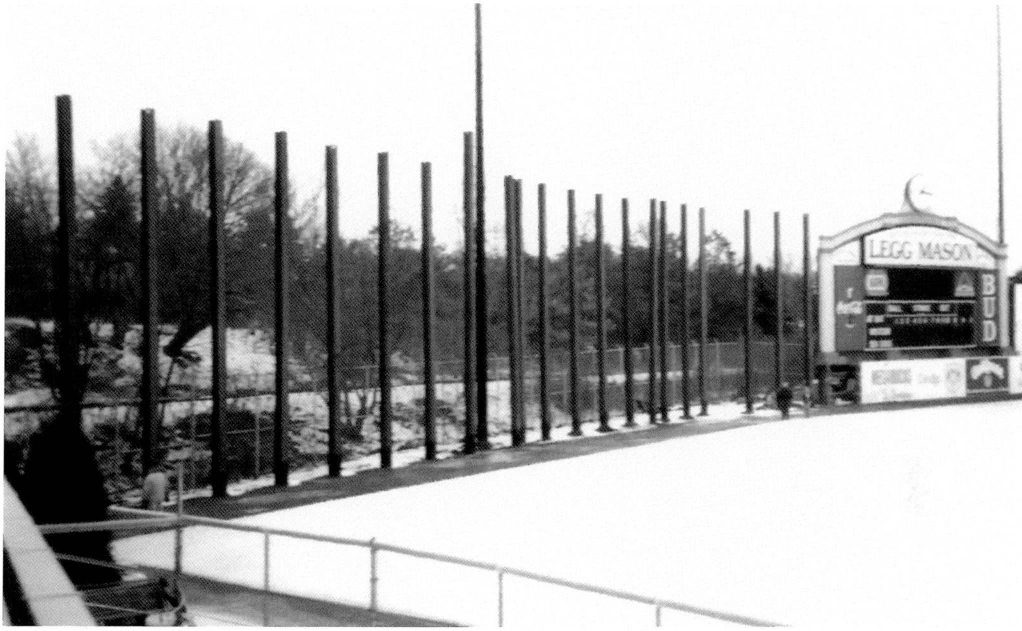

Not long after the Portland Sea Dogs announced their new affiliation agreement with the Boston Red Sox, Sea Dogs owner Dan Burke made one of his own. Burke wanted to do something special to commemorate the Sea Dogs and Red Sox becoming affiliation partners. Burke funded the construction of a large green left field wall resembling the Green Monster at Fenway Park. Construction on the wall began almost immediately. However, because of the railroad track that runs right behind it, the Sea Dogs cannot build additional seating atop the wall like the monster seats in Boston. (Courtesy of Joel Marsden.)

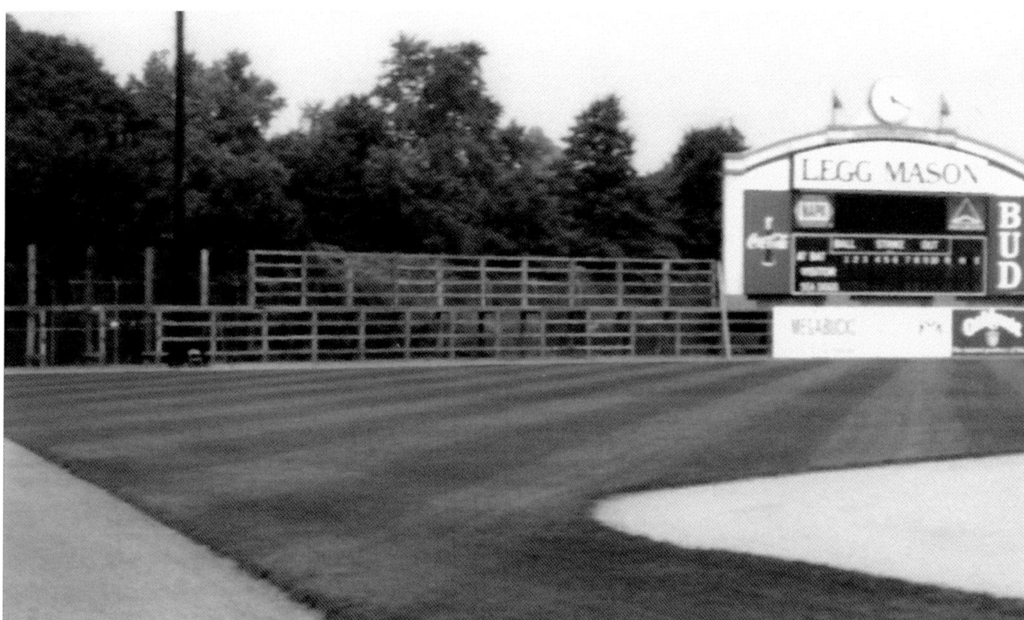

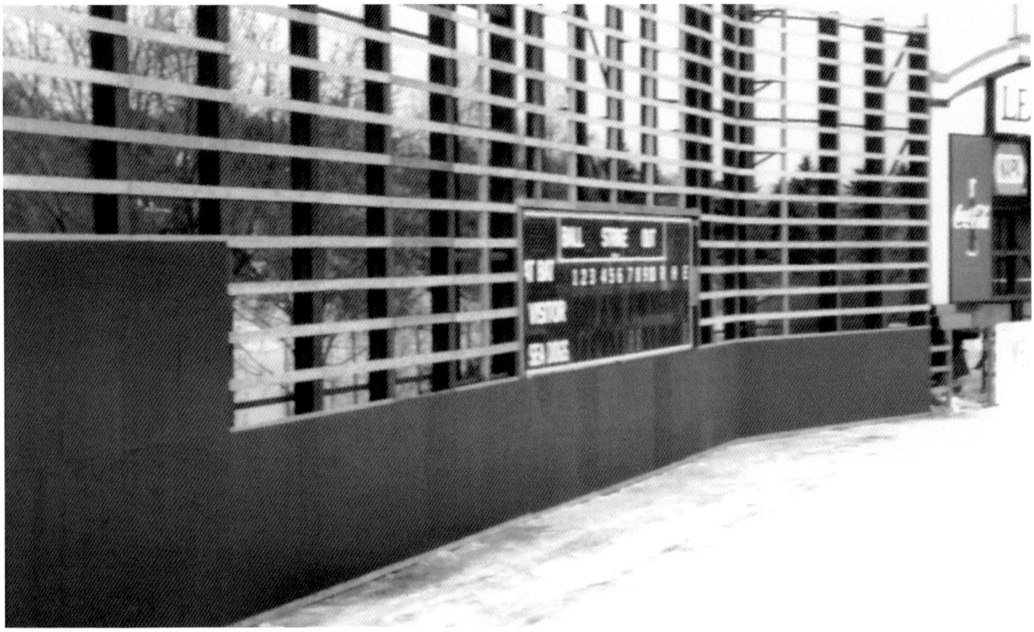

Unlike its Bostonian twin, the Sea Dogs' wall was constructed from wood, as opposed to Fenway Park's hard plastic. Although both walls are green, only upon closer inspection does one notice that Portland's wall is much darker. Also differing from the Green Monster is the scoreboard. The Green Monster's scoreboard operates manually and from inside the wall. Portland's operates electronically. An astute eye will notice along both sides of the scoreboard are the initials of both Dan Burke and his wife in Morse code. This is just like the Green Monster at Fenway. Along its scoreboard are the Morse code initials of former Boston Red Sox owner Tom Yawkey and his wife. (Courtesy of Joel Marsden.)

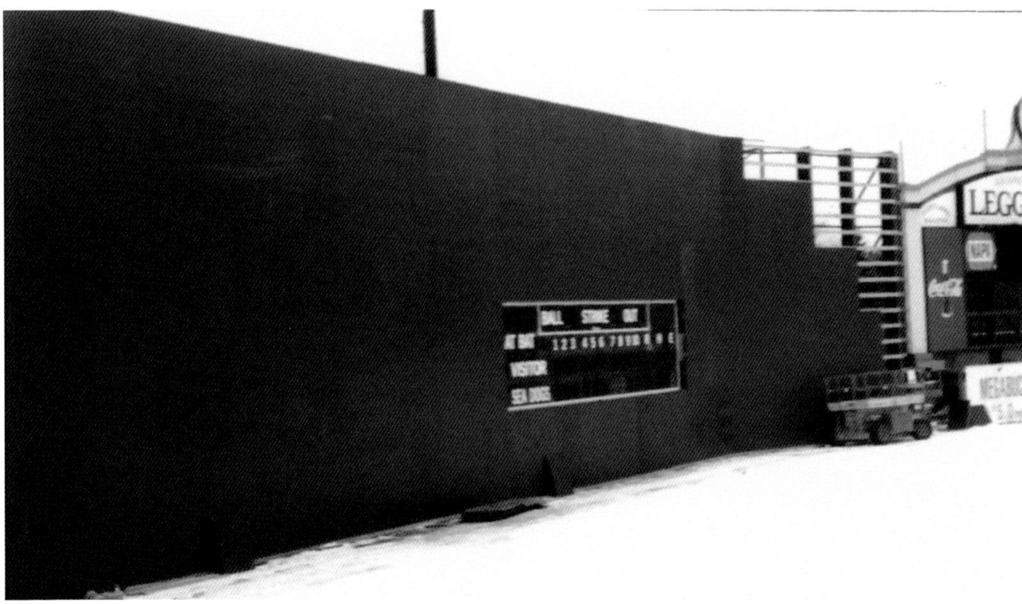

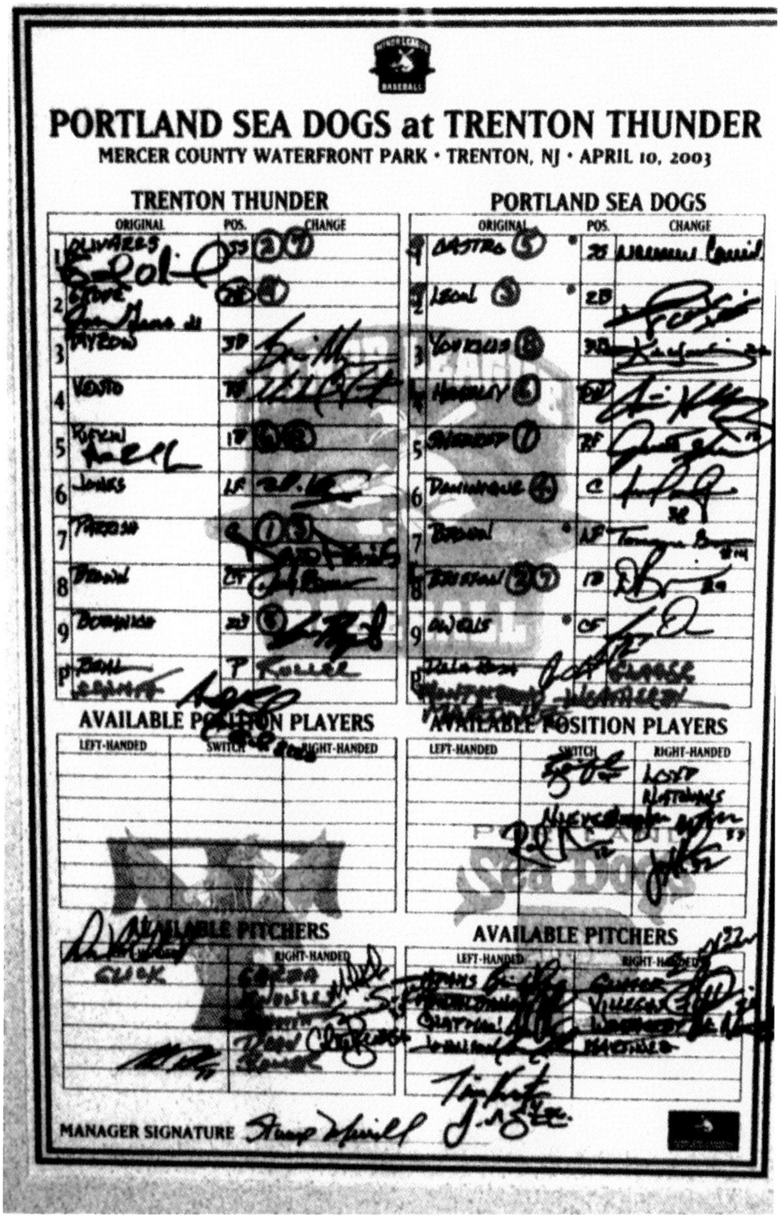

The winter of 2002–2003 was exciting but long for the Portland Sea Dogs organization and fans of the Sea Dogs. Both the fans and the organization eagerly counted down the days until opening day and the Sea Dogs played their first game as a Boston Red Sox affiliate. April and opening day finally arrived. Unfortunately, Mother Nature was not a fan. The Eastern League postponed the entire first week of the 2003 season because of snow. The Sea Dogs finally took the field in, ironically of all places, Trenton, New Jersey, former home of Boston's Eastern League affiliate, the Trenton Thunder. The starting lineup for Portland included future Red Sox star Kevin Youkilis making his debut with the Sea Dogs at third base. Portland lost to the New York Yankees' new affiliate 4-1. (Courtesy of Melanie Aber.)

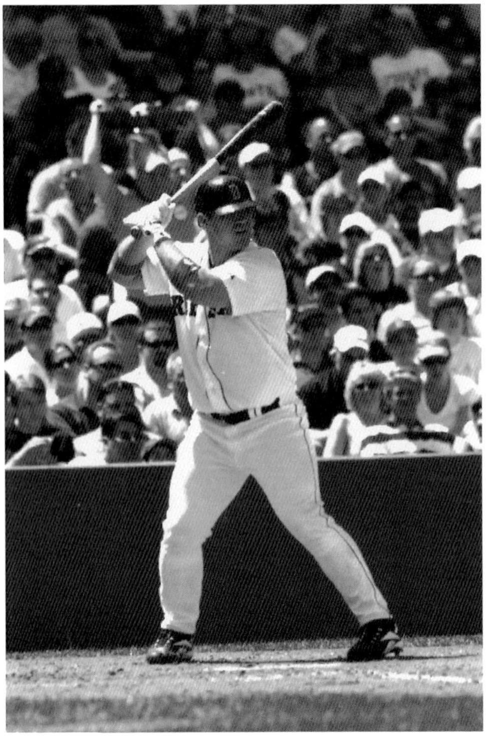

Kelly Shoppach was a top prospect in the Red Sox organization before being traded to Cleveland in the deal that brought Coco Crisp to Boston. Shoulder surgery limited Shoppach to only 92 games; however, he batted .282 with 12 homers and drove in 60. Nicknamed "Shop Vac" for his abilities behind the plate, Eastern League managers selected Shoppach as Best Defensive Catcher for 2003. (Courtesy of Brian Babineau, Boston Red Sox.)

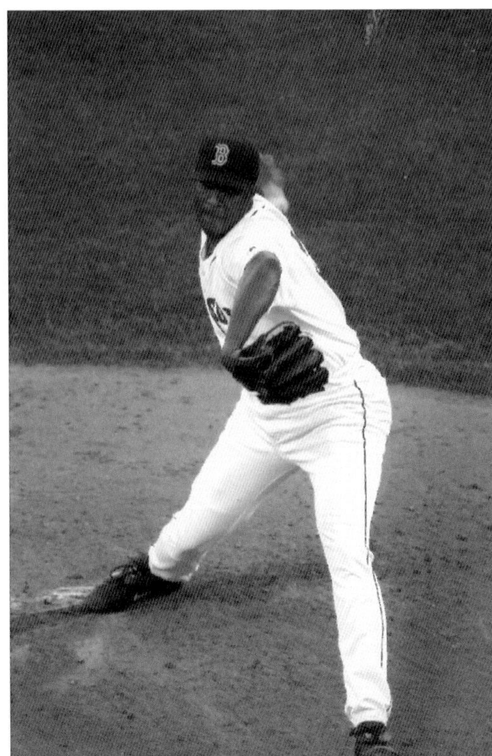

Veteran pitcher Pedro Astacio made his big-league debut in 1992 with the Los Angeles Dodgers. Since then, the well-traveled pitcher has pitched for the Colorado Rockies (1997–2001), Houston Astros (2001), New York Mets (2002–2003), Boston Red Sox (including a stint with the Sea Dogs, 2004), Texas Rangers (2005), San Diego Padres (2005), and the Washington Nationals (2006). (Courtesy of Steve Babineau, Boston Red Sox.)

In only a brief tour of duty with the Portland Sea Dogs, Red Sox farmhand Anastacio Martinez went 3-1 with a 2.25 ERA. In 34 appearances with Portland (all in relief), Martinez recorded a team-high 14 saves prior to his trade to the Pittsburgh Pirates on July 22. A week later, the Pirates traded Martinez back to Boston. (Courtesy of Steve Babineau, Boston Red Sox.)

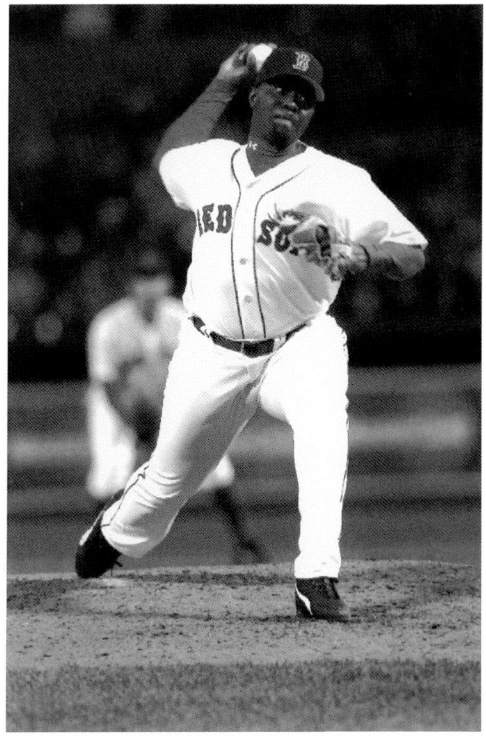

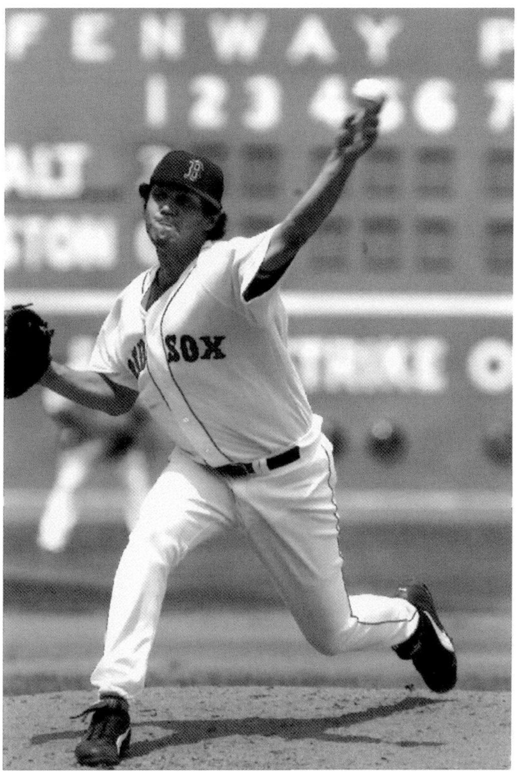

His tilting cap caused unknowing others to assume it must be a fashion statement. Abe Alvarez developed an infection in his left eye as an infant. When prescribed drops did not work, doctors prescribed a more aggressive prescription with a serious warning—it could cause blindness. Today the legally blind left-hander tips his cap to the side to balance the lighting in his blind eye. (Courtesy of Julie Cordiero, Boston Red Sox.)

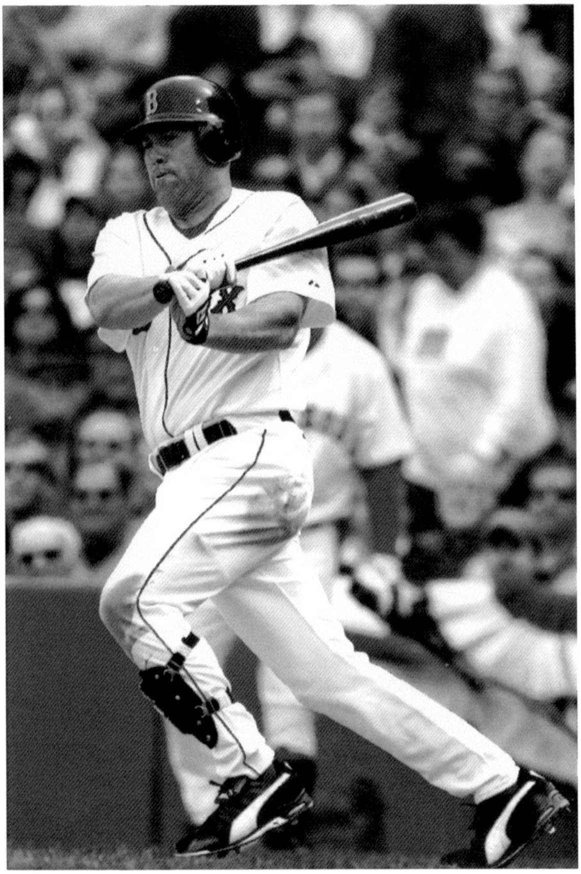

Kevin Youkilis was batting .327 with six home runs and 37 RBIs in 94 games with Portland when he received a promotion to Triple-A Pawtucket in late July. His .327 batting average is second-best all-time, and his .487 on-base percentage is best in franchise history. Additionally, Youkilis scored a run in eight consecutive games, crossing home plate 12 times during the streak. A Cape Cod League veteran, Youkilis is a fan favorite with the Sea Dogs. Below, the Cincinnati, Ohio, native takes time out to sign autographs for his fans. (Left, courtesy of Brita Meng Outzen, Boston Red Sox; below courtesy of the Sea Dogs.)

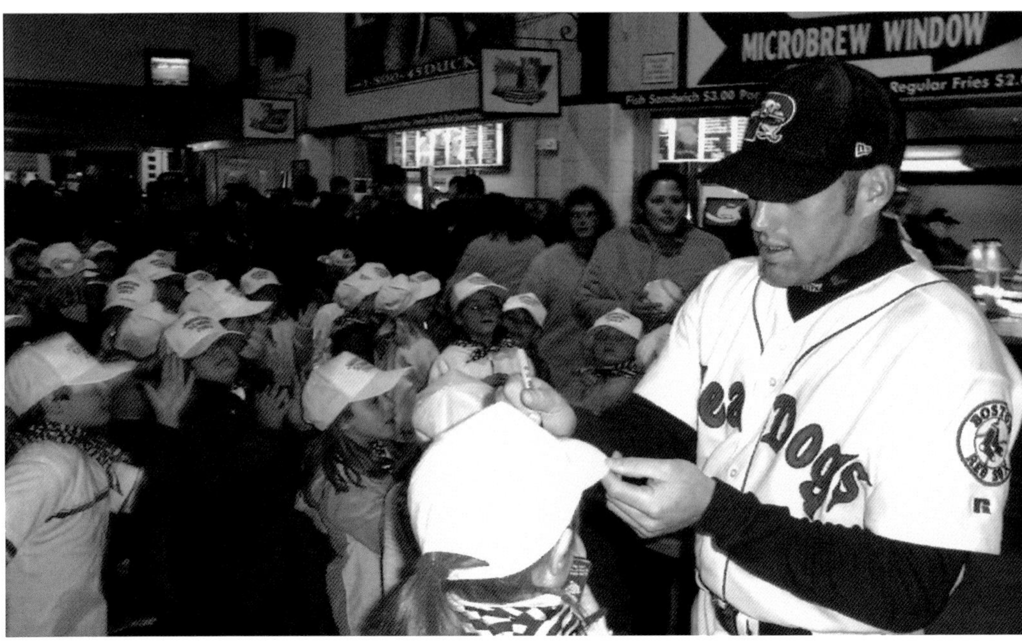

The Boston Red Sox promoted their top prospect shortstop Hanley Ramirez to the Sea Dogs in early August 2004. The highly anticipated Ramirez did not disappoint the organization or the fans. Ramirez batted .310, hit 5 home runs, and drove in 15 runs in only 32 games for the Sea Dogs. Additionally, Ramirez hit seven doubles and two triples and posted a .512 slugging and a .360 on-base percentage. The speedy 20-year-old also stole 12 bases. A major-league star in the making, Ramirez slides safely into third base during a game at Hadlock Field in 2004. (Right, courtesy of the Sea Dogs; below, courtesy of Melanie Aber.)

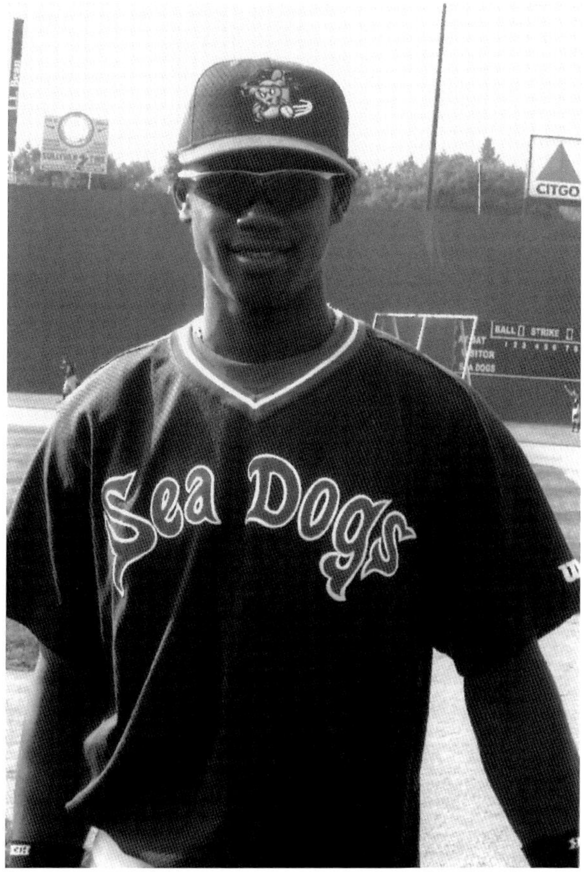

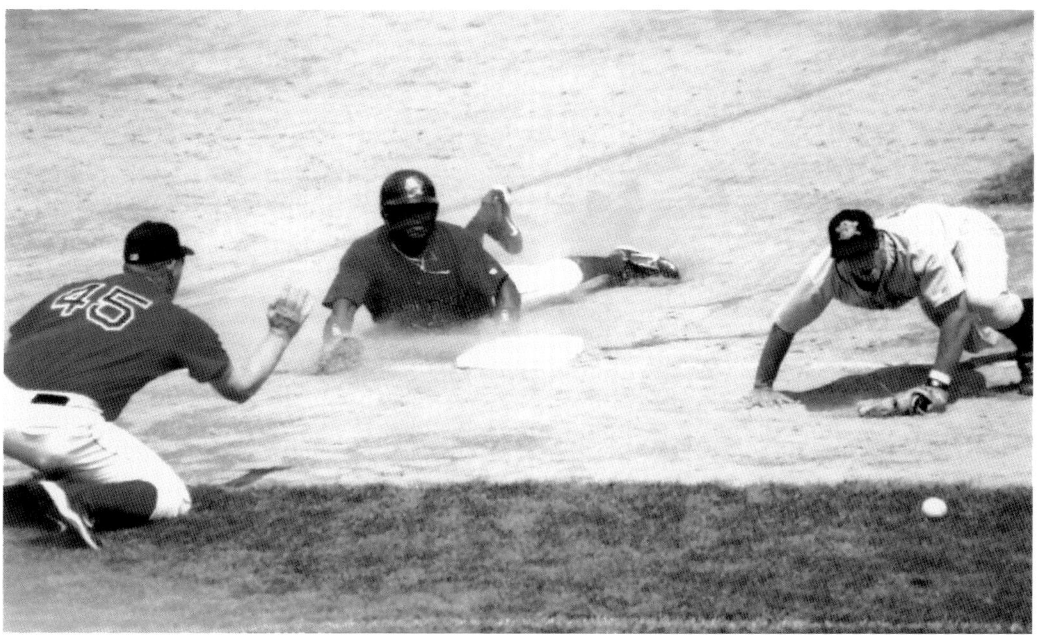

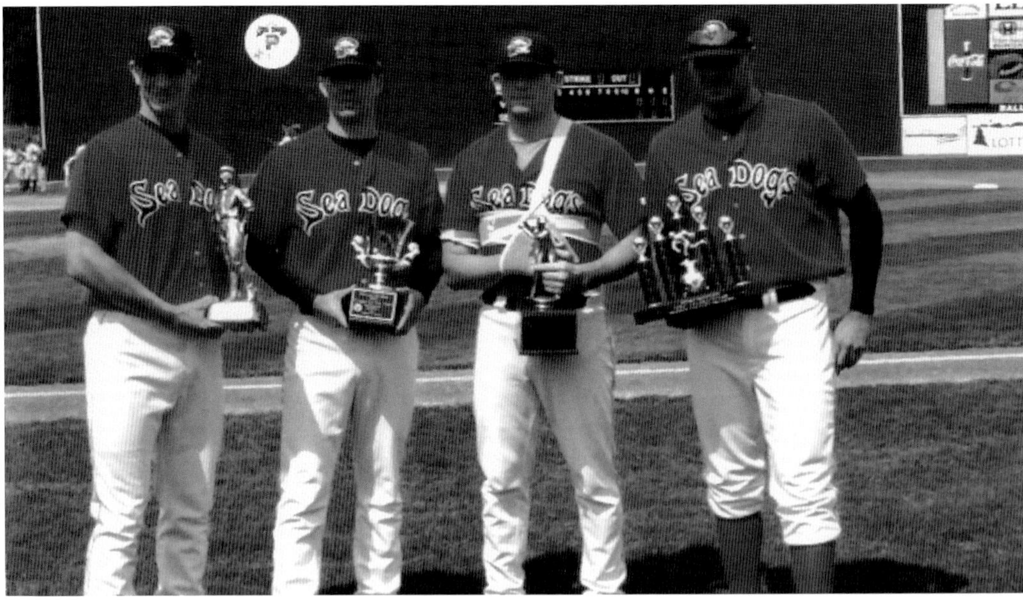

Although the organization selected the nominees, the fans of the Sea Dogs chose the winners of the annual Sea Dogs Team Awards. The 2003 season was the first opportunity for fans to vote on future Red Sox players. The 2003 winners are, from left to right, Jeremy Owens (MVP), James Johnson (Citizen of the Year), John Nathans (Tenth Player), and Josh Stevens (Pitcher of the Year). (Courtesy of the Sea Dogs.)

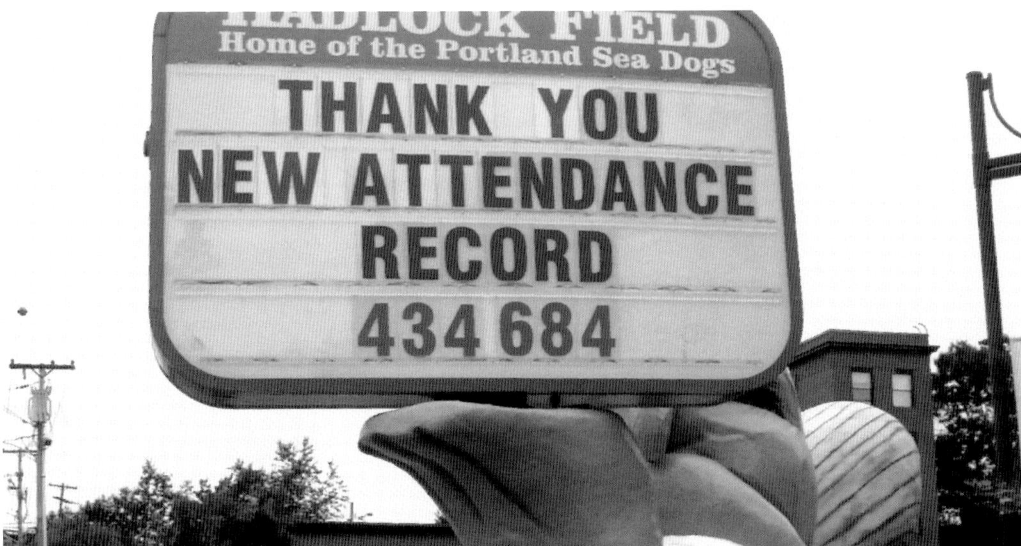

A few days before the start of the 2004 season, the Sea Dogs announced that preseason ticket sales were at an all-time high, reaching 250,000. At the end of April, the Sea Dogs welcomed their four-millionth fan in franchise history through the turnstiles. By season's end, the Sea Dogs broke their all-time attendance record as 434,684 fans come to Hadlock Field in 2004. (Courtesy of the Sea Dogs.)

6

Magic in the Moonlight (2005–2006)

That's my wish, Ray Kinsella. Is there enough magic out there in the moonlight to make this dream come true?
—Dr. Archibald "Moonlight" Graham, *Field of Dreams*

The stars in Portland twinkled a little brighter on July 13, 2005, when the Portland Sea Dogs and Hadlock Field hosted the 2005 Eastern League All-Star Game. The Sea Dogs coaching staff, led by Todd Claus, managed the Northern Division squad, which included a record seven Sea Dogs, to victory. Portland's all-stars lineup included Chris Durbin, Jon Lester, Brandon Moss, Jonathan Papelbon, Kenny Perez, Hanley Ramirez, and Jared Sandberg.

In September 2005, glory days returned to Portland.

The Sea Dogs reclaimed the Northern Division title and qualified for the playoffs for the first time in eight years. Again the Sea Dogs advanced but lost the Eastern League Championship Series.

In July 2006, the Sea Dogs welcomed their five-millionth fan in franchise history to Hadlock Field. The Sea Dogs were on pace to set another attendance record. By season's close, the Sea Dogs averaged a team record 6,358 fans per game.

On September 17, 2006, despite a second-place finish, the Portland Sea Dogs captured their first Eastern League championship. In a reverse of the previous season's championship series, Portland defeated the Akron Aeros, three games to two. It was Maine's first professional baseball championship in 91 years.

Eastern League Players of the Week from this era included Jared Sandberg, Brandon Moss, Chad Spann, and Jacoby Ellsbury. Eastern League Pitchers of the Week included David Pauley, Jonathan Papelbon, Jon Lester, Kason Gabbard, Phil Seibel, and Tommy Hottovy. Other Sea Dogs to earn honors during this period were Jon Lester (Eastern League Pitcher of the Year), Todd Claus (*Baseball America*'s Manager of the Year), and Hanley Ramirez (National League Rookie of the Year).

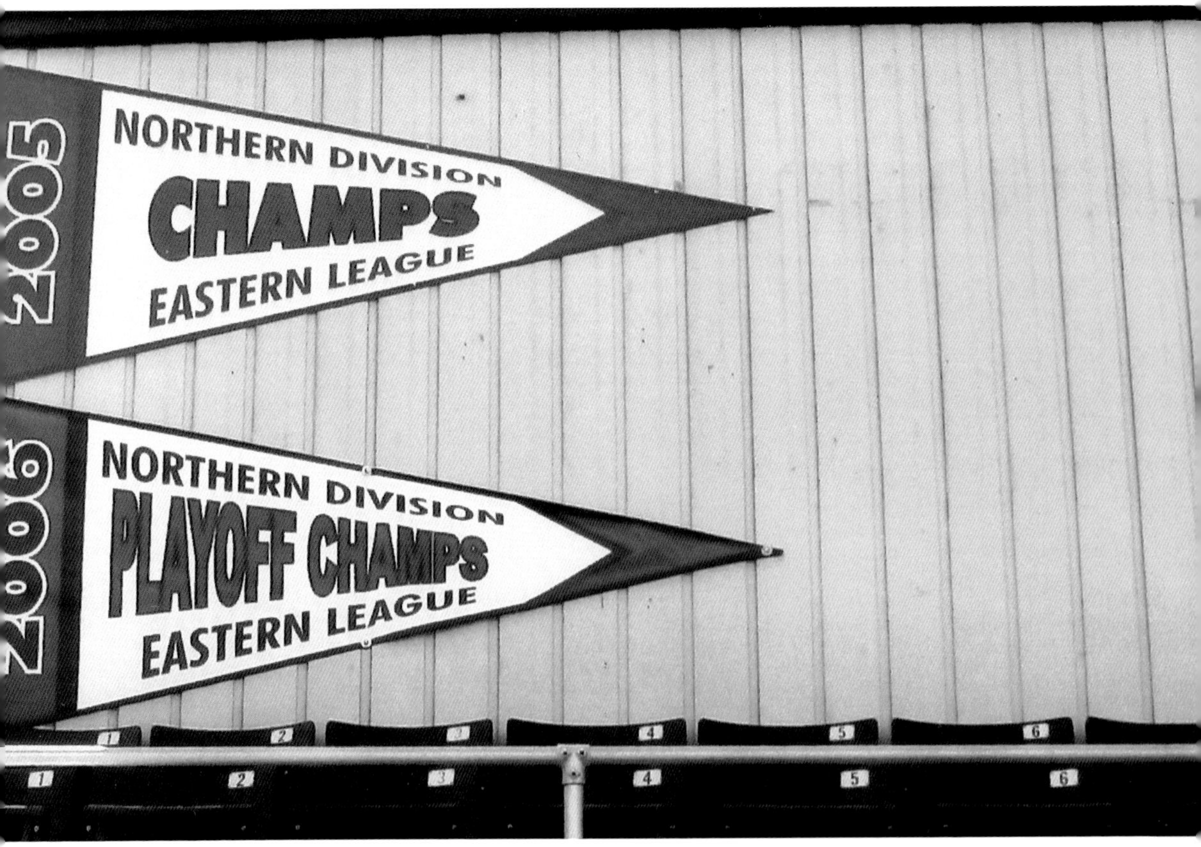

The 2005 Sea Dogs, playing under new manager Todd Claus, finished the season with a 76-66 record and reclaimed first place in the Northern Division after an eight-year absence. Portland defeated the Trenton Thunder three games to two, advancing to the Eastern League Championship Series. The Akron Aeros, winners of the Southern Division, defeated the Sea Dogs three games to one. The 2006 Sea Dogs finished the season with a 72-67 record and finished in second place. In a repeat of the 2005 postseason, the Sea Dogs defeated the Trenton Thunder in the first round to advance to the Eastern League Championship Series versus Akron. The Sea Dogs and Aeros again competed for the Eastern League title. On September 17, 2006, the Sea Dogs defeated the Aeros three games to two and captured their first Eastern League championship. It was Maine's first professional baseball championship in more than 90 years.

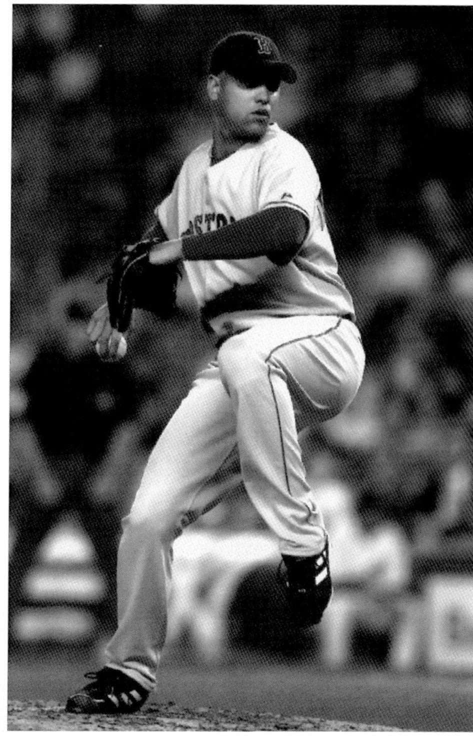

Boston native Manny Delcarmen, a graduate of West Roxbury High School, was a second-round draft pick by the Boston Red Sox in 2000. Delcarmen was the first draftee from a Boston public high school in more than 30 years. Five years after graduation, Delcarmen, the salutatorian of his graduating class, made his major-league debut for his hometown team on July 27, 2005. (Courtesy of Julie Cordiero, Boston Red Sox.)

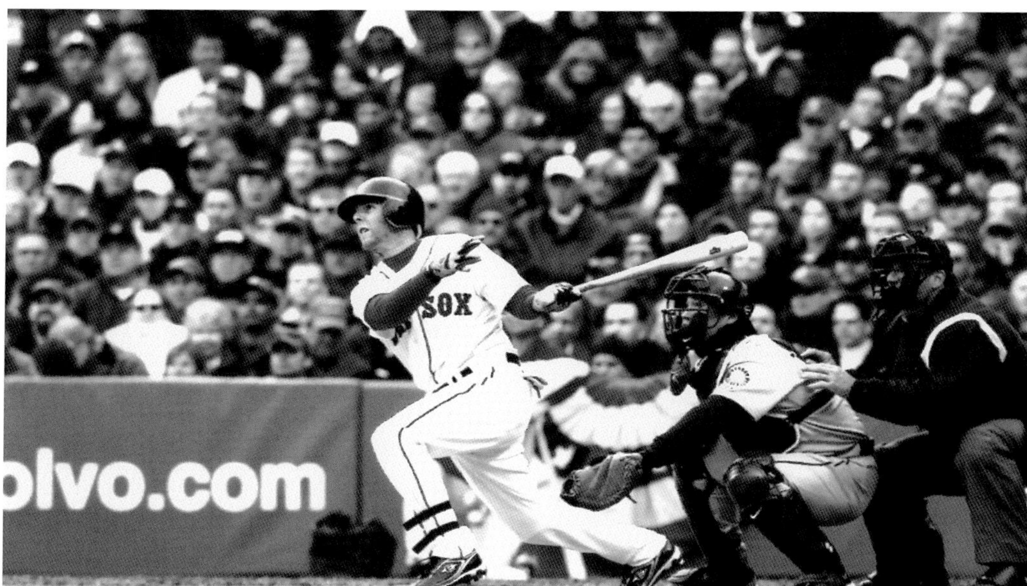

Scoring 35 runs in 66 games with Portland, Dustin Pedroia earned a promotion to Triple-A Pawtucket in late June 2005. At the time of his promotion, Pedroia was batting .324, with 8 homers and 40 RBIs. The infielder won Boston's Minor League Quality Plate Appearance Award for June, striking out only 10 times in 29 games (23 with Portland, 6 with Pawtucket.) (Courtesy of Brian Babineau, Boston Red Sox.)

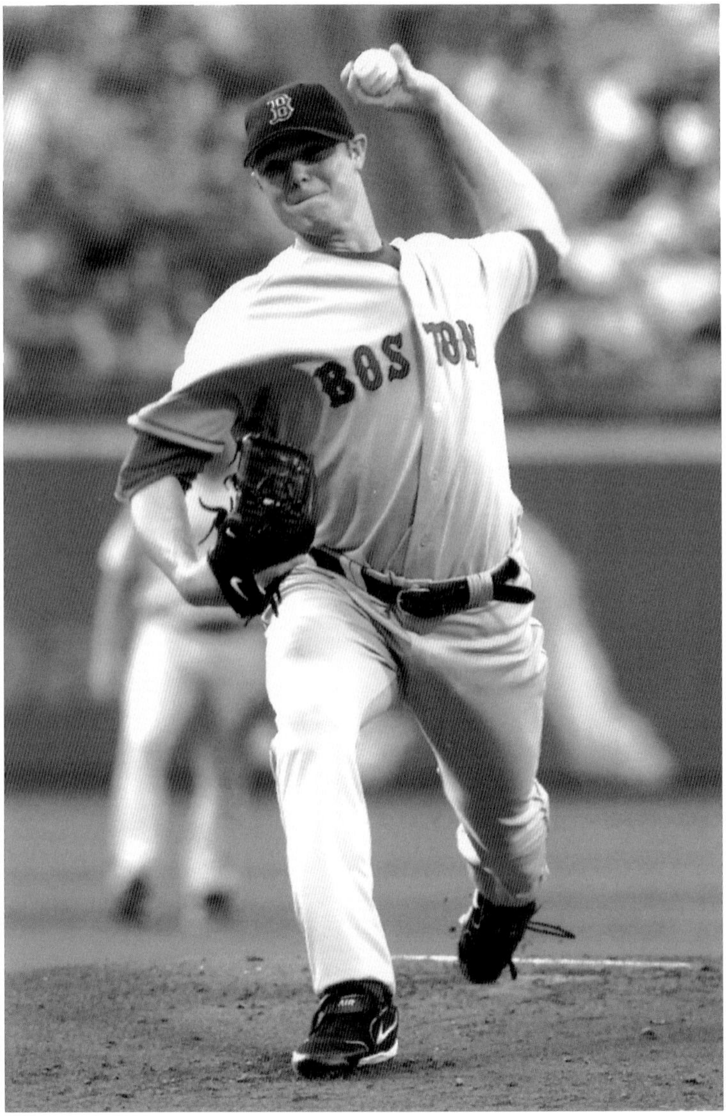

In a July game versus the New Hampshire Fisher Cats, Jon Lester pitched a complete game, a one-hitter, the second in Portland Sea Dogs history. In 2005, Lester was 11-6 with three complete games. He led the league with a 2.61 ERA and 163 strikeouts. His ERA established a new Portland single-season record, while his strikeouts are second best for a Sea Dogs pitcher in a season. The pitcher won Eastern League Pitcher of the Year honors, and the Red Sox selected Lester as the organization's Minor League Pitcher of the Year for 2005. Lester started Game 1 of both the Northern Division Championship Series and the Eastern League Championship Series, striking out 15 batters in 13 innings of work. In August 2006, doctors diagnosed the southpaw with a treatable type of anaplastic large cell lymphoma, ending Lester's outstanding rookie season with Boston. After treatment, doctors pronounced him cancer-free in December 2006. Lester took the mound for the first time in July 2007 against the Cleveland Indians. (Courtesy of Julie Cordiero, Boston Red Sox.)

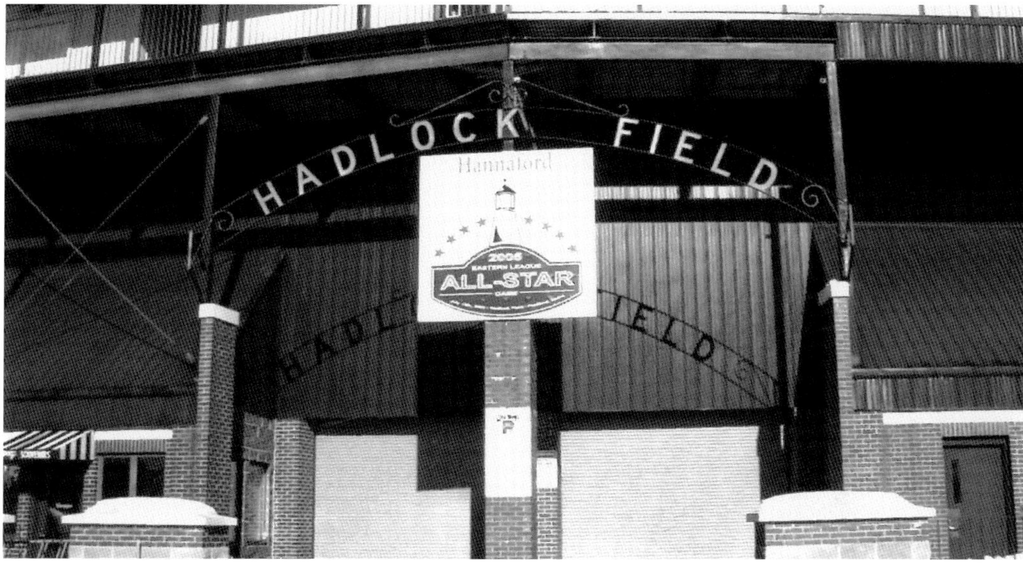

In late summer 2004, the Eastern League announced that Portland and Hadlock Field would play host to the 2005 Eastern League All-Star Game the following July. Todd Claus and his coaching staff managed the Northern Division team to a 9-6 victory. Portland players included Chris Durbin, Jon Lester, Brandon Moss, Jonathan Papelbon, Kenny Perez, Hanley Ramirez, and Jared Sandberg. Moss gave the Northern Division a 4-3 lead with a single in the third inning. Ramirez went two-for-three, stole two bases, and scored a run. In a game featuring five lead changes, Perez, replacing teammate Ramirez, broke a 6-6 deadlock with a two-out, two-run double in the bottom of the eighth inning. Pregame highlights included a home run derby and former president George H. W. Bush tossing out the ceremonial first pitch. (Above, courtesy of the Sea Dogs; below, courtesy of Melanie Aber.)

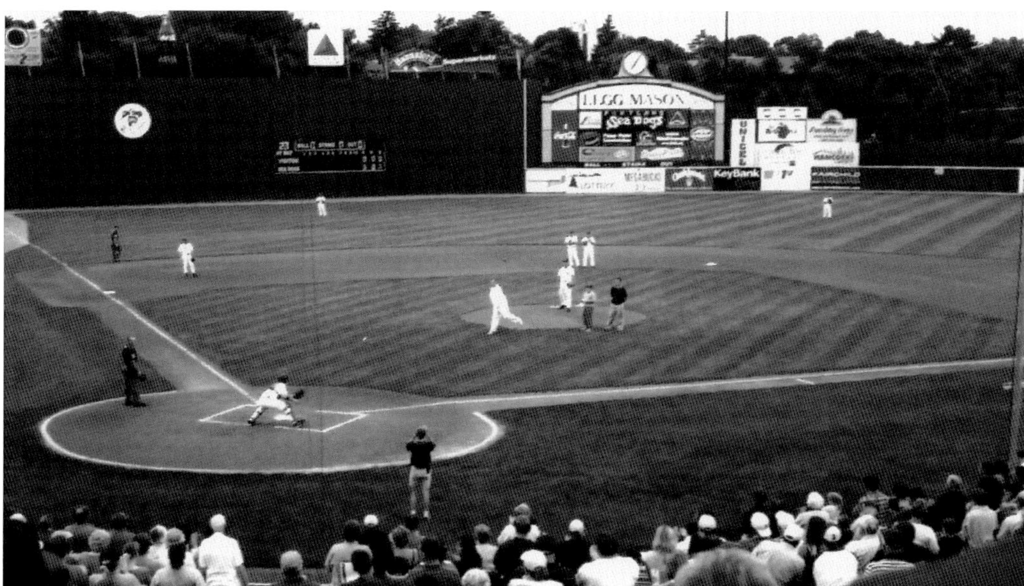

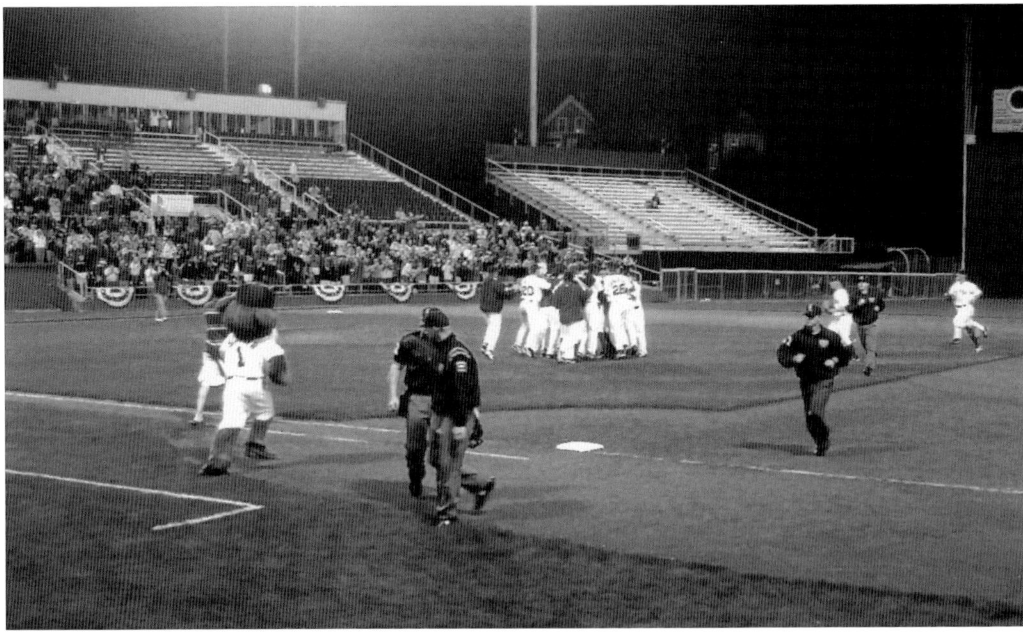

The Sea Dogs celebrate after defeating Northern Division rival the Trenton Thunder and winning their first Northern Division title since 1997. With the victory over Trenton, the Sea Dogs made their first appearance in the Eastern League Championship Series in eight seasons. The Sea Dogs lost to the Akron Aeros. The 2005 Portland Sea Dogs team included seven all-star players, a Sea Dogs record. The league recognized players Jared Sandberg and Brandon Moss and pitchers David Pauley, Jonathan Papelbon, and Jon Lester for Player and Pitcher of the Week honors during the 2005 season. (Above, courtesy of the Sea Dogs; below, photograph by Stewart Smith.)

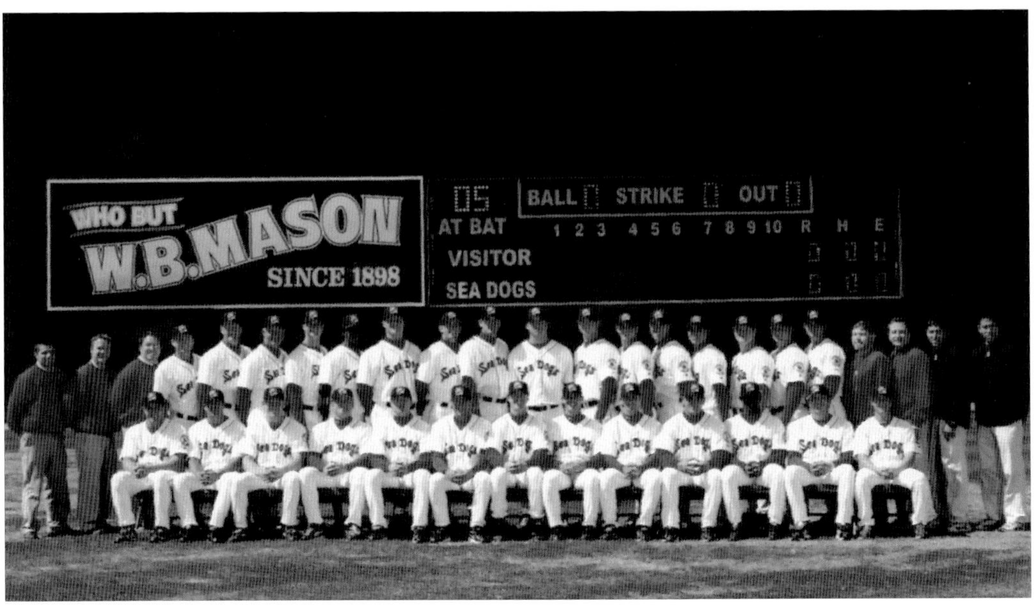

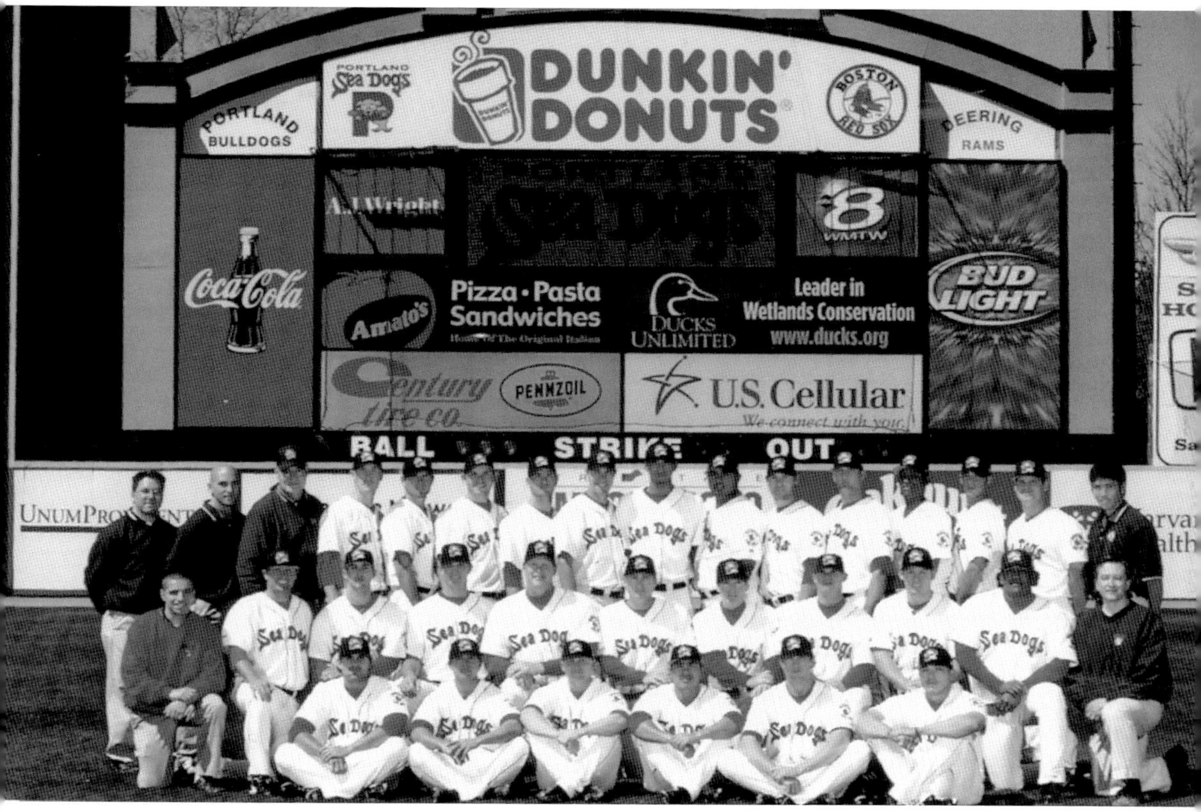

Manager Todd Claus returned to manage the Sea Dogs in 2006, after leading Portland to its first appearance in the Eastern League Championship Series since 1997. The 2006 Eastern League championship team included MVP Brandon Moss and top prospect and future major-league talent Jacoby Ellsbury. Like every minor-league team, the revolving door on talent continued to turn, and the 2006 season was no exception. Tyler Minges joined the team in late May and batted over .300 for the remainder of the season. Minor-league veteran Brian Myrow replaced Chad Spann after an ankle injury sidelined the third baseman for the rest of the season. Throughout the season, Portland's affiliation partner, the Boston Red Sox, featured 16 former Sea Dogs, including 7 players who played in Portland in 2006. Previous Sea Dogs players included Lenny DiNardo, Kason Gabbard, Devern Hansack, Craig Hansen, Gabe Kapler, David Murphy, and David Pauley. (Photograph by Stewart Smith.)

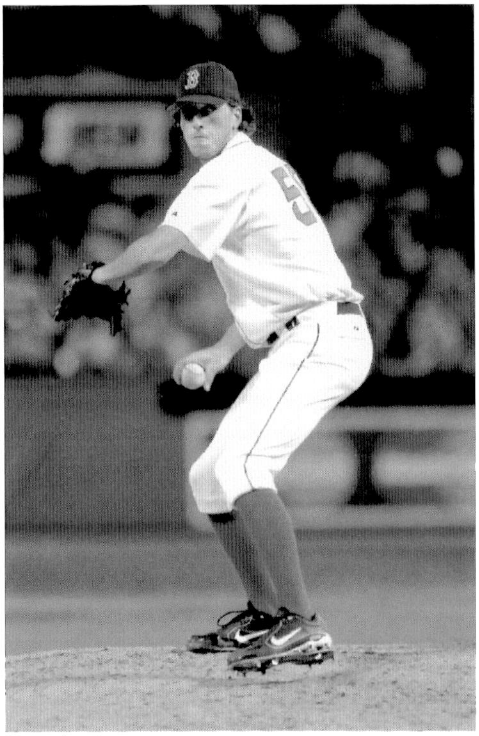

Craig Hansen surrendered the first run of his career in April 2006. Hansen set a franchise record by pitching 20.1 consecutive scoreless innings. However, Hansen did not hold the record for very long. Phil Seibel erased Hansen's name in the record book two months later when he pitched 22.2 innings before a runner crossed the plate. (Courtesy of Steve Babineau, Boston Red Sox.)

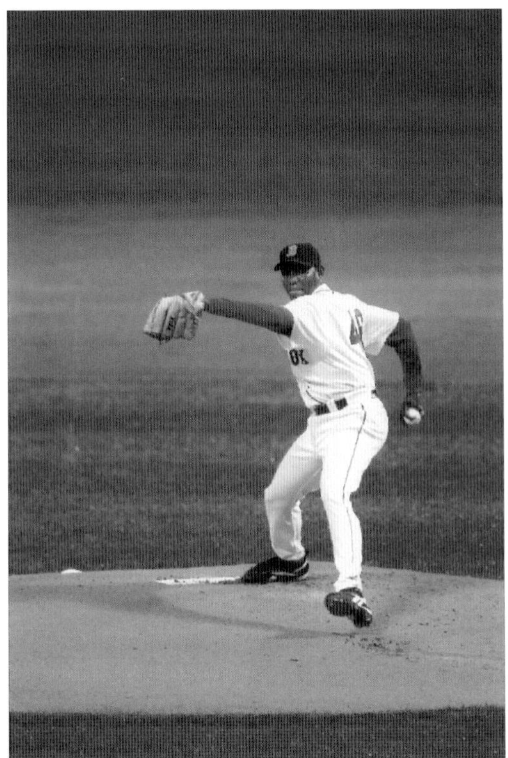

In 2006, Devern Hansack was the Sea Dogs leader in ERA (3.26), fifth best in Sea Dogs history for a single season. He also led the starting rotation in strikeouts with 124 in 2006. The fans selected Hansack as Sea Dogs Pitcher of the Year for 2006. (Courtesy of Steve Babineau, Boston Red Sox.)

Brandon Moss got off to a slow start in 2006, batting a dismal .178 in April. However, the slumping outfielder recovered and hit .352 in June and .327 in August. His league-leading 36 doubles established a new single-season Sea Dogs record. Moss was also the 2006 Sea Dogs leader in RBIs (83), runs scored (76), and hits (145). (Courtesy of Cindy Loo, Boston Red Sox.)

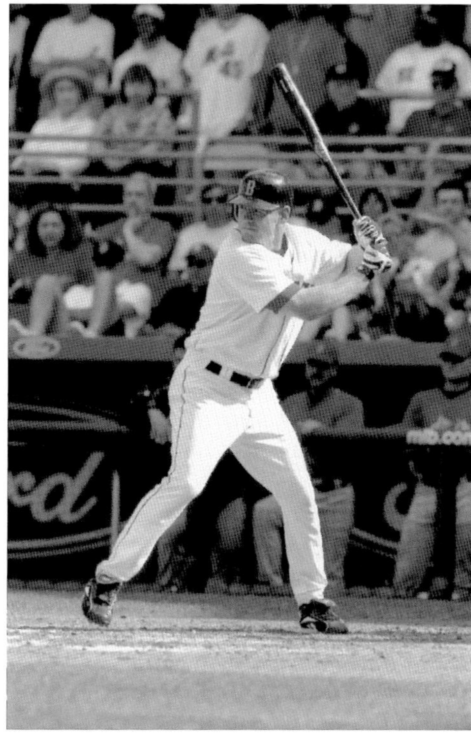

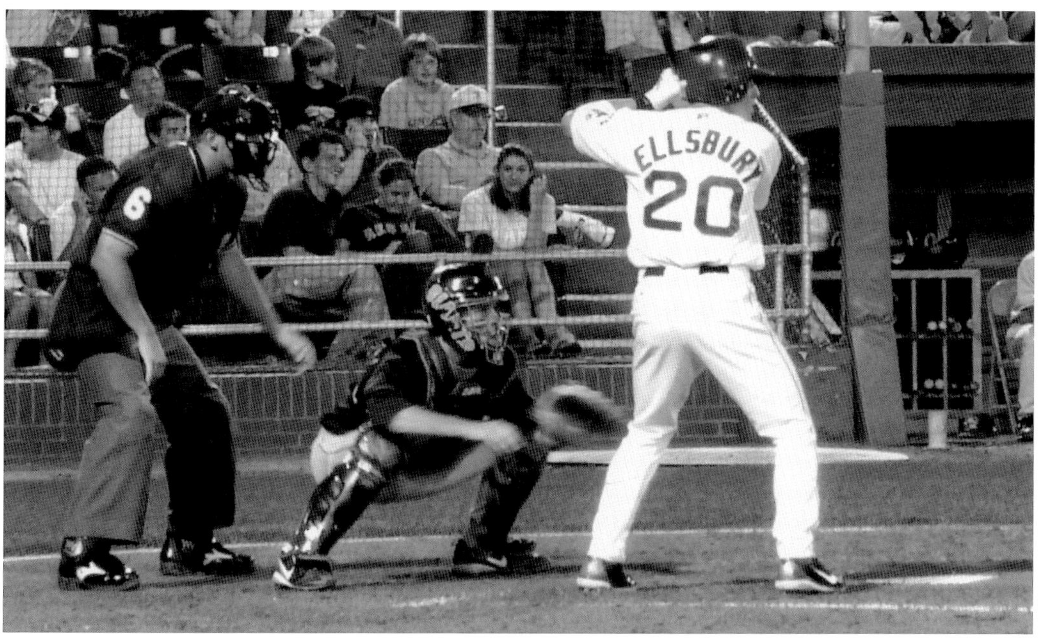

Promising Red Sox prospect Jacob Ellsbury joined the Sea Dogs in 2006. The center fielder quickly became one of the Eastern League's top defensive and offensive stars. Ellsbury hit .308 with three homers and 19 RBIs. The speedy Ellsbury is tied for the team lead in triples and is the team leader in steals with 16, despite only appearing in 50 games. (Courtesy of the Sea Dogs.)

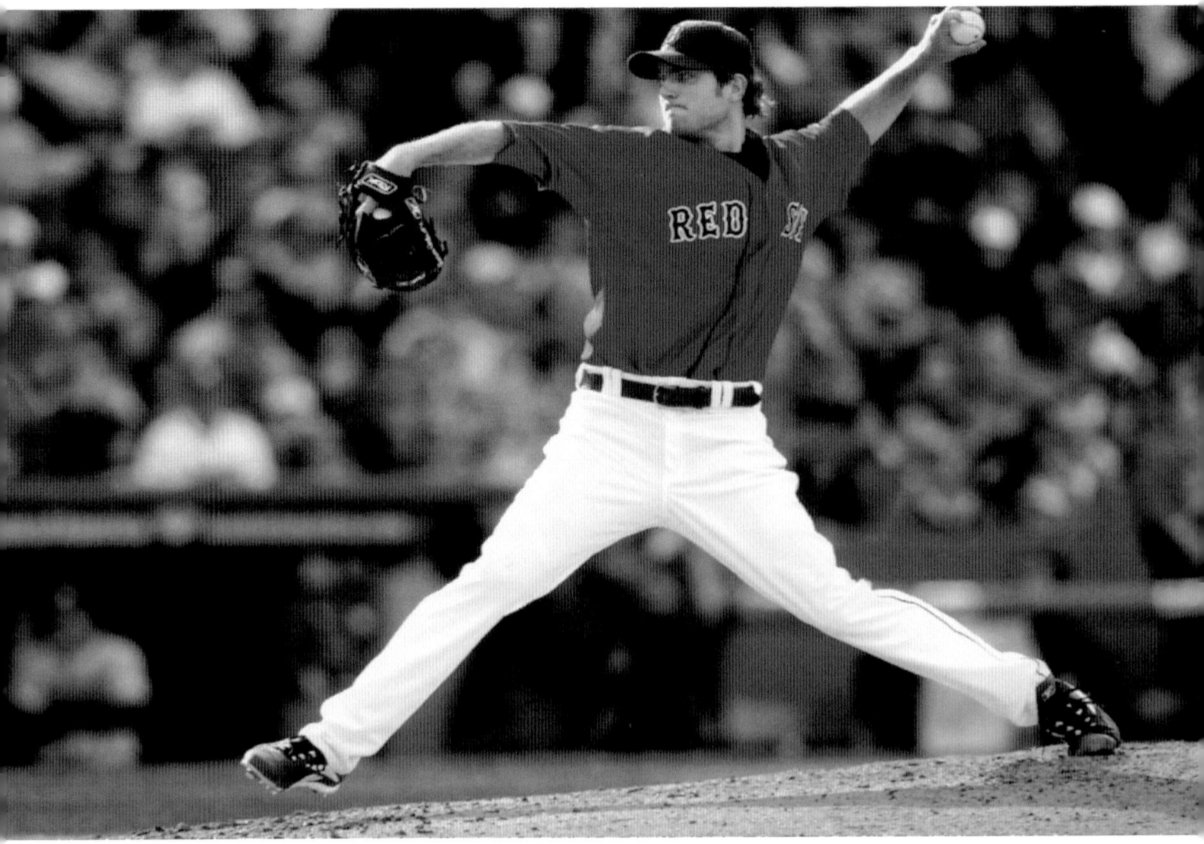

For Kason Gabbard, the 2006 season is one for the history books. Gabbard, along with teammates Devern Hansack, Manny Delcarmen, Lenny DiNardo, Craig Hansen, Jon Lester, and Jermaine Van Buren, made Boston Red Sox history in 2006. It was the first time in Red Sox history that seven pitchers earned their first major-league victory in the same season. The previous record was six pitchers in 1969. Gabbard's quick rise up the Boston organizational ladder began with the Sea Dogs and at Hadlock Field in 2006. The lefty won all five of his final starts before earning a promotion to Triple-A Pawtucket. Before leaving Maine for Rhode Island, Gabbard made Sea Dogs history. Gabbard became the fastest Sea Dogs pitcher to nine wins. His record-setting 9th victory came after his 13th, and final, start for the Sea Dogs. (Courtesy of Brita Meng Outzen, Boston Red Sox.)

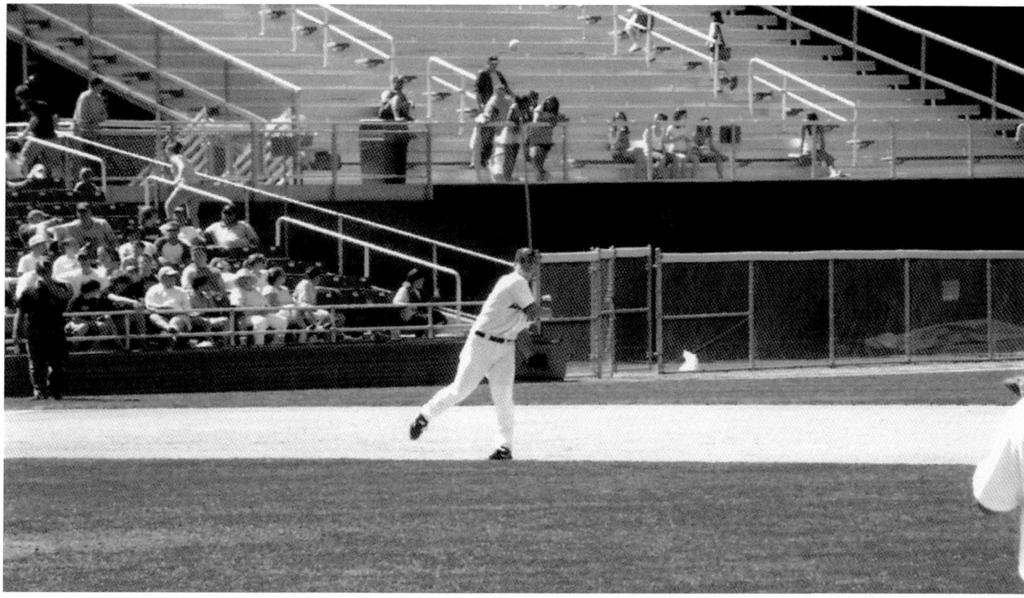

With an above-average glove and eye at the plate, Chad Spann methodically worked his way up the organizational ladder. In late July 2006, the third baseman led the Sea Dogs in batting average at .294 (fifth best in the Eastern League), with 10 homers and 50 RBIs. His season abruptly ended after he injured his left ankle in early August. (Courtesy of the Sea Dogs.)

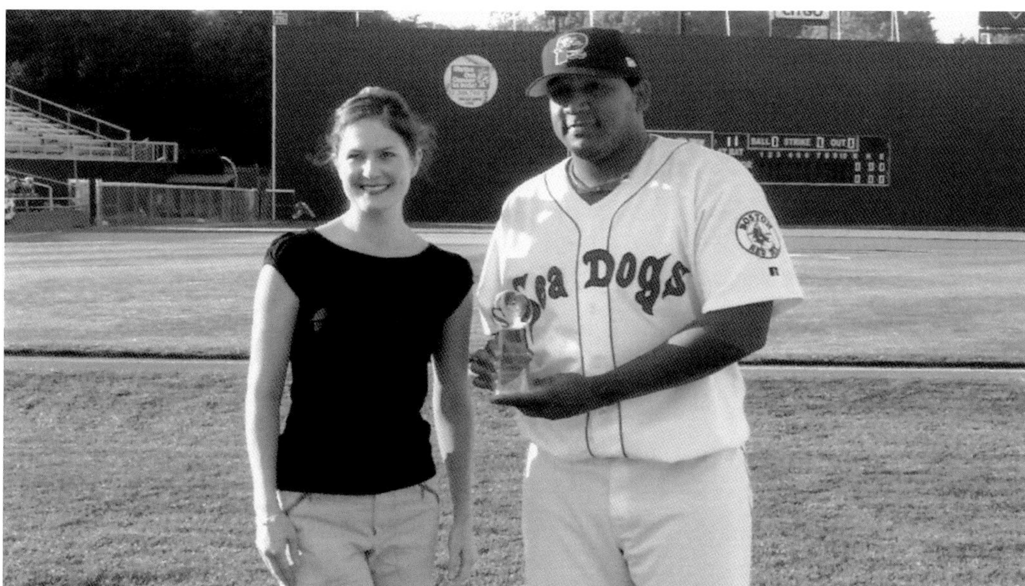

In 2004, Edgar Martinez struggled offensively and forced Boston's front office staff to question and reevaluate his big-league potential. Martinez began his transition from catcher to pitcher in July 2004. *At the Yard* magazine awarded the converted catcher its Diamond in the Rough Award for 2005 in a pregame ceremony. The Venezuelan saved 12 games in 2006 for the Sea Dogs, best on the team. (Courtesy of the Sea Dogs.)

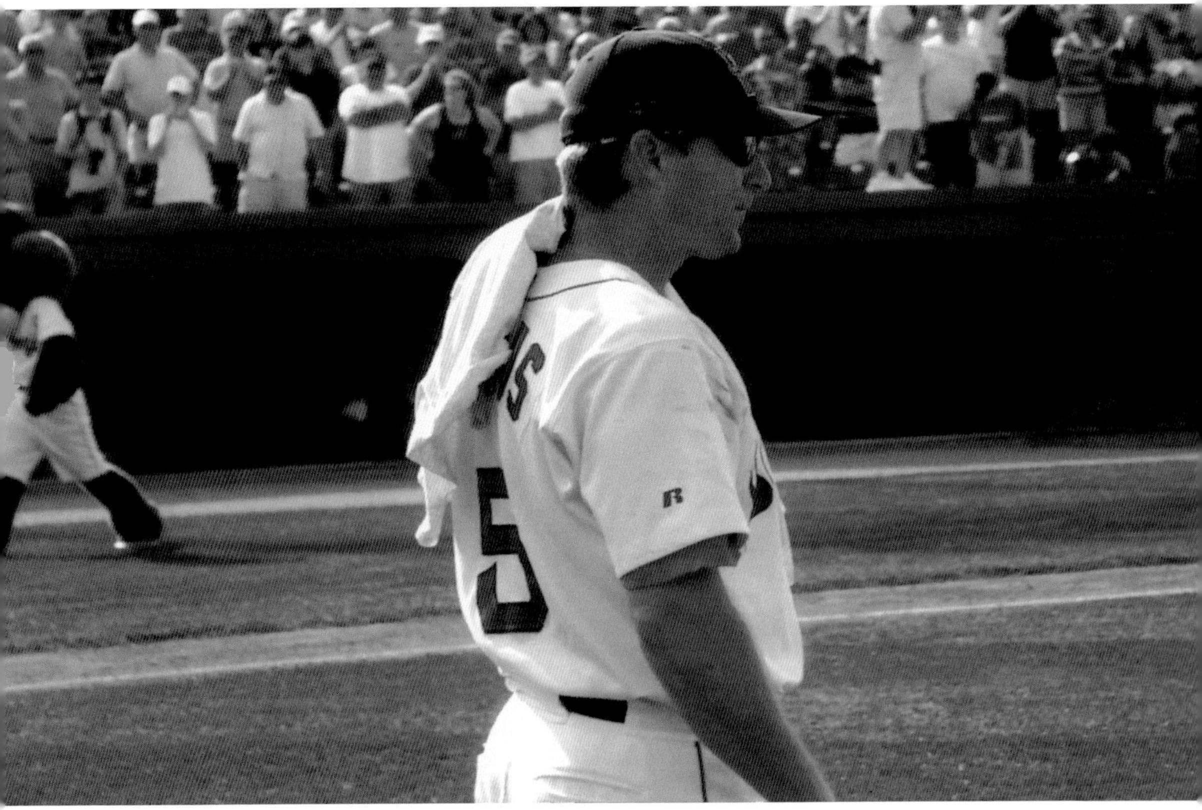

The Boston Red Sox named Todd Claus manager of the Portland Sea Dogs before the start of the 2005 season. The Sea Dogs, since becoming affiliation partners with the Red Sox in 2003, were coming off two mediocre seasons. In his first season, Claus and the Sea Dogs reclaimed the Northern Division title and returned to the postseason for the first time in years. The Sea Dogs advanced to the Eastern League Championship Series but lost to the Akron Aeros. Claus and his coaching staff led the Northern Division to victory in the 2005 Eastern League All-Star Game played in Portland. In 2006, Claus guided Portland to the franchise's first Eastern League championship over the Aeros. *Baseball America* named Claus 2006 Minor League Manager of the Year. The Red Sox awarded Claus and promoted him to major-league advance scout before the start of the 2007 season. (Courtesy of the Sea Dogs.)

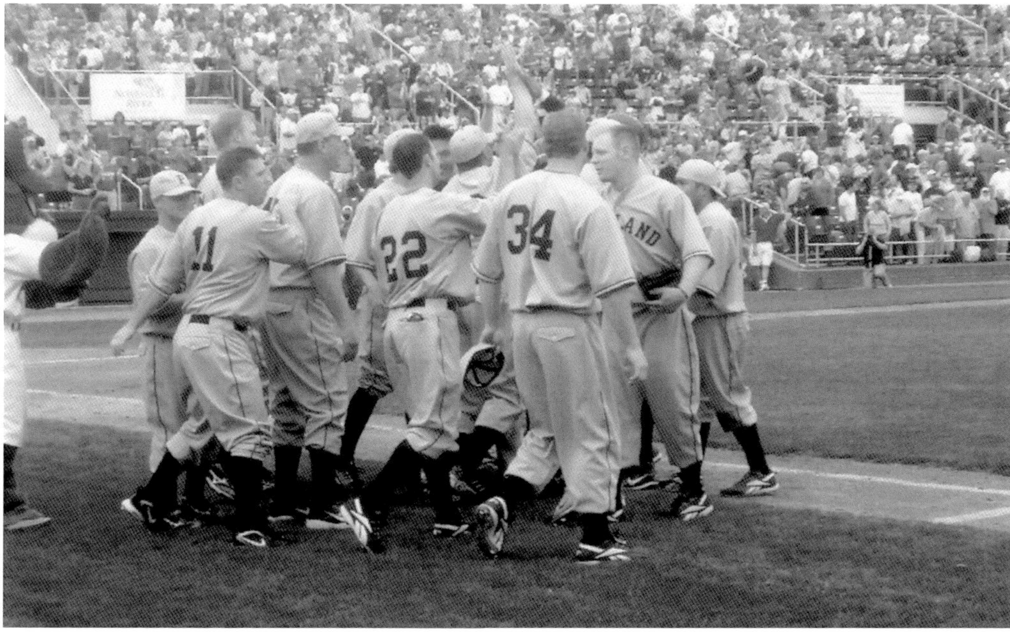

The Portland Sea Dogs closed out the 2006 regular season losing 38 of 63 games. The stretch included a demoralizing 10-game losing streak in early August. The streak denied the Sea Dogs a first-place finish. Nevertheless, and despite a second-place finish, the Sea Dogs qualified for the postseason for a second straight year. In a reprise of the 2005 Northern Division Championship Series, the Sea Dogs faced the Trenton Thunder for the Northern Division title. The Sea Dogs arrived in New Jersey and the 2006 postseason as the Eastern League's biggest underdogs. (Courtesy of the Sea Dogs.)

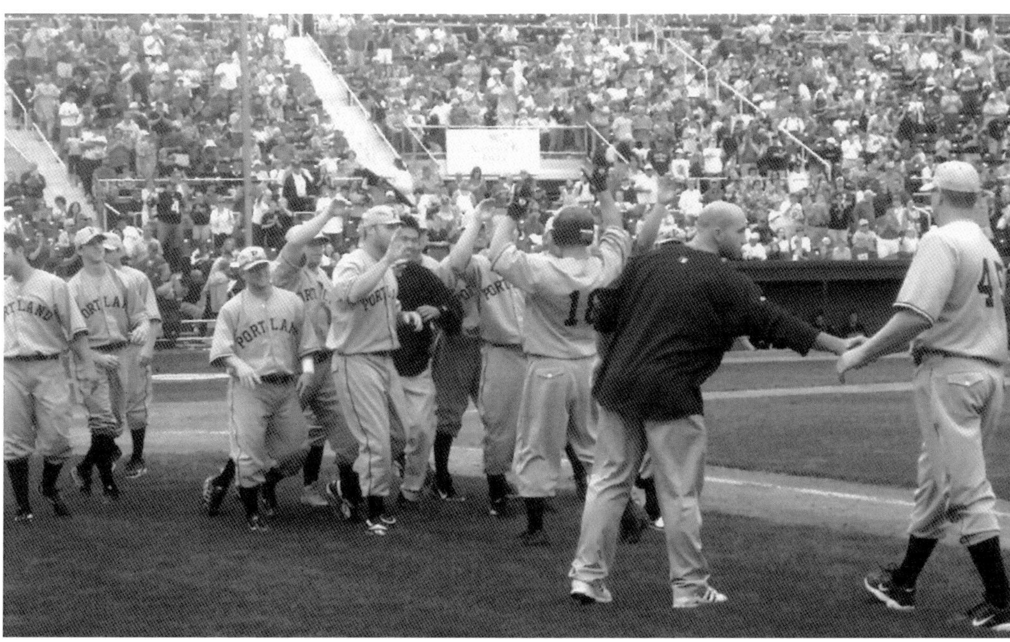

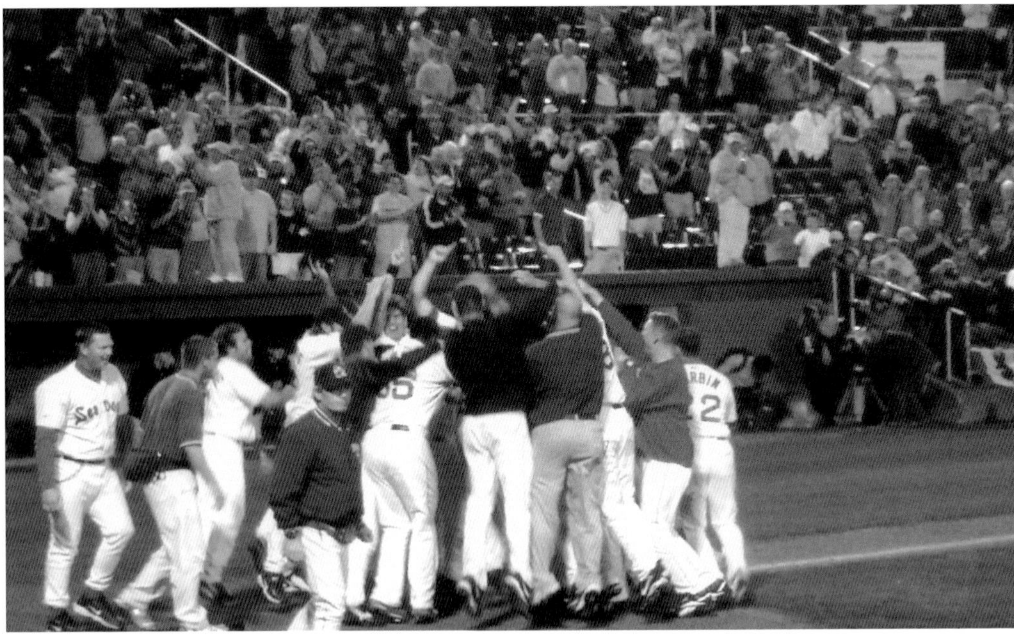

The Sea Dogs lost Game 1 of the Northern Division Championship Series to their rival, the Trenton Thunder, by the score of 3-1. The Sea Dogs rebounded and won Game 2 (10-3) and tied the best-of-five series at one apiece. George Kottaras made his Portland debut and, in Game 2, blasted a home run in his second at bat. The series shifted venues and headed to Portland and Hadlock Field. Portland took Game 3 with a 5-4 victory. In Game 4, the Sea Dogs defeated and eliminated Trenton in 10 innings 4-3. Portland took the series three games to one and moved one step closer to winning the Eastern League title. (Courtesy of the Sea Dogs.)

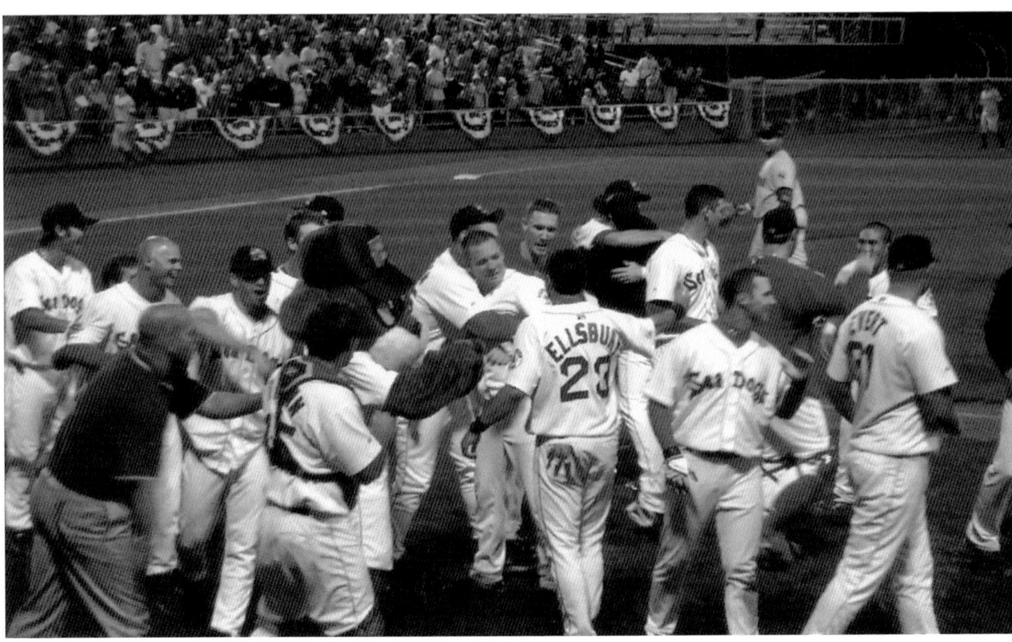

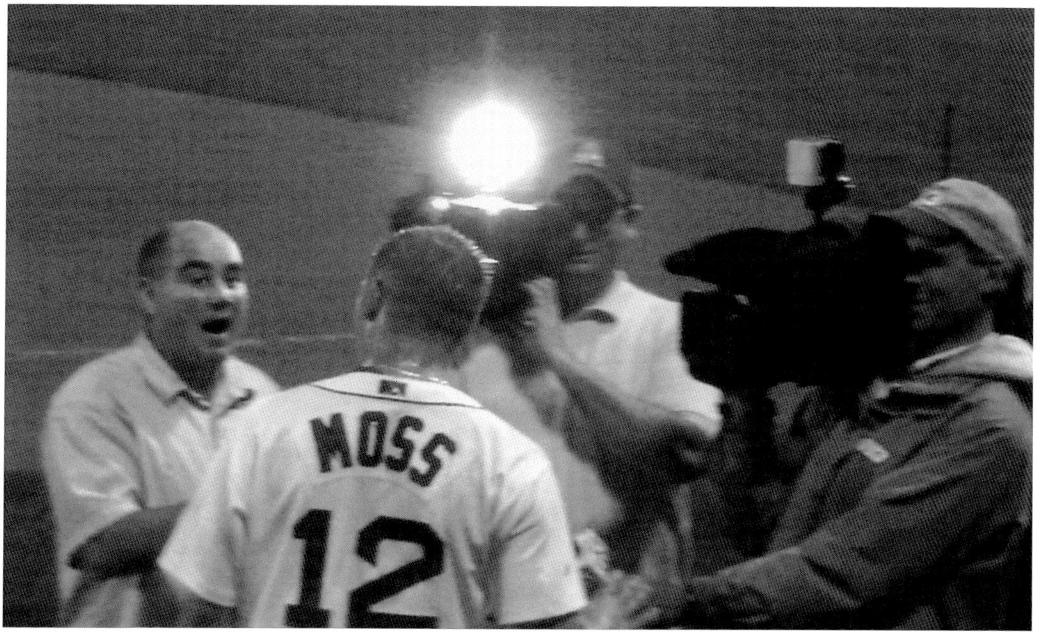

Brandon Moss talks with reporters following the Sea Dogs' Game 4 victory in the Northern Division Championship Series. Moss's walk-off home run in the bottom of the 10th inning clinched the Northern Division Championship Series for the Sea Dogs over the Trenton Thunder. The home run was Moss's second of the postseason. (Courtesy of the Sea Dogs.)

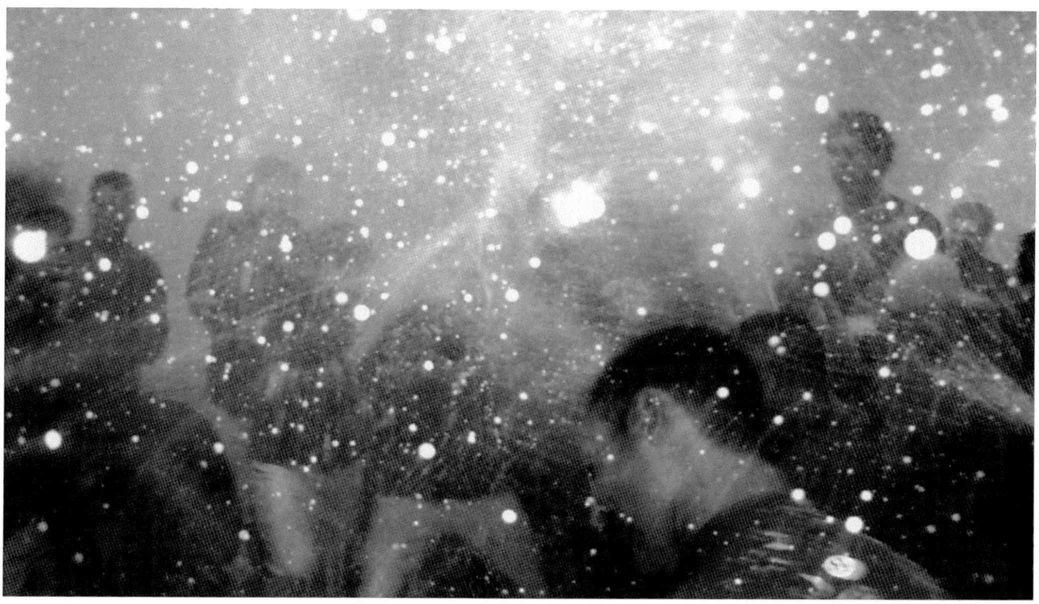

The Portland Sea Dogs celebrate their upcoming appearance in the Eastern League Championship Series. In a rematch of the 2005 Eastern League Championship Series, the Sea Dogs faced the Southern Division winner Akron Aeros for the Eastern League title. In 2005, the Sea Dogs lost the title, dropping three games out of four to the Aeros. (Courtesy of the Sea Dogs.)

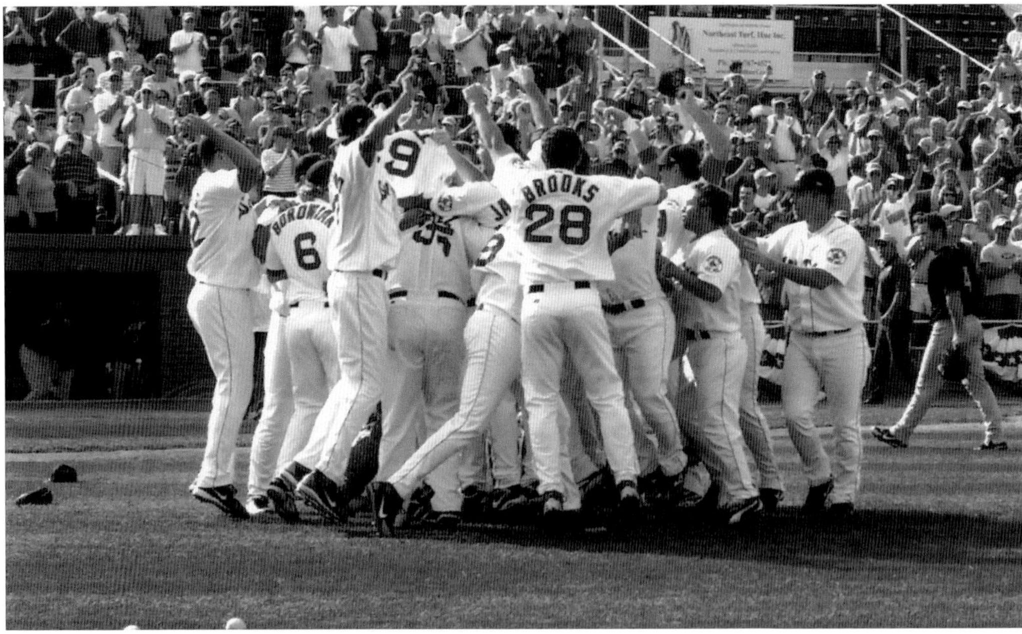

September 17, 2006, was a gorgeous autumn day in Portland. Over at Hadlock Field, the Portland Sea Dogs were hosts to a decisive Game 5 in their postseason series against the Akron Aeros. On the mound, Sea Dogs reliever Jon Searles recorded the final out of the 2006 championship series when Akron's Trevor Crowe flied out to left fielder Chris Durbin. The Sea Dogs won the series three games to two and captured their first Eastern League championship in their 13-year history with an 8-5 victory over the Aeros. (Courtesy of the Sea Dogs.)

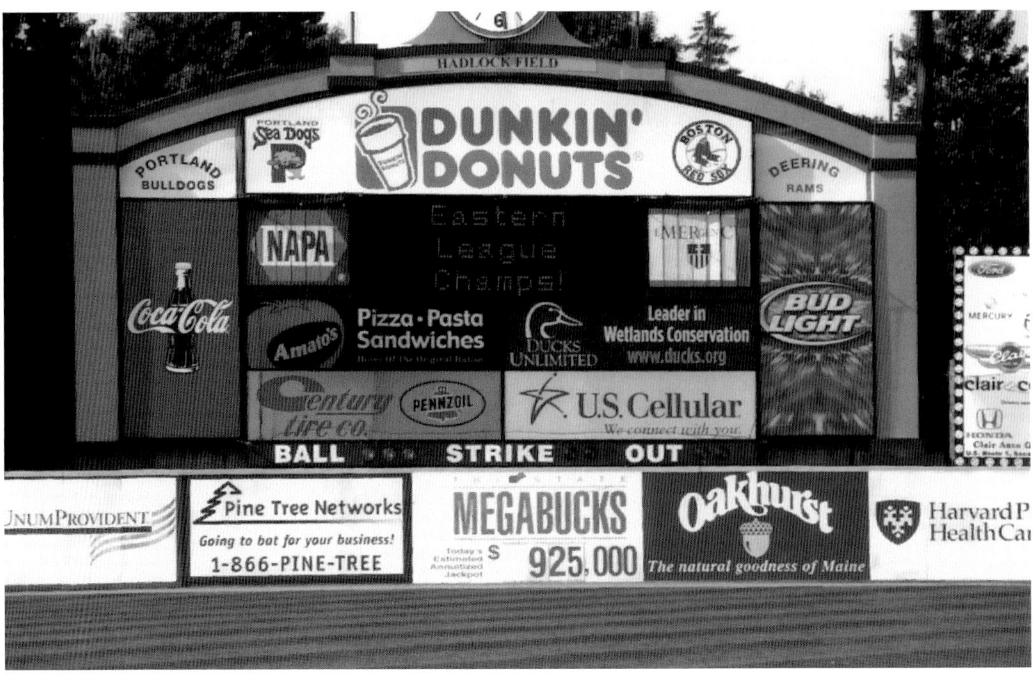

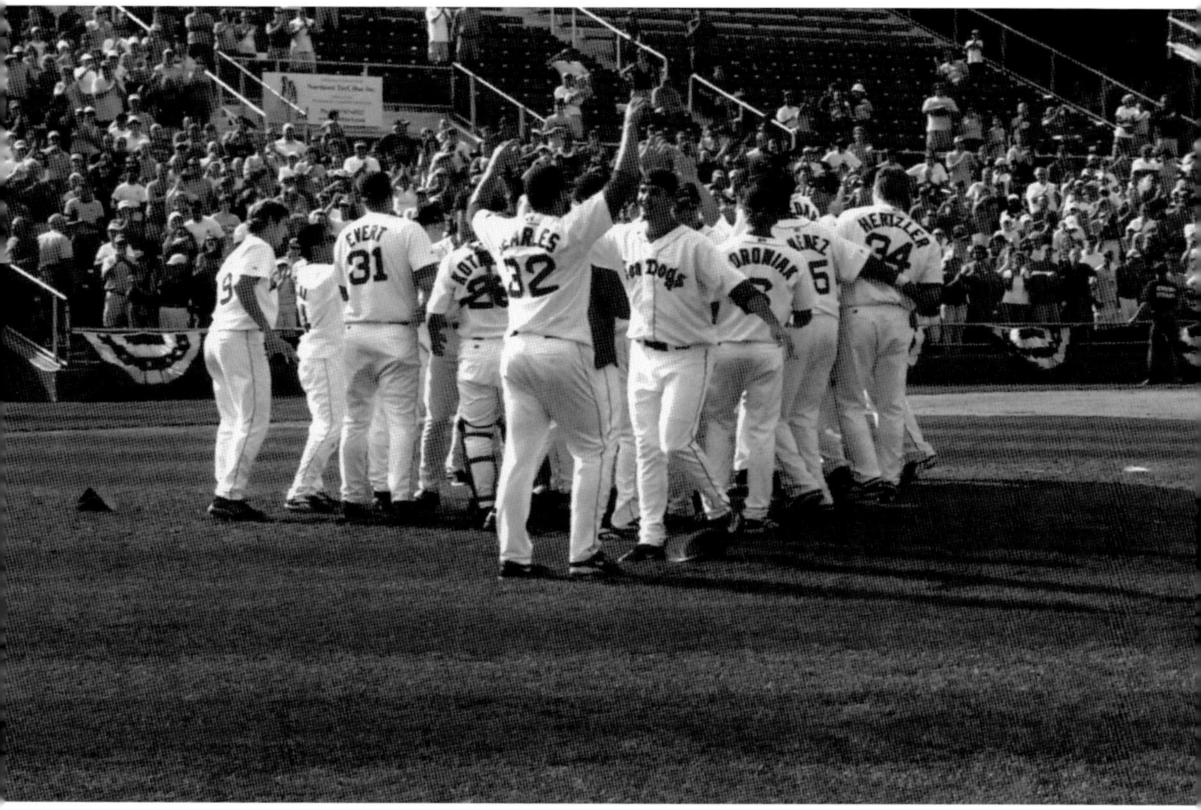

In Game 1, starter Devern Hansack got the win, and closer Edgar Martinez got the save as the Sea Dogs won 4-3 at Canal Park in Akron. The Sea Dogs won Game 2 with a 13-8 victory, and the series left Canal Park and Ohio behind and headed for Hadlock Field and Maine. After winning the first two games in the best-of-five series, Portland headed for home with a 2-0 series advantage and one game away from the Eastern League title. The Aeros shocked the Sea Dogs, winning the next two games. Despite a pair of home runs by birthday boy Brandon Moss, closer Barry Hertzler's blown save was the difference in Game 3 as Akron won 6-4. In Game 4, Akron's 6-5 victory tied the championship series at two apiece and forced a decisive Game 5. (Courtesy of the Sea Dogs.)

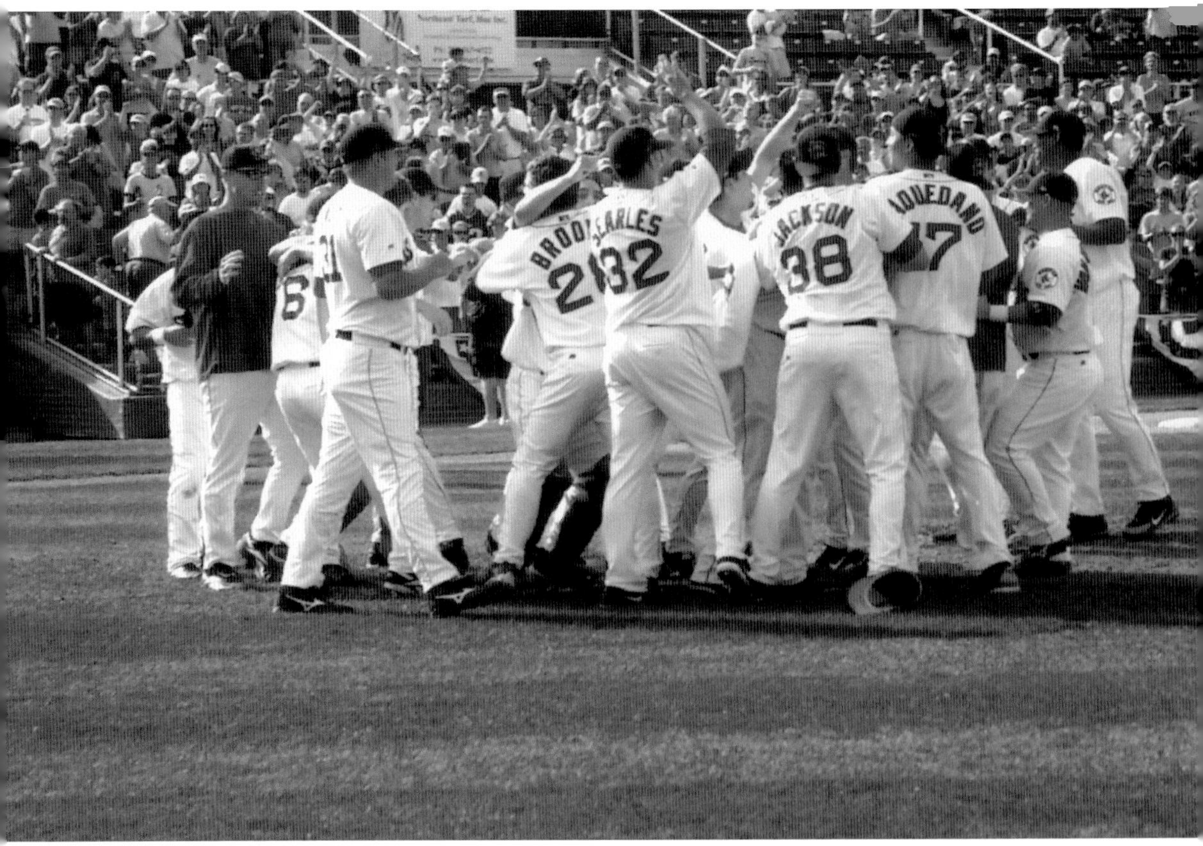

The fifth and final game of the 2006 season went to the Sea Dogs. The Sea Dogs struck first and struck early. Brian Myrow hit a two-run home run in the second inning off the Aeros' replacement starter Ronald Bay. Keoni De Renne cleared the bases with a three-run triple in the bottom of the third. Starter and Game 1 winner Devern Hansack returned to the mound in the fourth inning with a seven-run lead. Portland and Hansack coasted through the middle innings. Entering the top of the ninth with an 8-3 lead, Sea Dogs reliever John Searles gave up two runs before Chris Durbin caught the third and final out. The Portland Sea Dogs defeated the Akron Aeros in the fifth and deciding game, 8-5, and won the 2006 Eastern League Championship Series, three games to two. (Courtesy of the Sea Dogs.)

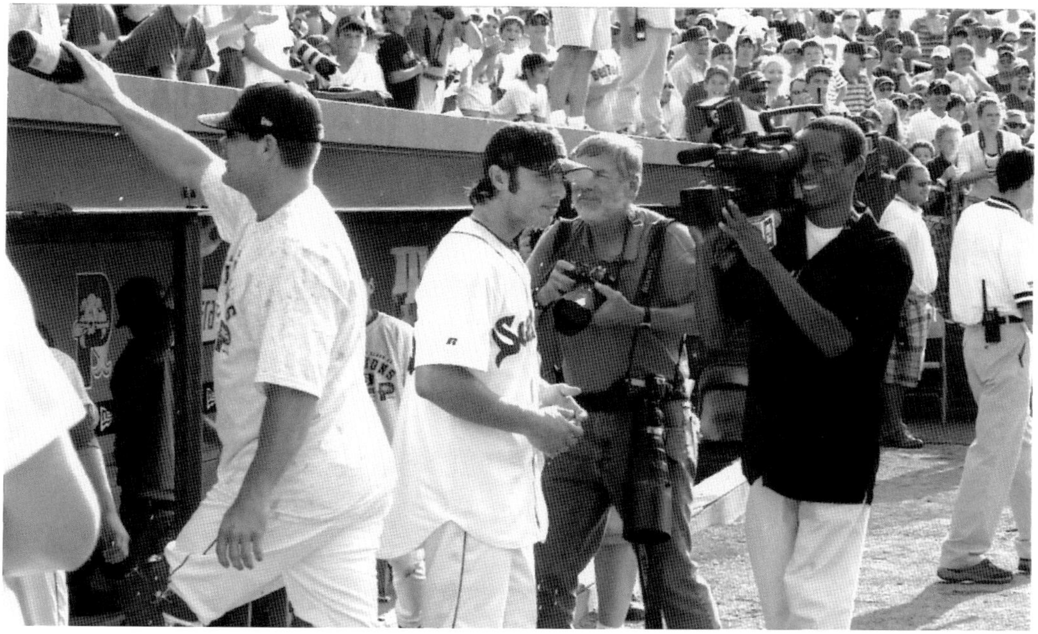

After the final out, victorious Sea Dogs players ran and gathered toward the center of the diamond. Players hugged and tossed their gloves in the air in celebration. Players popped open champagne bottles and champagne showered over all. Some players wandered over to the stands and over to the fans, who were all on their feet, and flipped their game-worn caps into the crowd. Slowly, the players regrouped and headed back toward the mound where they started passing around the No. 49 jersey belonging to missing, but not forgotten, closer Edgar Martinez. (Courtesy of the Sea Dogs.)

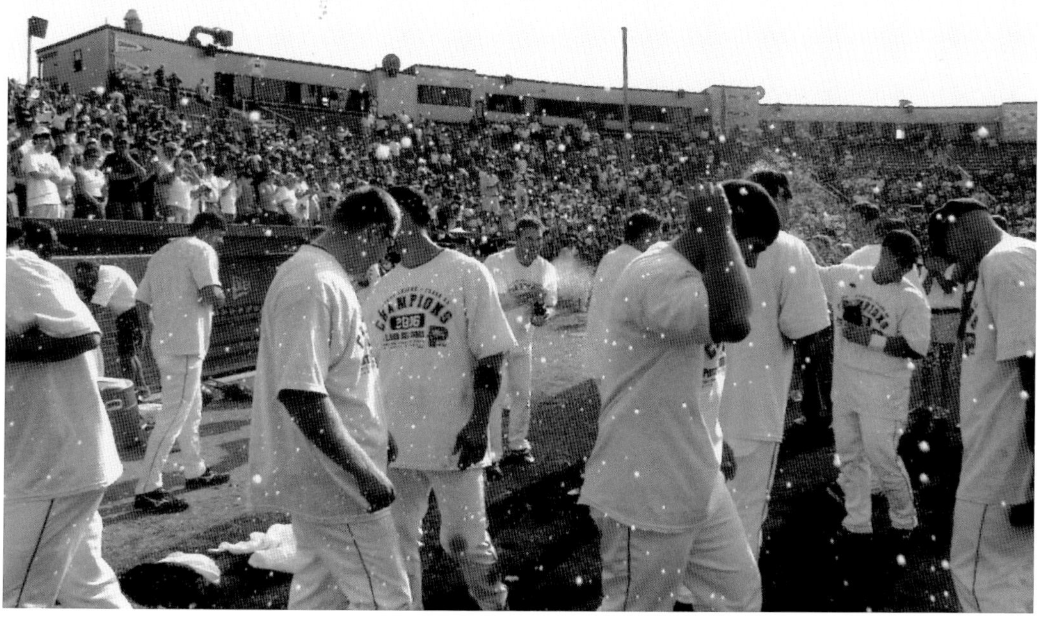

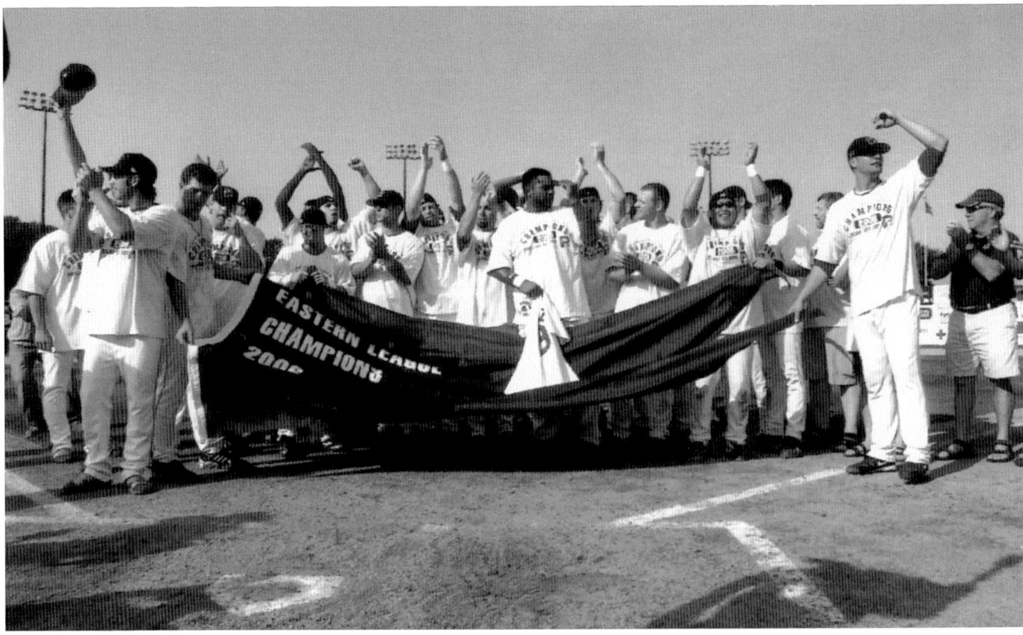

Sea Dogs players gather between the mound and home plate and grip the 2006 Eastern League championship banner. Front and center is Luis Jimenez, who holds the jersey of closer Edgar Martinez. Hours after his Game 1 save in Akron, Martinez found out his father had a heart attack and passed away. Martinez left the Sea Dogs before Game 2 and immediately headed back home to his native Venezuela to be with his family and to attend the funeral. The Sea Dogs closer missed the remainder of the series, but his teammates did not forget him. (Courtesy of the Sea Dogs.)

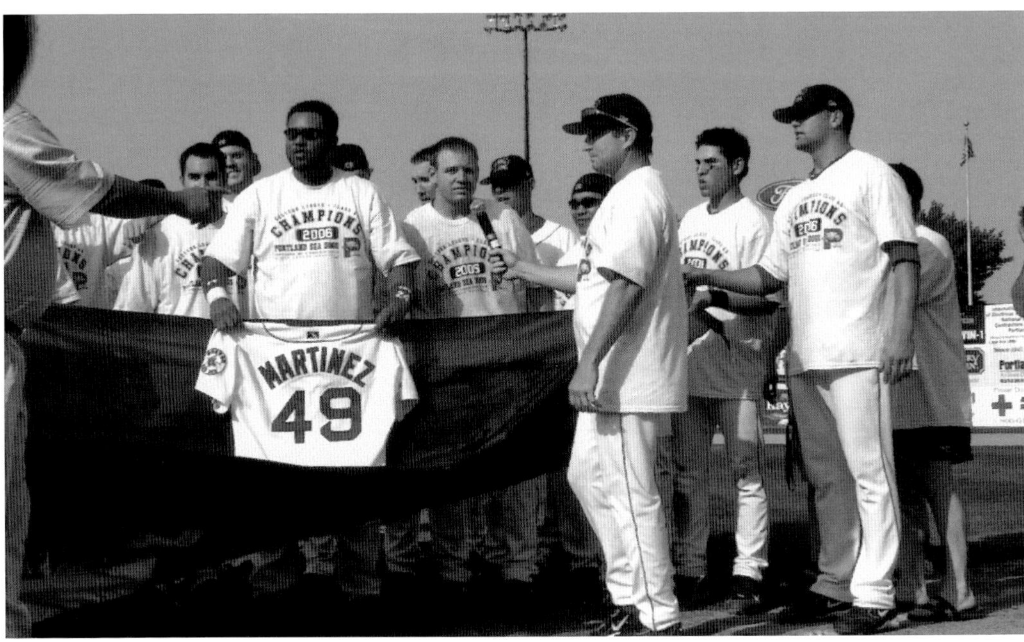

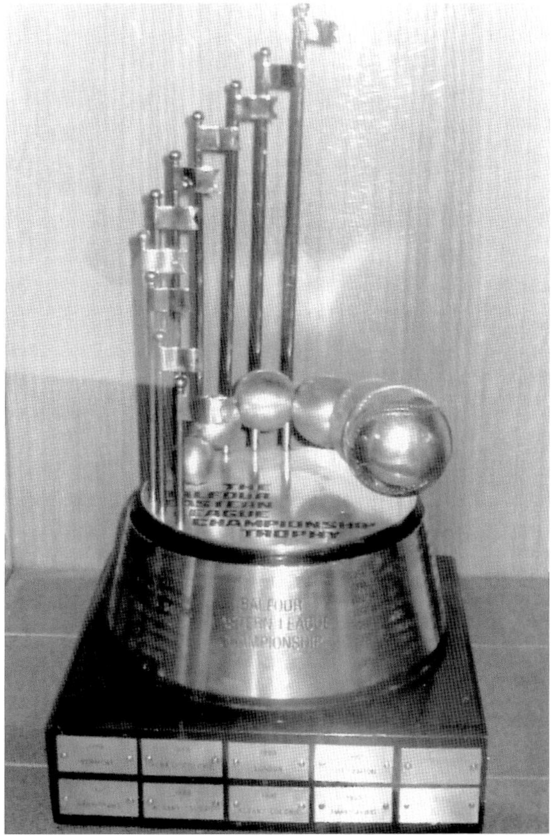

Except 2001, when the championship series was cancelled because of the terrorist attacks on September 11, the Balfour Eastern League Championship Trophy has been presented to the winning team. Recent winning teams include defending 2005 and 2003 champions Akron, New Hampshire (2004), and Norwich (2002). The Sea Dogs, losers of the 1996, 1997, and 2005 Eastern League Championship Series, defeated the Aeros to win the 2006 title. Eastern League president Joe McEacharn shakes manager Todd Claus's hand right before vice president and assistant general manager Jim Heffley hands over the trophy. (Below, courtesy of the Sea Dogs.)

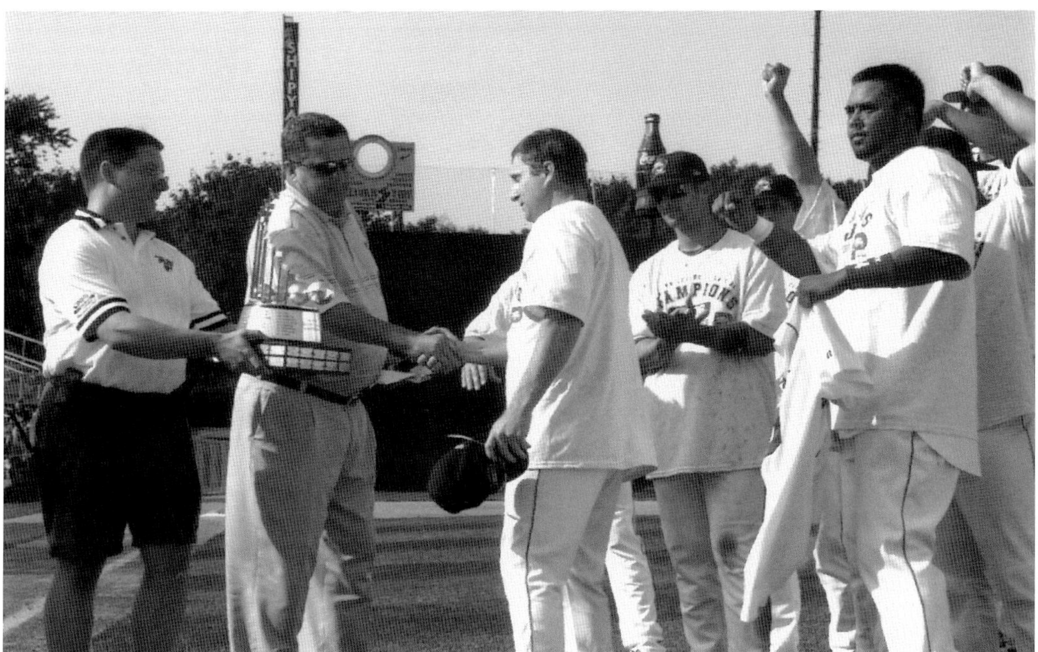

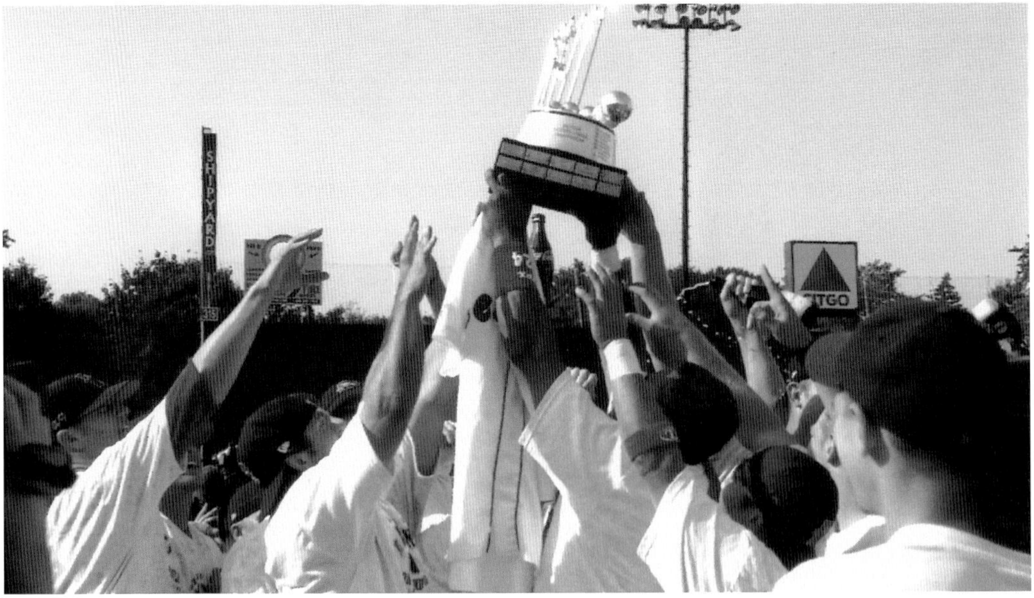

"I'm not entirely sure what a sauerkraut ball is," Portland mayor James Cohen quipped, "but I'm confident I'll soon find out." Before the start of the Eastern League Championship Series, Cohen and Akron mayor Don Plusquellic engaged in a friendly wager. Cohen would also enjoy one dozen hamburgers and brownies if the Aeros lost. If Portland lost, Cohen promised to send a dozen lobsters. (Courtesy of the Sea Dogs.)

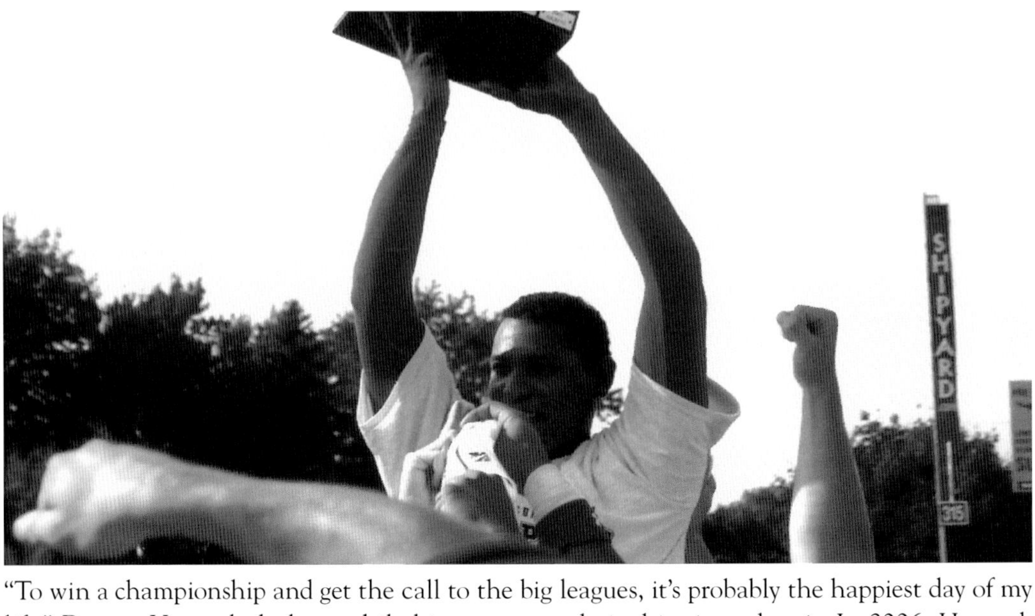

"To win a championship and get the call to the big leagues, it's probably the happiest day of my life," Devern Hansack declares while his teammates hoist him into the air. In 2006, Hansack returned to baseball following a two-year absence. Hansack won the deciding game of the Eastern League Championship Series. Immediately following the game, Hansack got the call; he would be heading for Boston. (Courtesy of the Sea Dogs.)

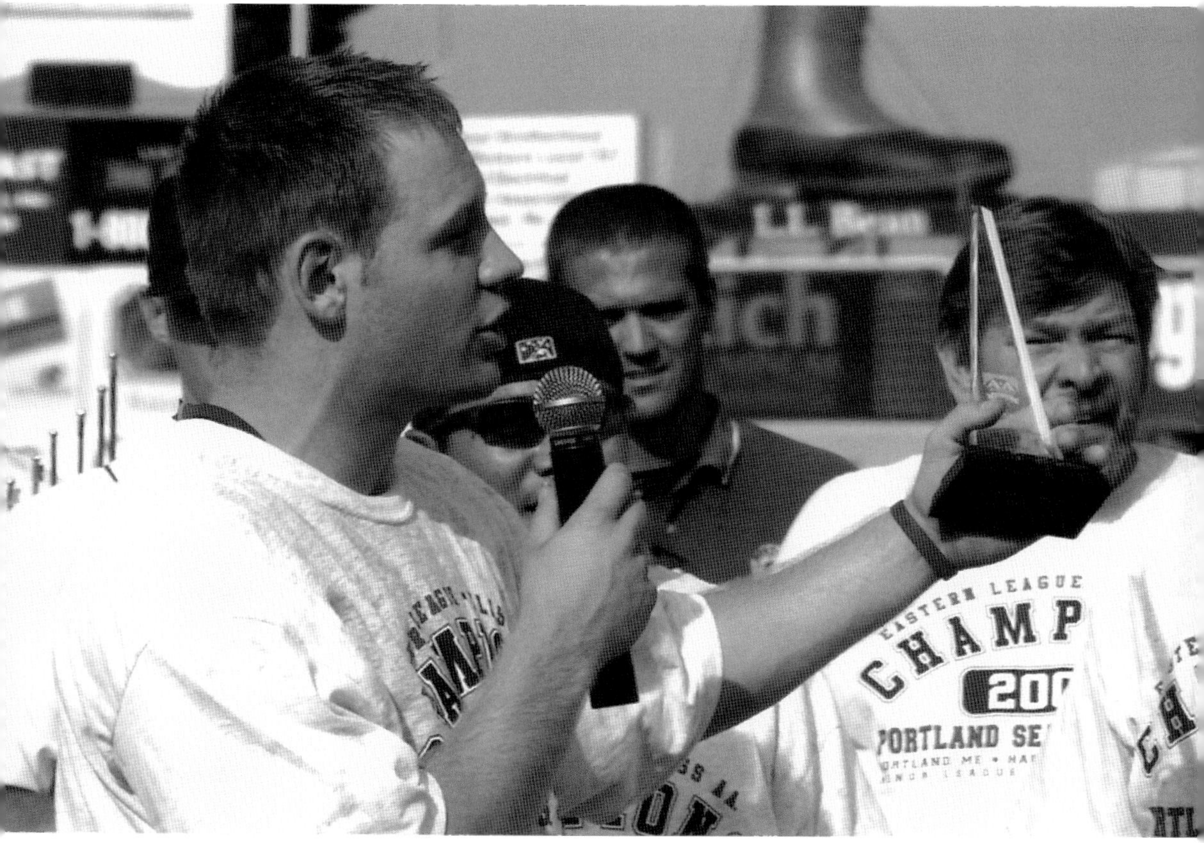

The Eastern League selected Brandon Moss as the MVP of the 2006 Eastern League playoffs. During the Sea Dogs' playoff run, the right fielder batted .361 with five home runs. He drove in 10 runs and scored nine times in nine games. Moss registered a .425 on-base percentage and a .806 slugging percentage. In the heartbreaking Game 4 loss against the Aeros, Moss celebrated his 23rd birthday by hitting a pair of home runs. In the same game, Moss made the defensive play of the game. Moss snagged a ball hit deep into right field, right before crashing into the wall that leads into the Sea Dogs' bullpen to end the fourth inning. It was Moss's game-winning home run in the Northern Division Championship Series versus the Trenton Thunder that allowed Portland to advance to the Eastern League Championship Series against the Akron Aeros. (Courtesy of the Sea Dogs.)

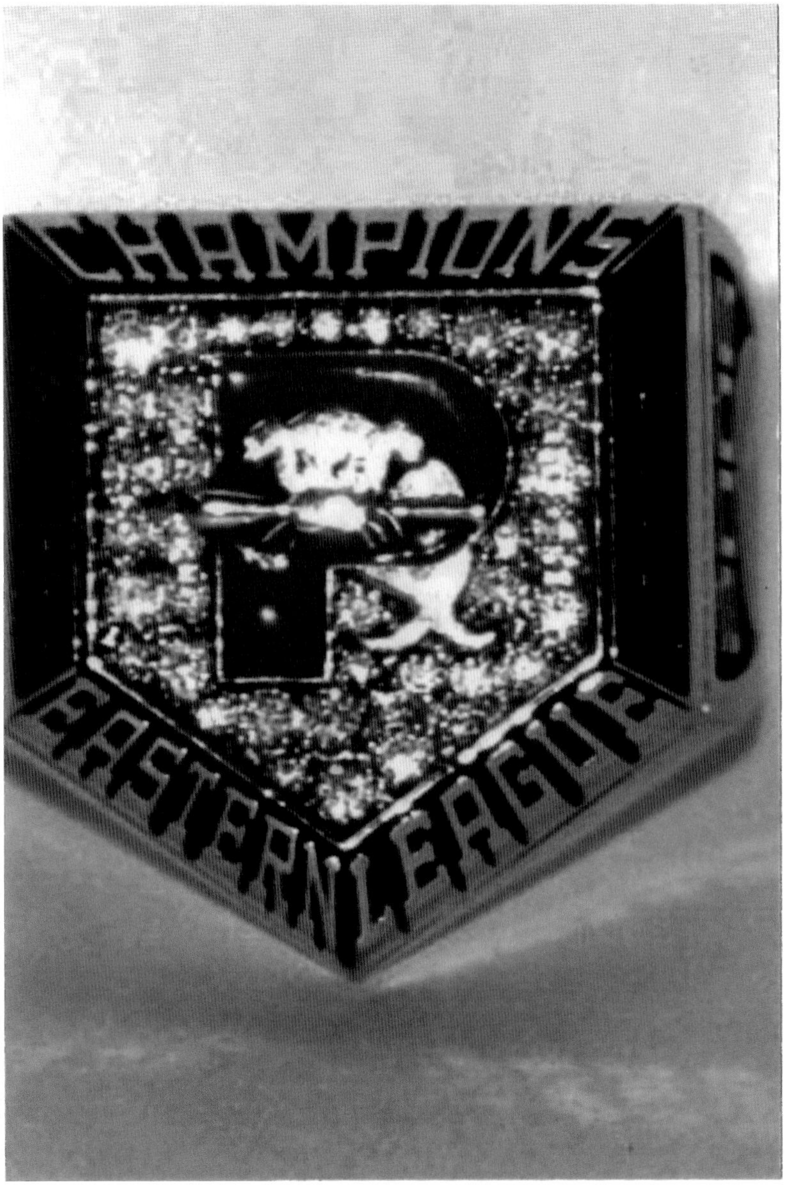

Intergold Limited designed and made the Portland Sea Dogs Eastern League championship rings. Major League Baseball championship clienteles of the Canadian-based company include the 2006 World Series champion St. Louis Cardinals, the Florida Marlins (2003), and the Anaheim Angels (2002). Other baseball championship teams include the 2006 American League champion Detroit Tigers, the 2005 National League champion Houston Astros, and the St. Louis Cardinals' ring in 2004. In a highly anticipated and twice-postponed opening day, Portland Sea Dogs players, team personnel, and front office staff received their championship rings. The rings were given out in a special on-field ceremony before the start of the game. The Pawtucket Red Sox also held a ring ceremony on opening day for all the former Sea Dogs players who were currently playing for the Pawtucket Red Sox. (Courtesy of the Sea Dogs.)

7

The Chance to Stare Down a Pitcher

I never got to bat in the major leagues. I would have liked to have had that chance. Just once. To stare down a big league pitcher . . . make him think you know something he doesn't. That's what I wish for . . . to feel the tingling in your arm as you connect with the ball. To run the bases, stretch a double into a triple and flop face first into third, and wrap your arms around the bag.

—Dr. Archibald "Moonlight" Graham, *Field of Dreams*

Between 1994 and 2006, the Portland Sea Dogs sent 137 players up to the big leagues. Two World Series MVPs, nine major-league all-stars, two Rookies of the Year, and a Rookie of the Year runner-up have called Portland home.

MVPs Livan Hernandez and Josh Beckett, Rookies of the Year Hanley Ramirez and Dustin Pedroia, and Rookie of the Year runner-up Jonathan Papelbon made stops in Portland. Charles Johnson, Edgar Renteria, Alex Gonzalez, Luis Castillo, Brad Penny, A. J. Burnett, and all-time Sea Dogs favorite Kevin Millar (twice) have also made stops in Portland.

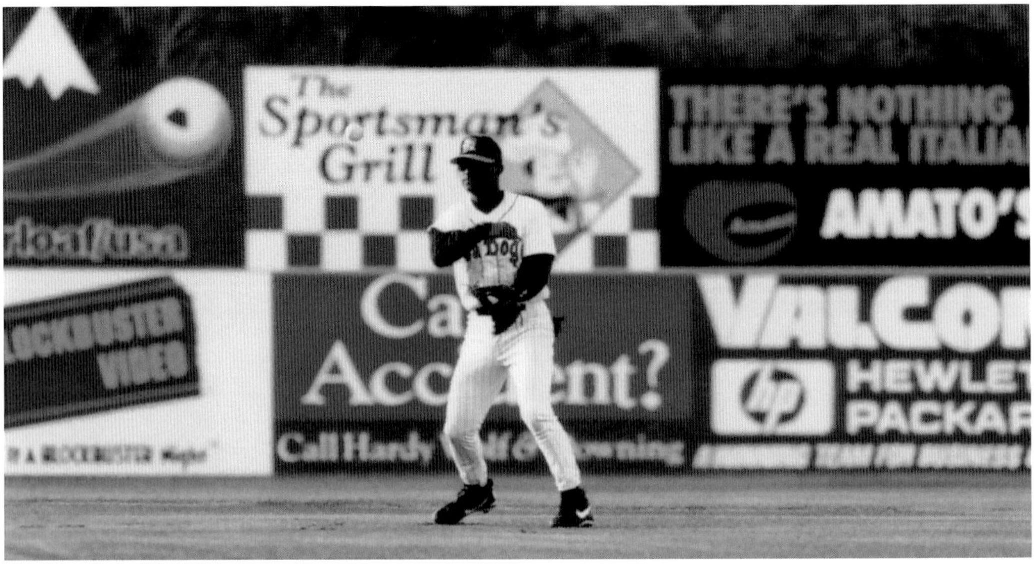

Dominican Republic native Luis Castillo recorded a hit in 35 straight games in 2002, the longest in history by a Latino player. In the field, the second baseman and three-time Gold Glove recipient set a then major-league record of 143 games (2006–2007) without committing an error. Castillo, a three-time all-star with the Marlins, was a member of both Florida World Series championship teams in 1997 and 2003. (Photograph by Stewart Smith.)

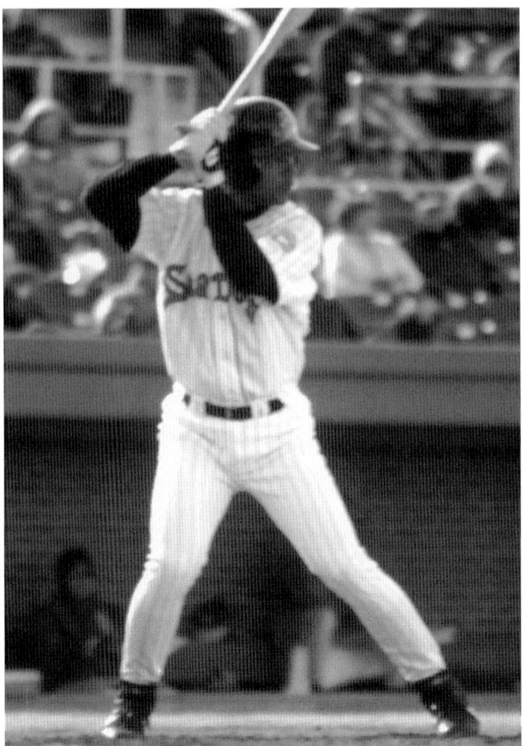

Alex Gonzalez played a pivotal role in the 2003 World Series against the New York Yankees. In Game 4, Gonzalez hit a walk-off, game-winning home run in the 13th inning. The Marlins won 4-3 and tied the series at two. The following night, Gonzalez hit a two-out, game-tying double. In the sixth and deciding game, Gonzalez slid around Yankee catcher Jorge Posada, scoring the insurance run. (Photograph by Stewart Smith.)

On May 12, 2001, former Sea Dogs starting pitcher Allan James (A. J.) Burnett made Major League Baseball history. Burnett, despite walking nine batters, pitched a 3-0 no-hitter versus the San Diego Padres at Jack Murphy Stadium in San Diego. Burnett donated his cap and a game-used baseball to the National Baseball Hall of Fame in Cooperstown, New York. (Photograph by Stewart Smith.)

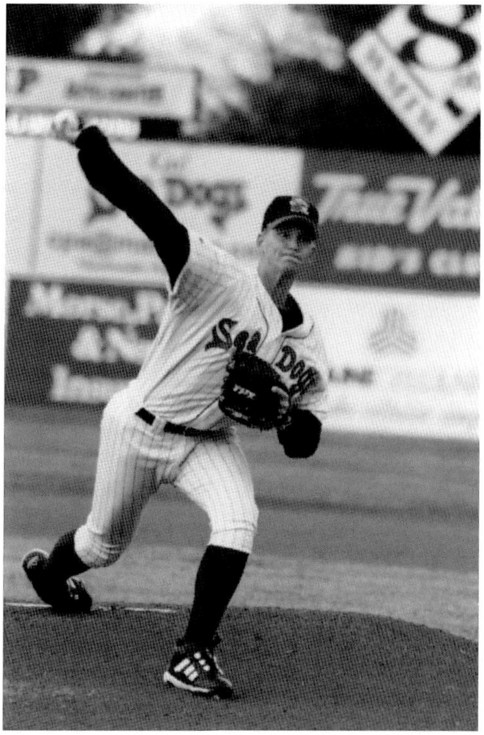

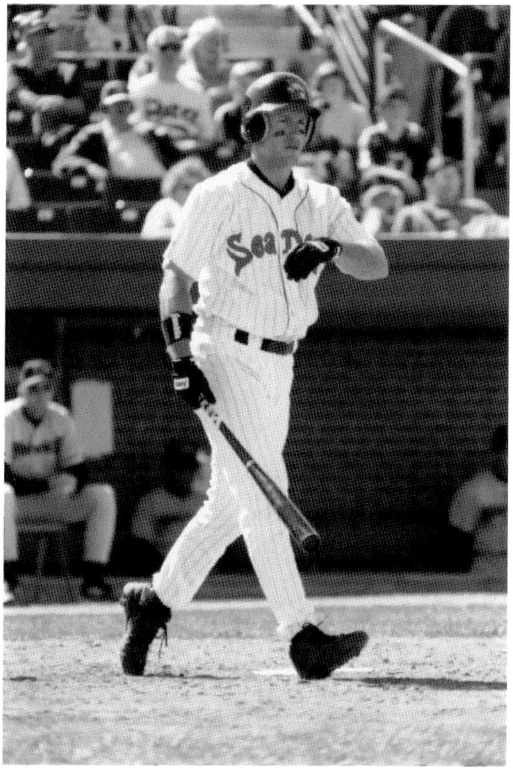

Two former Portland Sea Dogs teammates reunited in 2005. The Chicago White Sox acquired infielder/outfielder Ross Gload from the Colorado Rockies following the 2002 season and signed outfielder Pablo Ozuna prior to the 2005 season. Gload and Ozuna played together on the 2000 Sea Dogs team. (Photograph by Stewart Smith.)

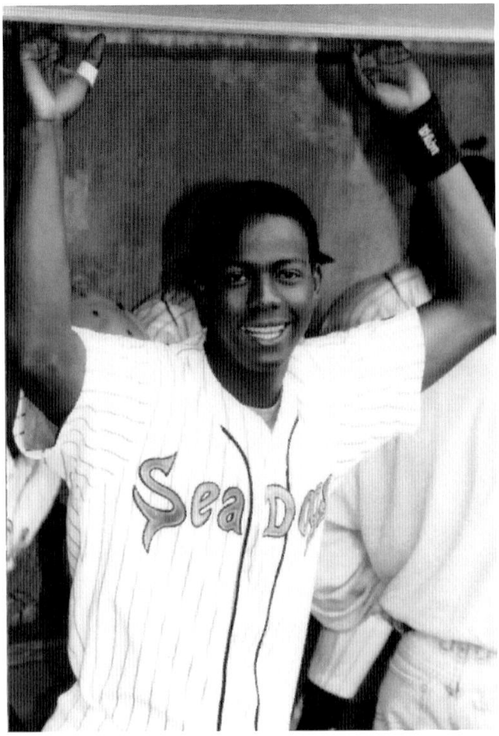

In 1997, the Florida Marlins, in defeating the Cleveland Indians, became the fastest expansion team ever to play in and win the World Series. The world champions included several former Sea Dogs on its roster, including shortstop Edgar Renteria (left) and the young Cuban pitcher Livan Hernandez (below). Both players played key roles in the Marlins' road to victory. On November 4, 1997, only days after his World Series–winning hit, Renteria received the San Carlos Cross of the Order of the Great Knight, his native Colombia's highest honor. At age 22, Hernandez became the youngest pitcher to win a World Series Game 1. Major League Baseball chose Hernandez, only two years removed from his defection to the United States from Cuba, as the series MVP. (Photographs by Stewart Smith.)

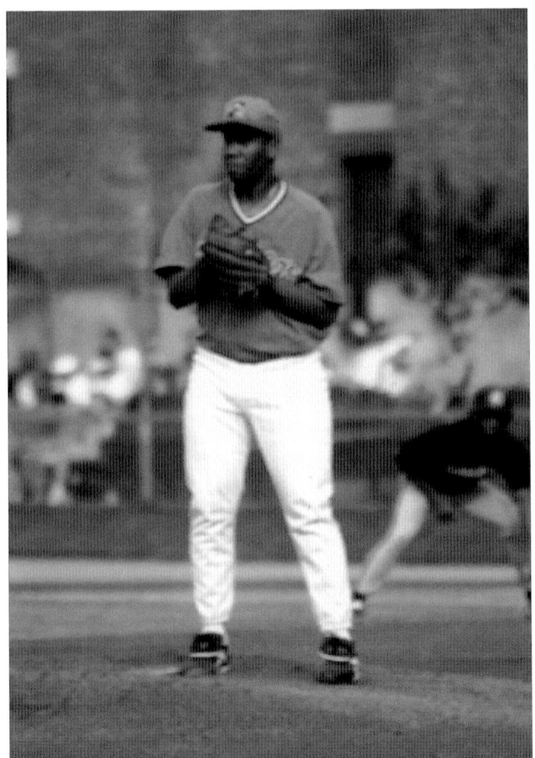

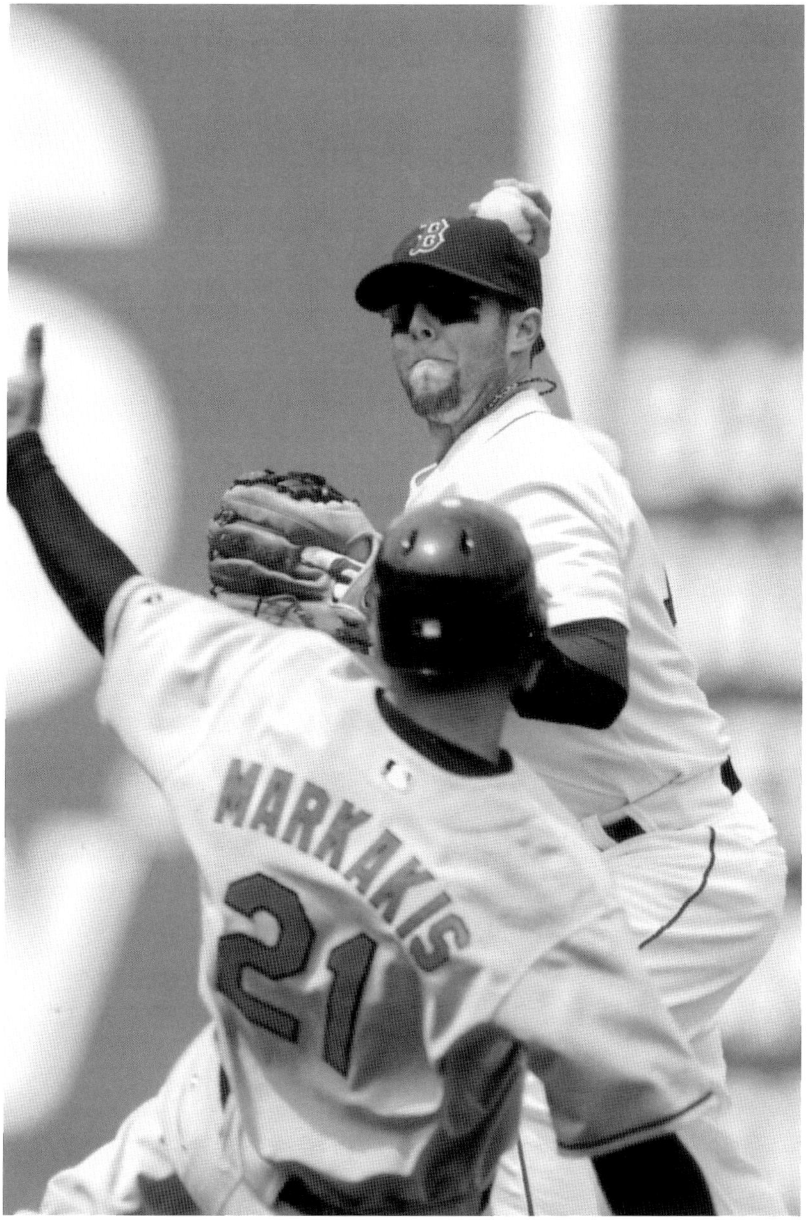

For a second straight season, the Baseball Writers of America selected a former Sea Dog for Rookie of the Year. Second baseman Dustin Pedroia followed in the footsteps of former teammate and current Florida Marlins shortstop Hanley Ramirez, who nabbed National League Rookie of the Year honors in 2006. In 139 games with Boston in 2007, Pedroia batted .317 with eight homers and 50 RBIs. Pedroia, the Red Sox's second-round selection in the 2004 draft, was the American League Rookie of the Month for May and won Player of the Week honors for the week of May 28–June 3. Pedroia was the sixth Boston Red Sox player to be named as the American League's top rookie and the first since Nomar Garciaparra in 1997. (Courtesy of Steve Babineau, Boston Red Sox.)

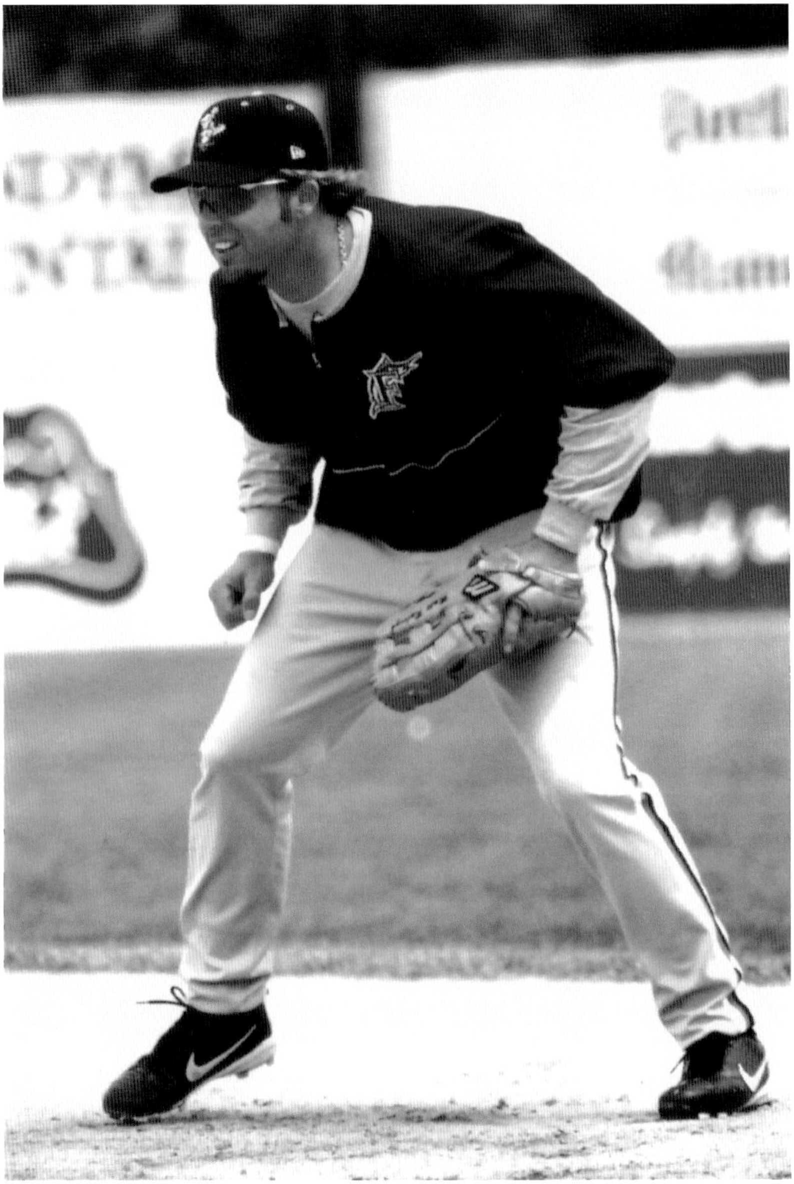

Portland inducted all-time fan favorite Kevin Millar and Bob Ganley into the Sea Dogs Hall of Fame in 2006. Heading into the 2007 season, Millar ranked as Portland's franchise record holder in 14 different offensive categories. The first baseman/outfielder played in 268 games for the Sea Dogs, batting .328 with 51 homers and 220 RBIs. In 1997, Millar put up what many consider the best season in Eastern League history. Millar led the league with a .342 batting average and 131 RBIs. However, his 32 homers are second best and five short of preventing him from winning the first Triple Crown in league history. After the season concluded, the Eastern League named Millar the league's MVP. After five seasons with the Marlins, Millar returned home to New England, signing with the Boston Red Sox in 2003. Millar hit the 10,000th home run in Fenway Park history in 2003. In 2004, he won a World Series ring. (Courtesy of the Sea Dogs.)

The two "streakiest" players in minor-league baseball history both played for Portland. From May 12 to July 28, 2003, Kevin Youkilis reached base in 62 straight games before his promotion to Pawtucket. With Pawtucket, Youkilis extended his streak, ending at 71 games. From July 12 to August 30, 1997, Kevin Millar reached base in 46 straight games. Millar's minor-league streak ended at 71 games with Triple-A Calgary in 1999. (Courtesy of the Sea Dogs.)

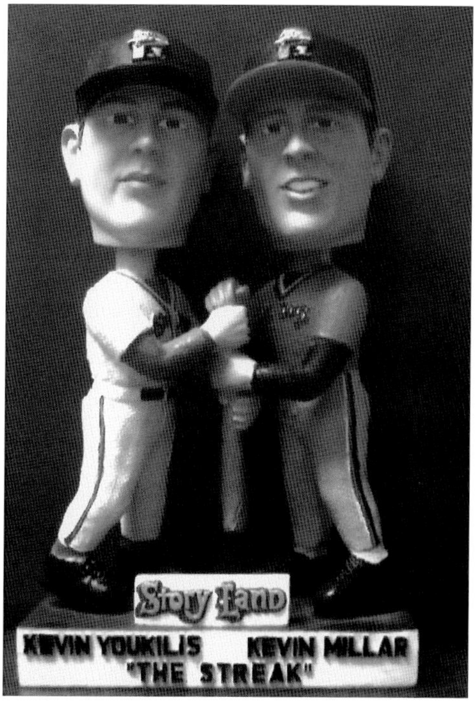

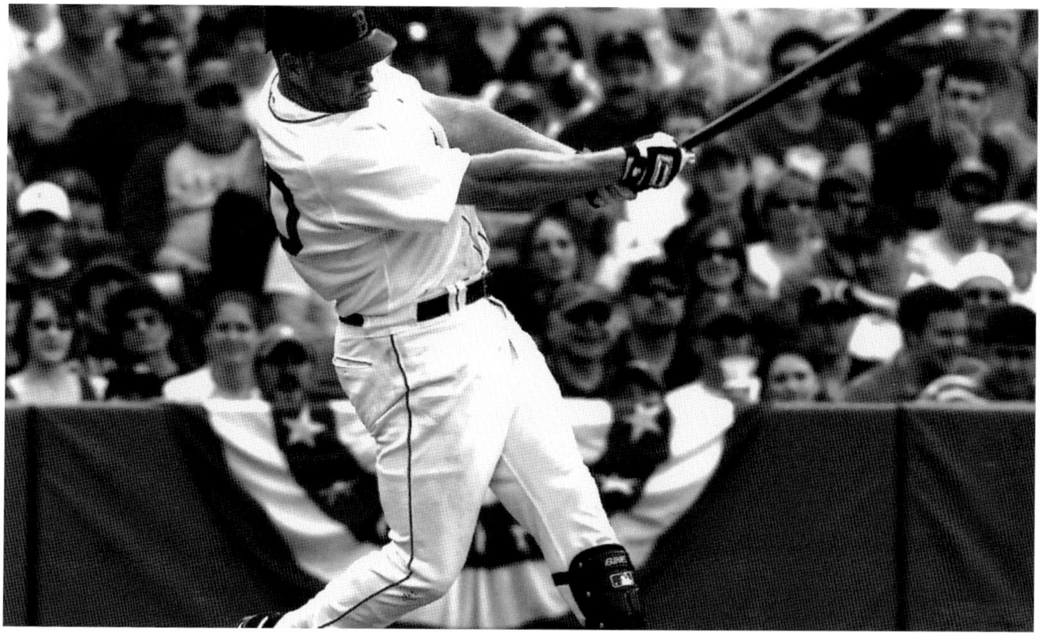

Active in the community was fan favorite and former Sea Dog Youkilis. In 2006, Youkilis started a program he calls Lil' Youks. The ticket program invited patients from the Home for Little Wanderers and the Massachusetts General Hospital Teen Oncology Support Group. Youkilis also helped raise money for Locks of Love, Canine Companions for Independence, and Christmas at Fenway. (Courtesy of Brian Babineau, Boston Red Sox.)

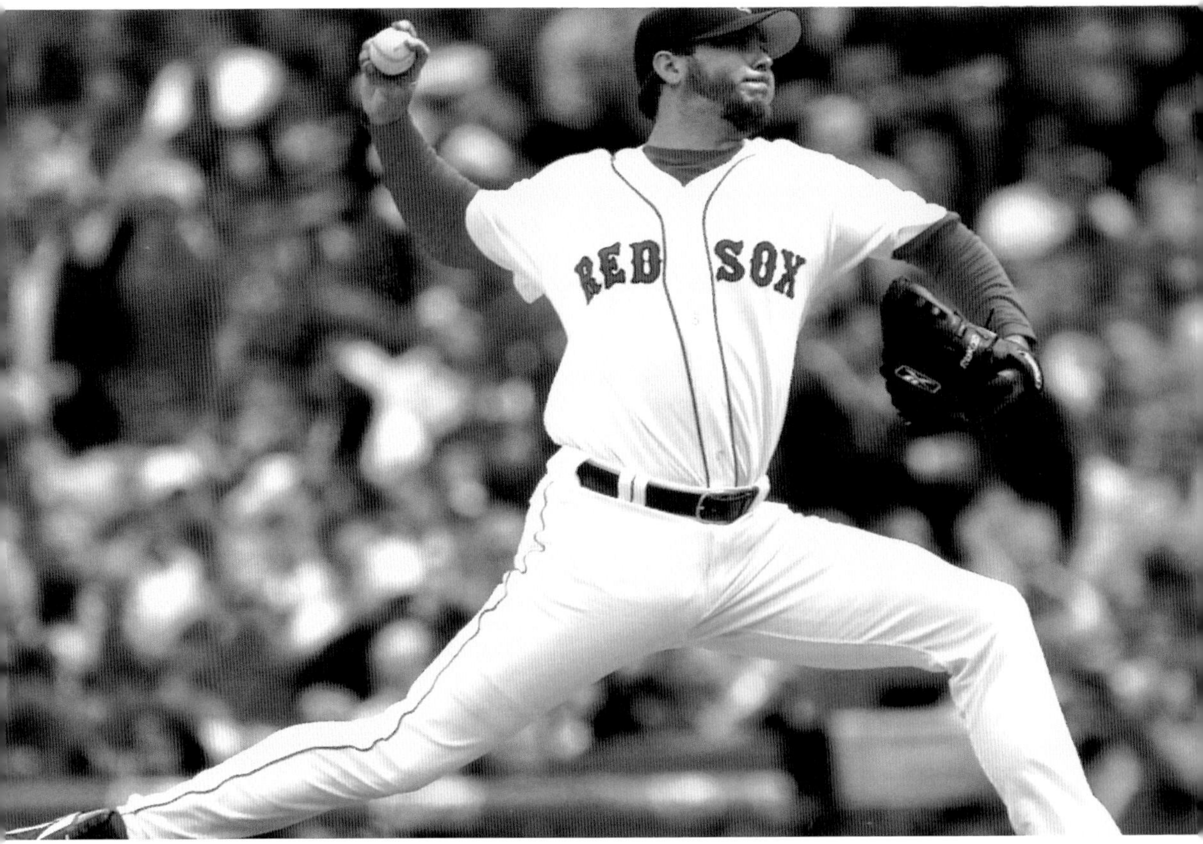

Part of the enjoyment in cheering for a minor-league team is watching potential talent blossom into major-league stars. In recent years, Sea Dogs fans have had the opportunity to see two future World Series MVPs don a Sea Dogs uniform. Cuban defector Livan Hernandez won in 1997 for his pitching performance over the Cleveland Indians. In 2003, the Florida Marlins defeated the New York Yankees and won their second World Series championship. Pitching on only three days' rest, Josh Beckett tossed a complete game shutout to help the Marlins win the sixth and deciding game of the World Series at Yankee Stadium. Major League Baseball named Beckett the series MVP as he established himself as one of the top postseason pitchers. (Courtesy of Julie Cordiero, Boston Red Sox.)

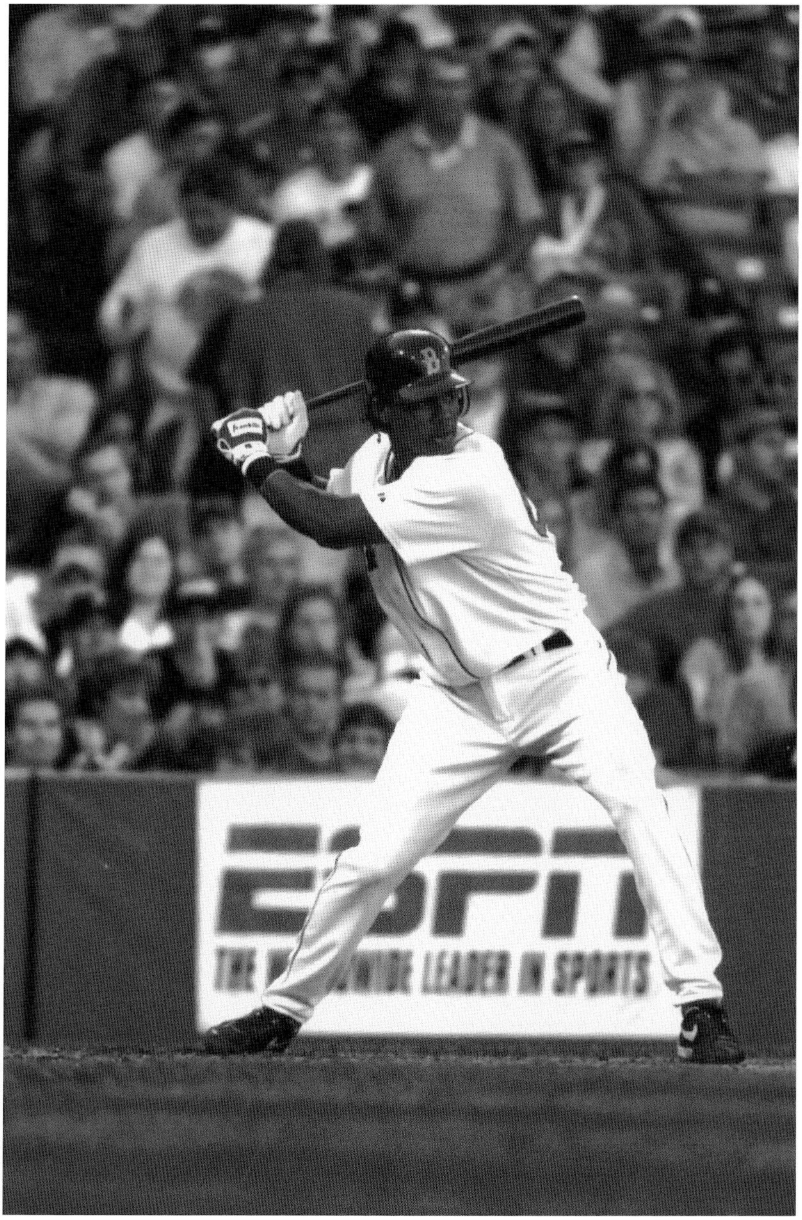

Hanley Ramirez, a former Boston Red Sox top prospect, quickly became one of the more electrifying players in the National League. In his rookie season with the Florida Marlins, Ramirez led all rookies with a .292 batting average, including 185 hits, 119 runs, 46 doubles, 11 triples, and 51 stolen bases. Ramirez also smacked seven leadoff home runs, a Marlins record. He became the first National League rookie to score 110-plus runs and steal 50-plus bases. His stellar season earned him 2006 Rookie of the Year honors. In a strange reversal of fortune, Beckett and Ramirez, two former Sea Dogs, were part of a seven-player deal that sent Ramirez to the Marlins and Beckett to the Red Sox on Thanksgiving Day 2005. (Courtesy of Brita Meng Outzen, Boston Red Sox.)

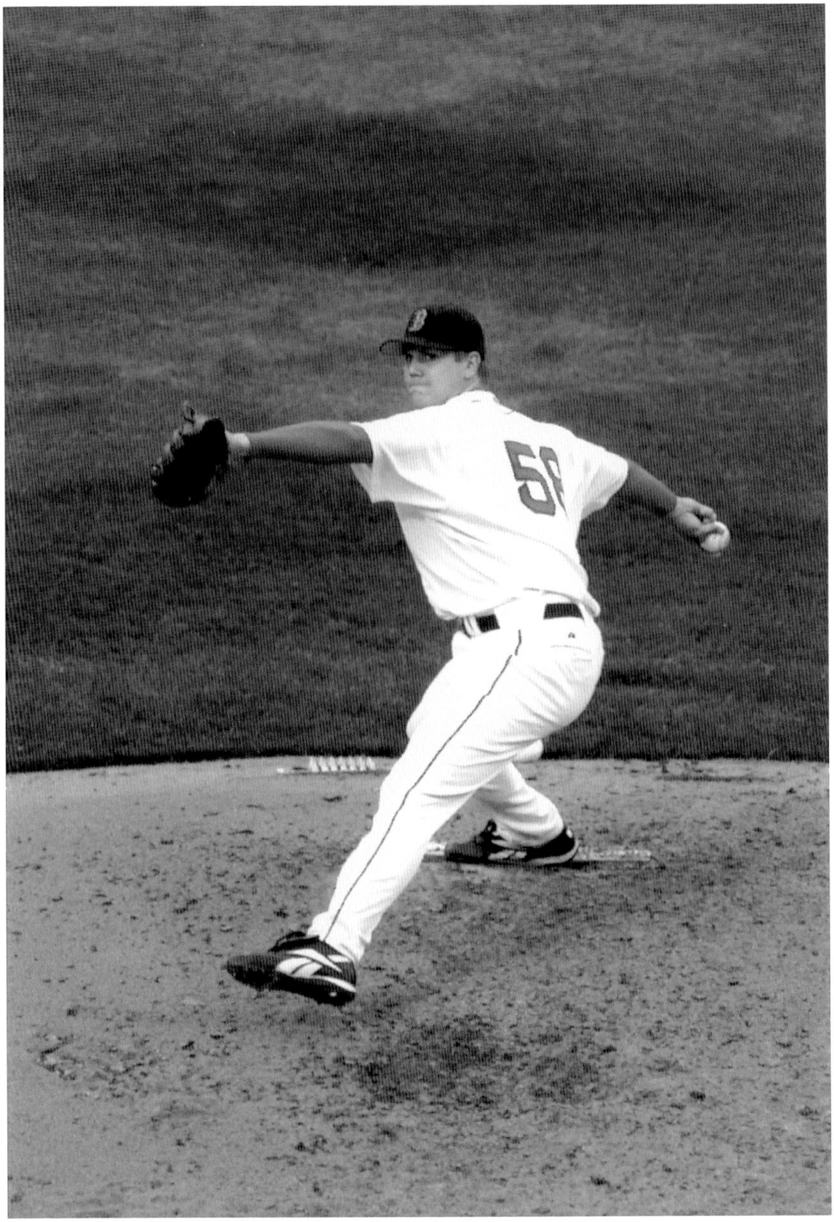

After incumbent closer Keith Foulke was ineffective in his comeback from an injury-plagued 2005 campaign, Jonathan Papelbon inherited the role of closer. In only the second game of the 2006 season, Papelbon registered his first career save against the Texas Rangers. Papelbon closed out the 2006 season with one of the most dominating seasons ever recorded for a rookie pitcher. In 68 innings of work, Papelbon saved 35 games (26 by the all-star break) and struck out 75 batters. Opposing batters hit only a minuscule .167. Papelbon was runner-up for American League Rookie of the Year honors. Former Eastern League rival and current Detroit Tigers starting pitcher Justin Verlander grabbed the honor instead. (Courtesy of Steve Babineau, Boston Red Sox.)

8

A Place where Dreams Come True

Is this heaven?
It's Iowa.
Iowa? I could have sworn this was heaven.
Is there a heaven?
Oh Yeah. It's the place where dreams come true.

—John and Ray Kinsella, *Field of Dreams*

Record-breaking attendance figures, a showcase and training ground for future major-league talent, a city institution: it may not be heaven or Iowa, but it is Hadlock Field.

Found along the Atlantic coast in downtown Portland, Hadlock Field is conveniently found off Interstate 295, the state's most heavily traveled road. Nestled between Fitzpatrick Stadium and the "Expo," or Portland Exposition building, construction of Hadlock Field began in the early 1990s, when baseball returned to the city after a 45-year absence.

A former high school baseball diamond, Hadlock Field consisted of a chain-link fence, lights, and bleachers for about 1,200 fans when the Sea Dogs took up residency.

More than a decade later, the fence is gone and in its place a monster. The lighting has improved, and more than five million fans have watched a game.

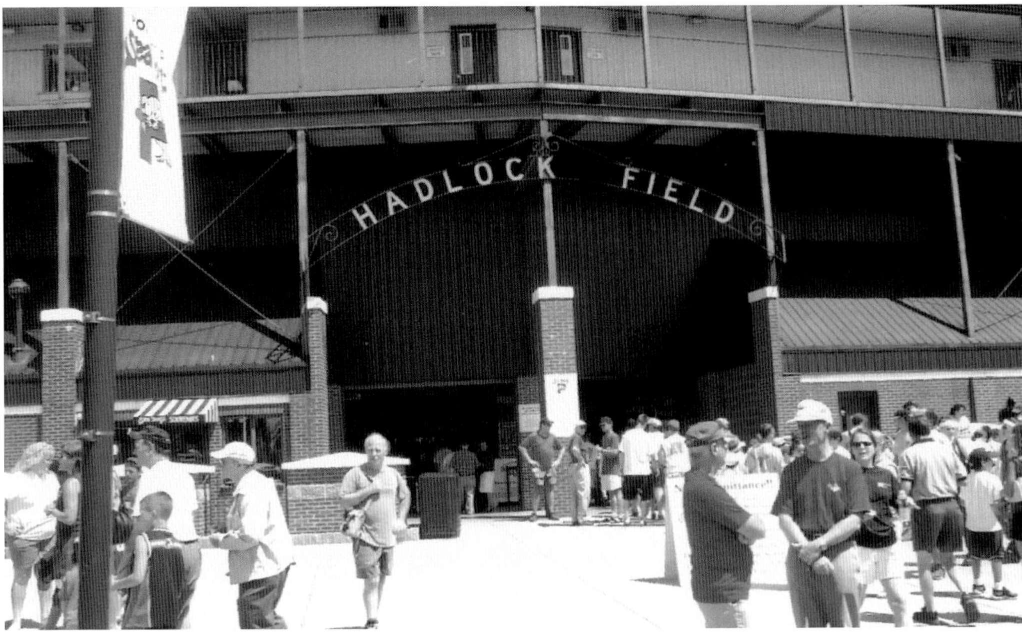

Named after Edson B. Hadlock Jr., former baseball coach for Portland High School, Hadlock Field, formerly Portland Stadium, was the playing grounds for high school baseball games. The name change to Hadlock Field followed Hadlock's retirement after 29 years of coaching. After Hadlock's passing the winter before, the city refurbished and renamed the aging ball field Edson Hadlock Memorial Field in May 1985. (Courtesy of the Sea Dogs.)

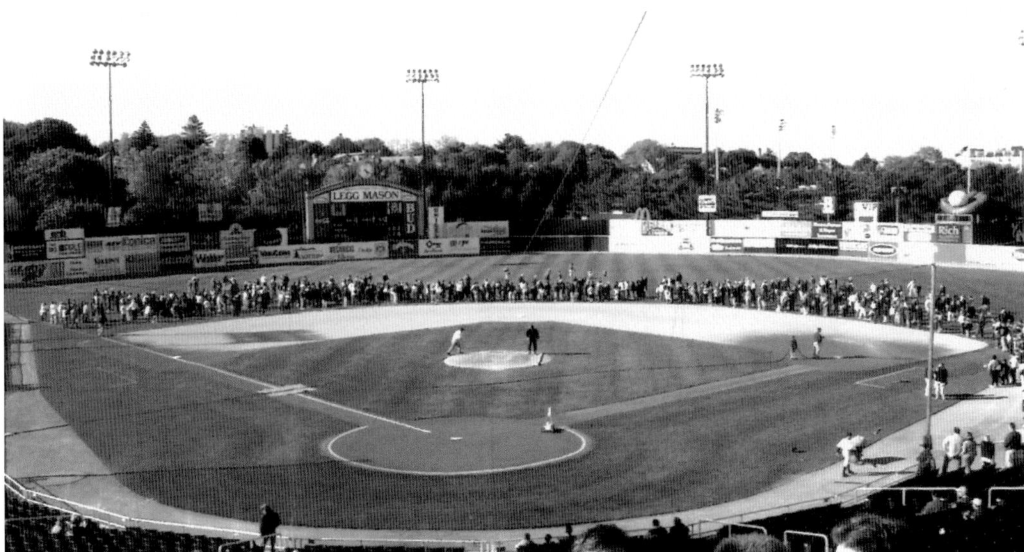

Seven months after the Eastern League selected Portland as home to one of two Eastern League baseball teams, the Sea Dogs held groundbreaking ceremonies at Hadlock Field in May 1993. The Eastern League scheduled the Sea Dogs to play ball beginning in April 1994, giving the city less than a year to upgrade the facility to Double-A standards. (Courtesy of the Sea Dogs.)

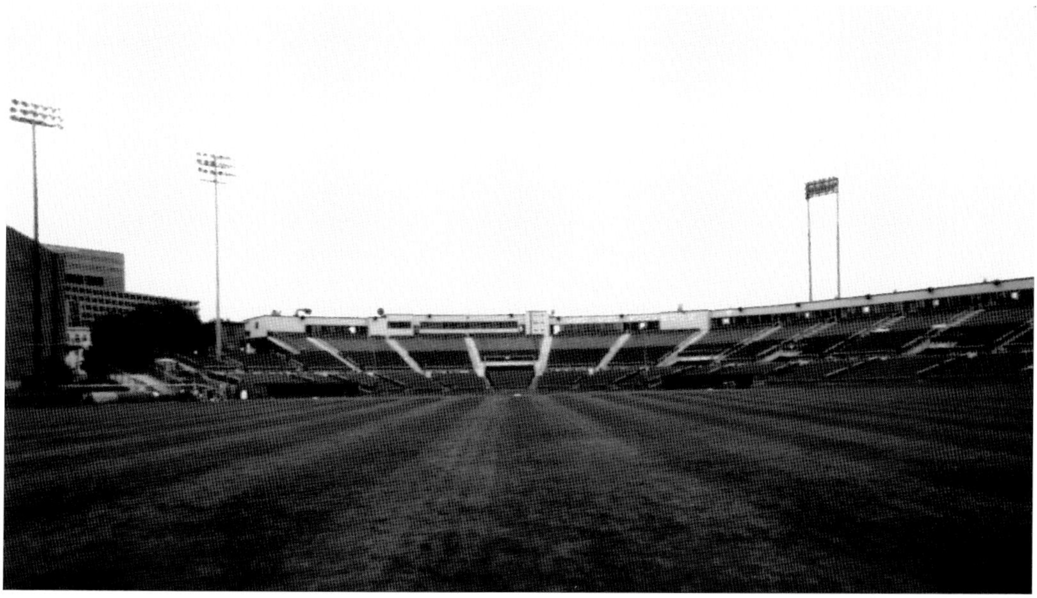

No one sees, but hears, one of the more unforgettable aspects of Hadlock Field. Constructed out of aluminum, the primary seating bowl sits atop the main concourse. A Sea Dogs rally call consisting of fans' stomping feet, while perhaps not aesthetically pleasing to one's eardrums down below, is now a signature feature of the ballpark.

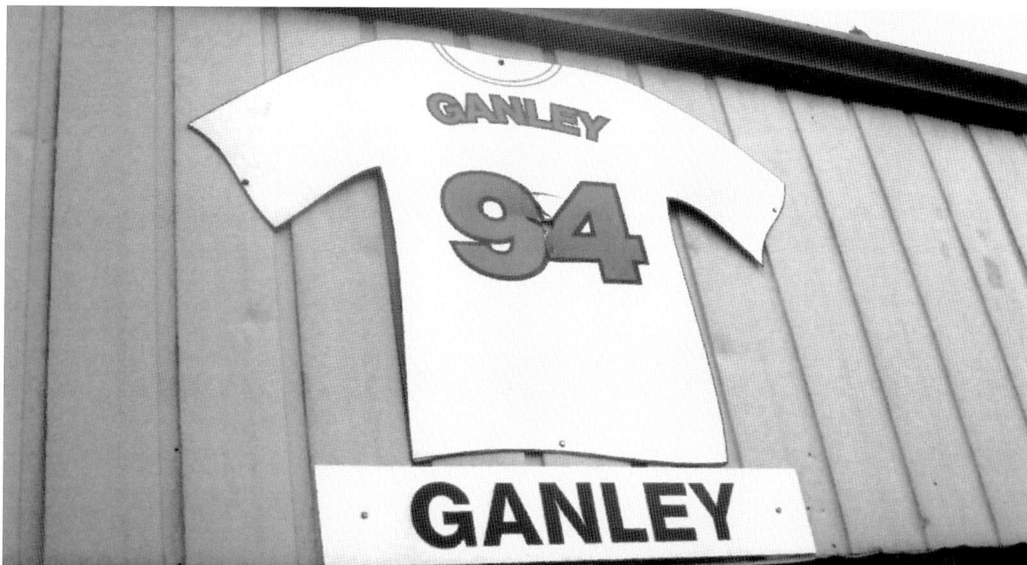

On April 9, 2001, Portland dedicated the skybox closest to Portland City Hall the Ganley Box in honor of Portland city manager and Sea Dogs booster Bob Ganley. Ganley, who passed away during the off-season, was a driving force in bringing the Sea Dogs to Portland. Ganley's No. 94 jersey represents the first year the Sea Dogs played ball in Portland and at Hadlock Field. (Courtesy of the Sea Dogs.)

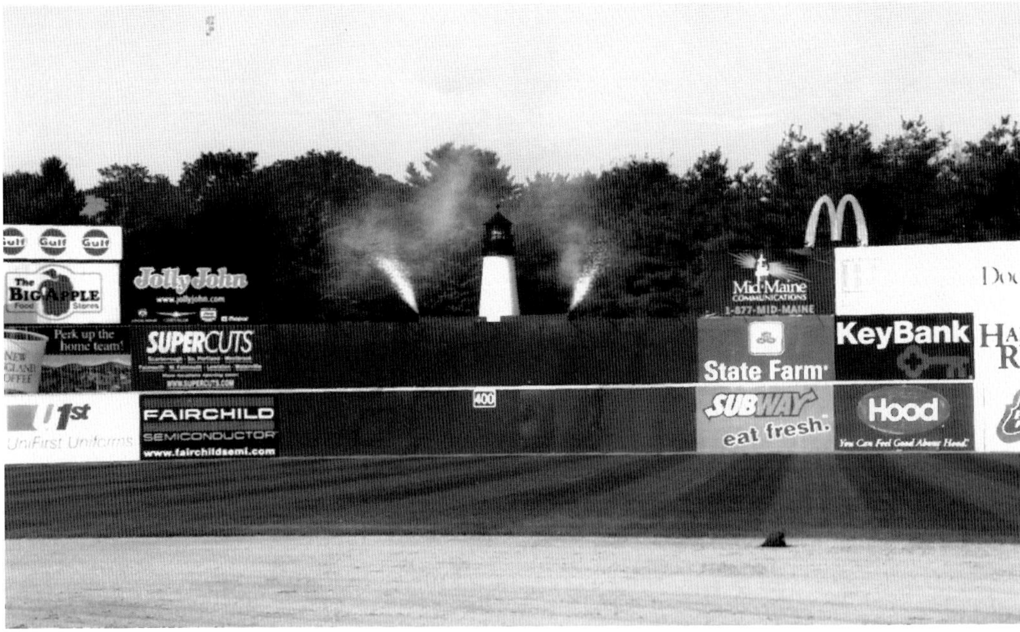

One of Hadlock Field's first and most distinctive gimmicks pays homage to Maine's maritime and lighthouse history. Rising from the "fog" is a 18-foot replica of neighboring town Cape Elizabeth's Portland Head Light. Signaling the lighthouse's ascent from behind the center field wall is a deep and bellowing foghorn. Once fully risen, fireworks shoot from the sides and the light spins. The lighthouse rises after every Sea Dogs home run and every Portland victory. Nicknamed "Burke's Beacon" after its first appearance in honor of Portland Sea Dogs owner Dan Burke, the modest Burke quickly abolished the moniker. (Courtesy of the Sea Dogs.)

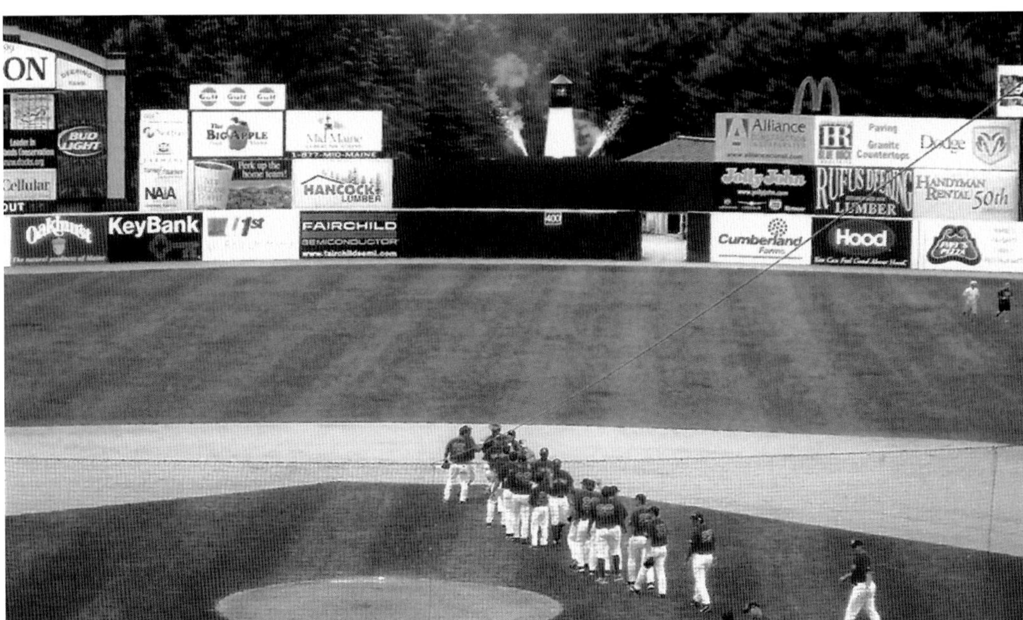

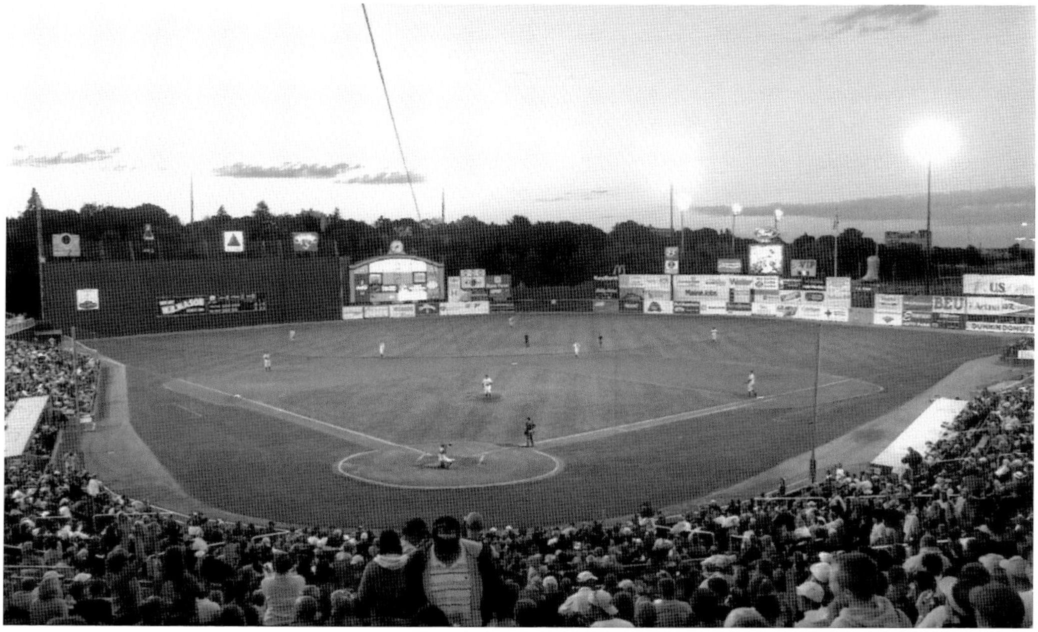

At the end of the 2002 season, the Sea Dogs announced that they severed ties with the Florida Marlins. They also announced they inked a new player development contract with the Boston Red Sox. The switch in affiliation partners not only brought a new crop of hopeful major-league talent to Hadlock Field but also brought cosmetic changes to the ballpark. Dan Burke, owner of the Sea Dogs, commemorated the union by funding changes to Hadlock Field's skyline. He began by renaming all the skyboxes after former Red Sox greats. (Courtesy of the Sea Dogs.)

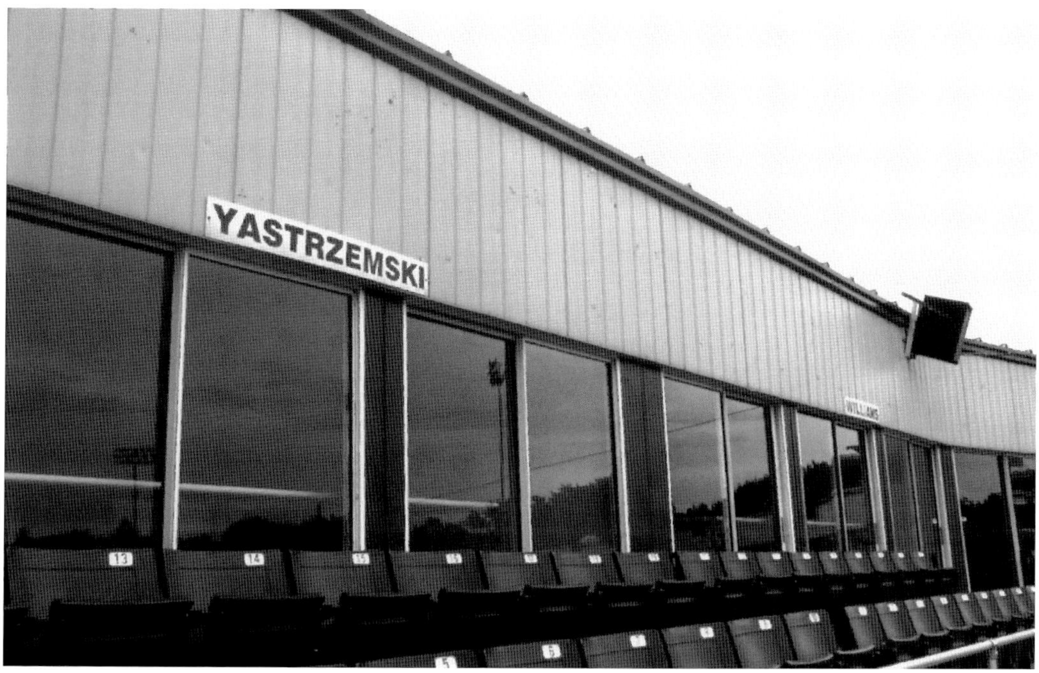

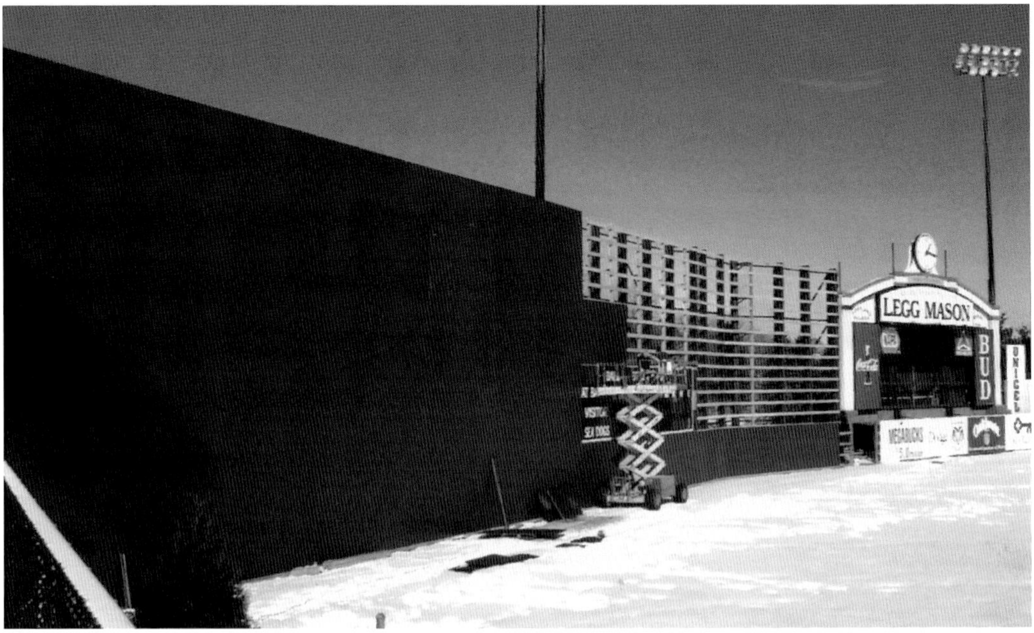

For inspiration, Burke looked to Portland's new affiliation partner and Fenway Park. Burke funded the construction of a miniature Green Monster. Like the team nickname, the naming of the mini wall was left to the citizens of Portland and fans of the Sea Dogs to decide. The winner was the Maine Monster. Like its Bostonian twin, the Maine Monster stands 37 feet high, and like its predecessor, the Maine Monster contains a screen to entrap home run balls. Although the Maine Monster mimics the Green Monster's height, it falls short in length at 160 feet (versus the Green Monster's 240 feet). Completing its similarity, though smaller than their Fenway counterparts, are a miniature Coca-Cola bottle and Citgo sign that sit atop the wall. (Courtesy of the Sea Dogs.)

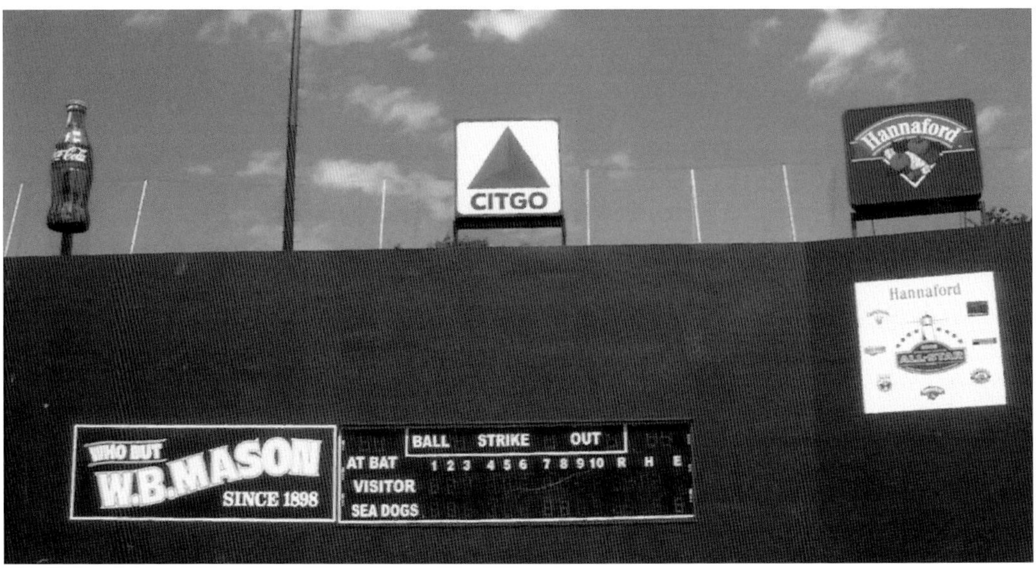

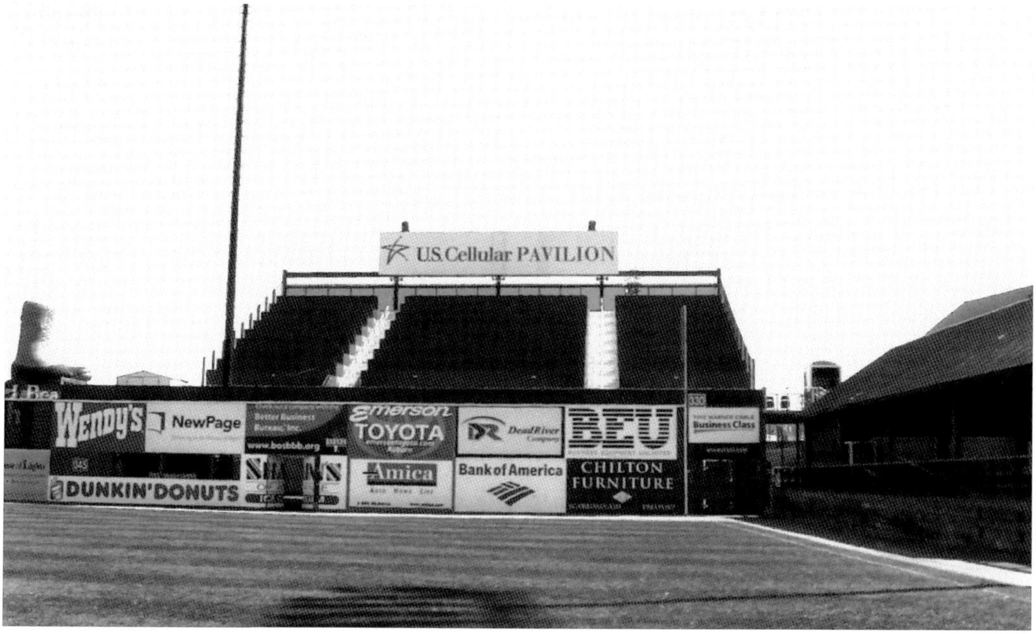

Because of the railroad tracks that run right behind the Maine Monster, the Sea Dogs are unable to build seats atop it. Instead, Portland built 393 seats above the home bullpen. The countertop-style seats are similar to Fenway Park's Monster Seats. Unique to minor-league baseball, the Sea Dogs promote the seats as the only seats at Hadlock Field where one can catch a home run ball. The Sea Dogs call their new seating area the U.S. Cellular Pavilion. Here is a view of the game and the new playing surface installed before opening day 2006, from the pavilion seats. (Below, courtesy of the Sea Dogs.)

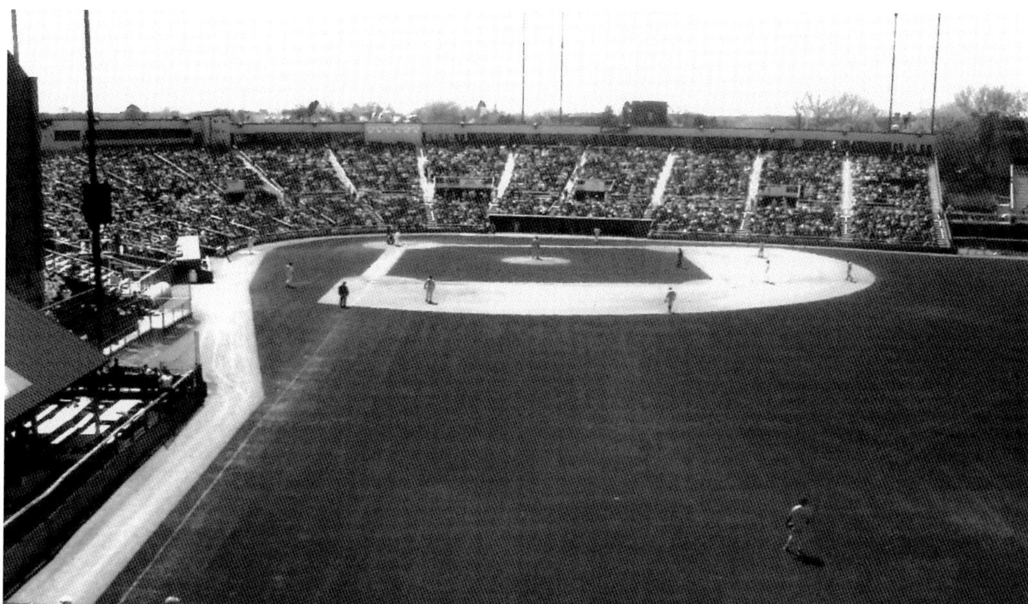

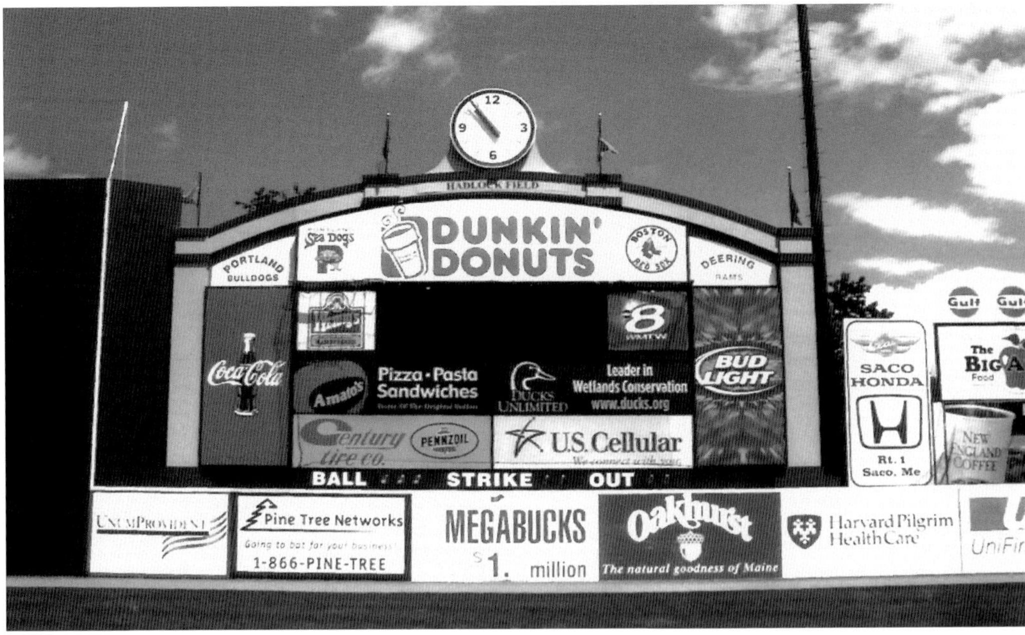

Securely nestled between the Maine Monster and the center field wall is the Dunkin' Donuts (previously Legg Mason) scoreboard. One of the only remaining features from opening day 1994, the scoreboard pays homage to logo-covered outfield fences, a staple in minor-league ballparks from Maine to California and everywhere in between. (Courtesy of the Sea Dogs.)

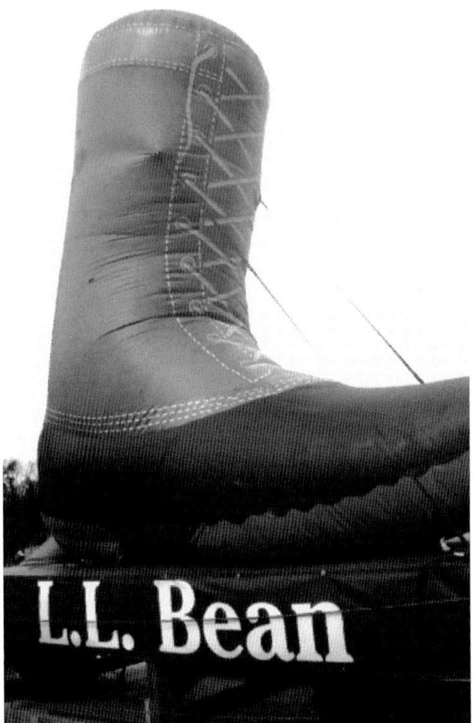

One of the more prominent features at Hadlock Field is the large, inflatable L. L. Bean boot. Founded in 1912 by Leon Leonwood Bean, L. L. Bean is one of the country's leading outdoor equipment and apparel companies. The one-man operation has grown into a global business with annual sales of $1.5 billion. Just down the road from its original store, L. L. Bean calls Freeport, Maine, home.

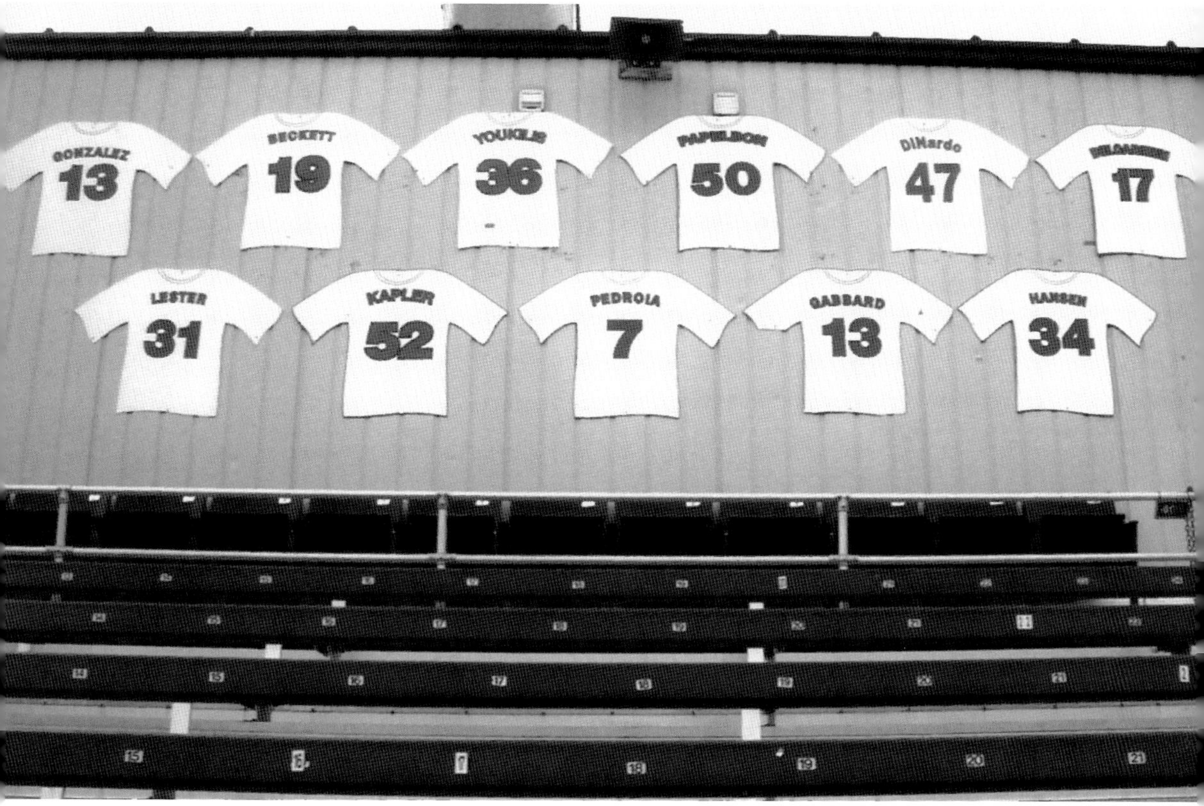

Hanging above the seats from home plate and down the third-base line are the Sea Dogs jerseys. The jerseys pay tribute to former Sea Dogs players who are currently playing on the Boston Red Sox (the Sea Dogs' major-league parent). The jerseys feature the former player's name and Sea Dogs number. Constantly in a state of flux, at one time, 11 jerseys were on display. These Sea Dogs jerseys belonged to, from left to right, (first row) Jon Lester (No. 31), Gabe Kapler (No. 52), Dustin Pedroia (No. 7), Kason Gabbard (No. 13), and Craig Hansen (No. 34); (second row) Alex Gonzalez (No. 13), Josh Beckett (No. 19), Kevin Youkilis (No. 36), Jonathan Papelbon (No. 50), Lenny DiNardo (No. 47), and Manny Delcarmen (No. 17). At the start of the 2007 season, eight player jerseys were on display. Former players included Beckett, Delcarmen, Devern Hansack (No. 29), Hansen, Lester, Papelbon, Pedroia, and Youkilis. (Courtesy of the Sea Dogs.)

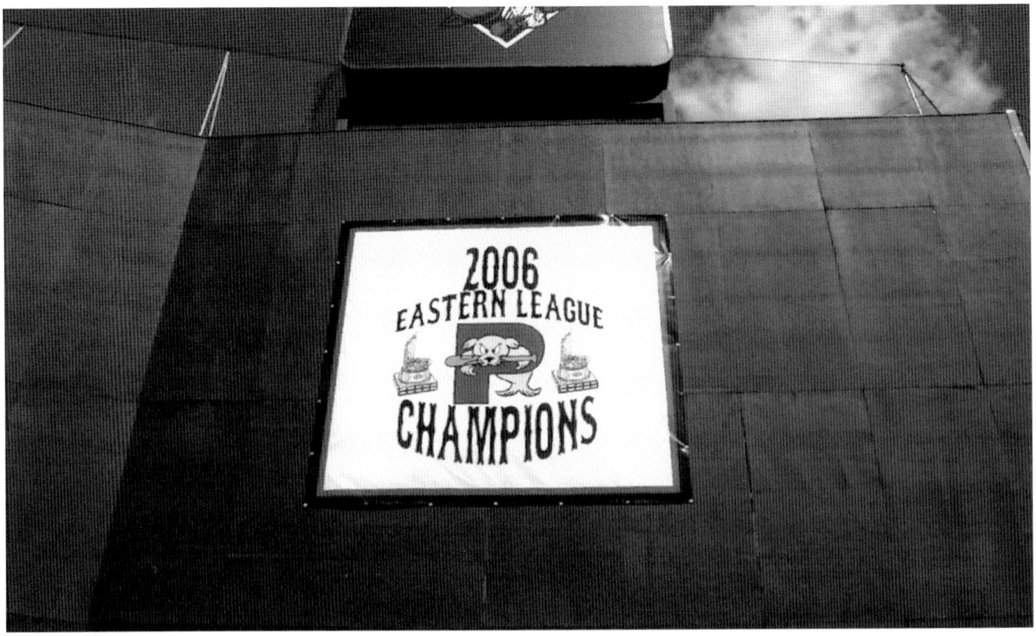

When the Sea Dogs returned to the Eastern League Championship Series in 2006, it was the fourth time in the team's 13-year franchise history. The Sea Dogs entered the series hoping to bring the city of Portland and the state of Maine their first title in nine decades. The Boston Red Sox, Portland's affiliation partner since the 2003 season, had not had a Double-A champion since the 1980s. Their previous winner was the New Britain Red Sox, winners of the Eastern League title in 1983. To commemorate the Sea Dogs' 2006 Eastern League championship victory, and new to Hadlock Field for 2007, were the 2006 Eastern League championship banner and stadium pennant.

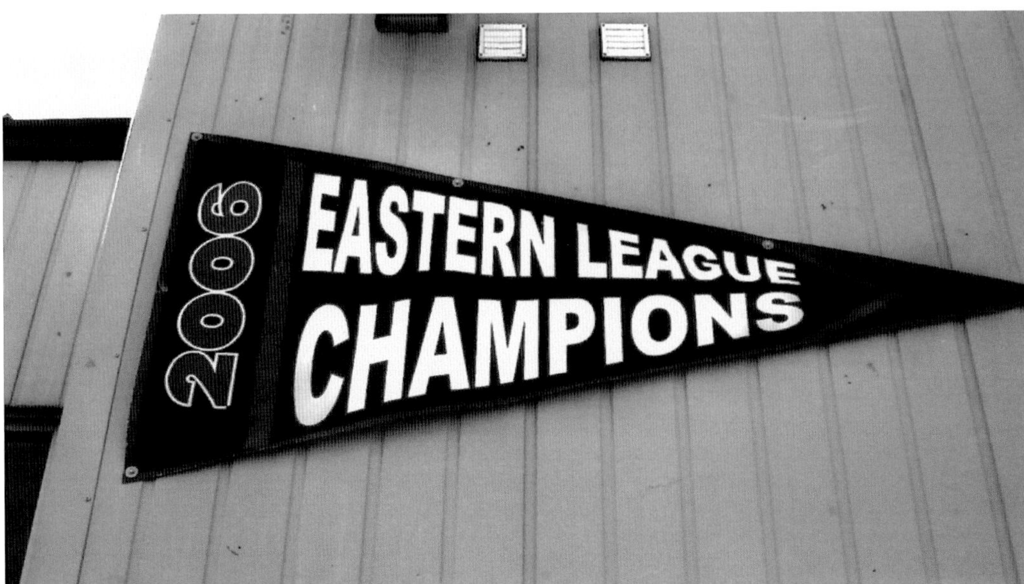

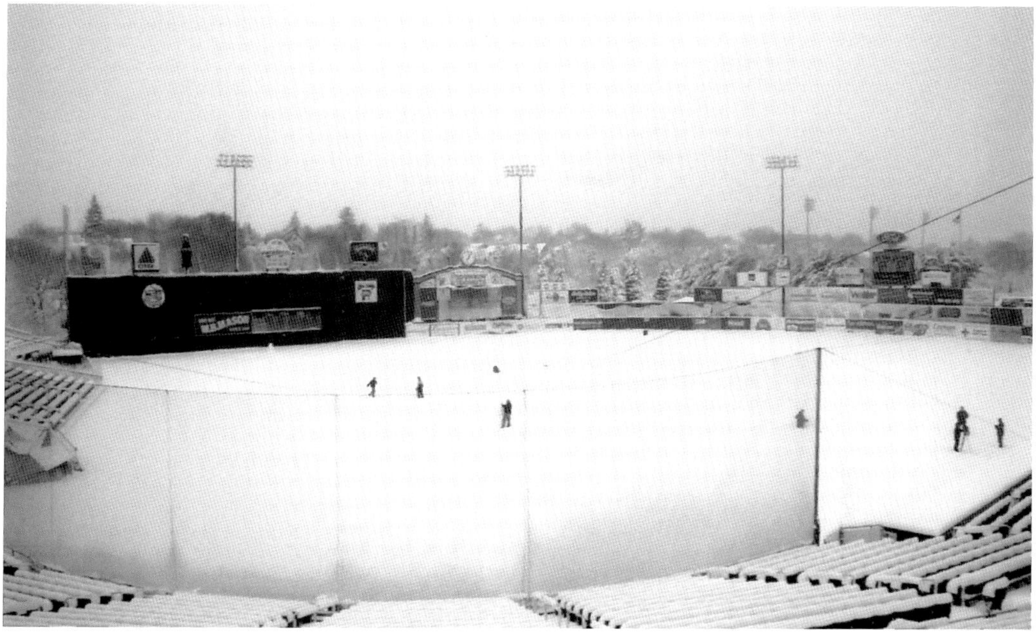

In 2007, the Sea Dogs declared April 27 as opening day, again. Earlier in the month, inclement weather erased 7 out of the first 10 home games. On the first opening day of the 2007 season, Mother Nature buried Portland under a 12-inch blanket of snow, cancelling the game. Opening day part two was scheduled for April 16, when Portland returned home for a brief series against the Trenton Thunder. The Sea Dogs rescheduled opening day festivities for the first game of the series. After a powerful nor'easter slashed the Maine coastline, Portland postponed the game (and opening day) again, until the end of April when the Sea Dogs come back home. Nobody ever claimed Mother Nature is a baseball fan. (Courtesy of the Sea Dogs.)

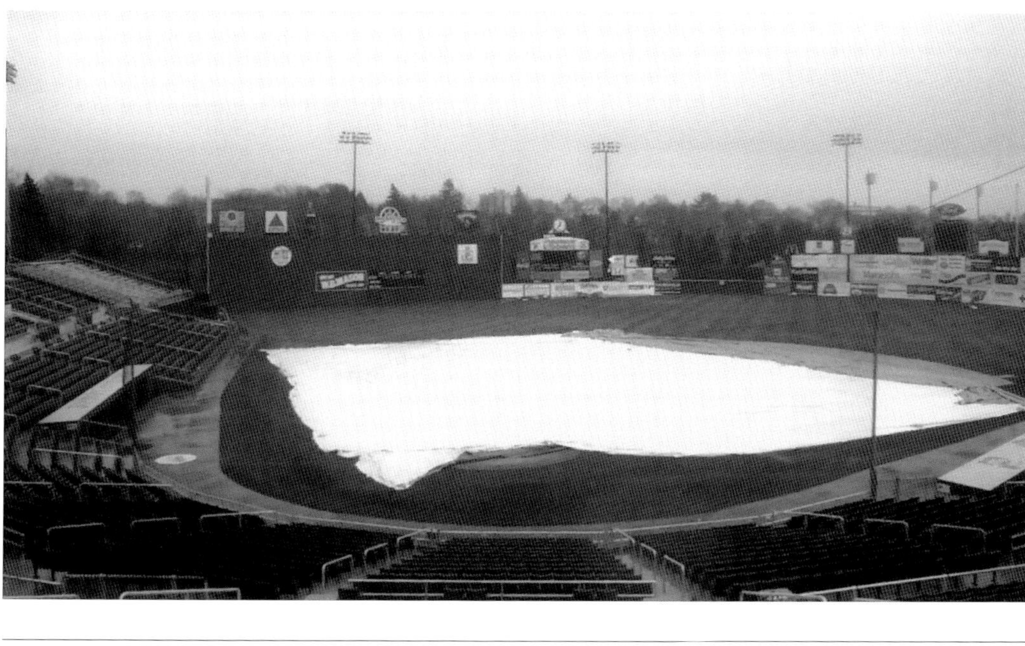

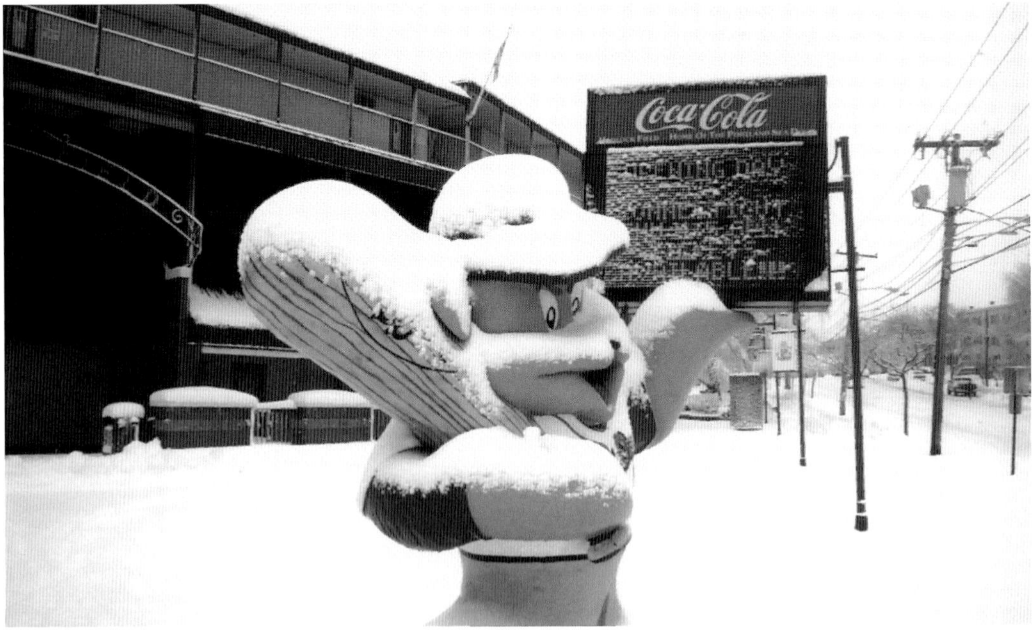

A spring snowstorm walloped the Midwest, burying several cities, such as Cleveland, under a foot of snow before it headed to New England and Maine. The snowstorm cancelled and postponed major- and minor-league baseball games (including several opening days) from the Midwest to the Atlantic coast. In Maine, cities from Bangor to Portland found themselves digging out from under a foot of snow. Heavy snows buried the Slugger statue outside the entrance of Hadlock Field on opening day 2007. After the heavy snows forced the Sea Dogs to cancel and postpone opening day versus Connecticut, the "Snowville Nine" come out to play. (Courtesy of the Sea Dogs.)

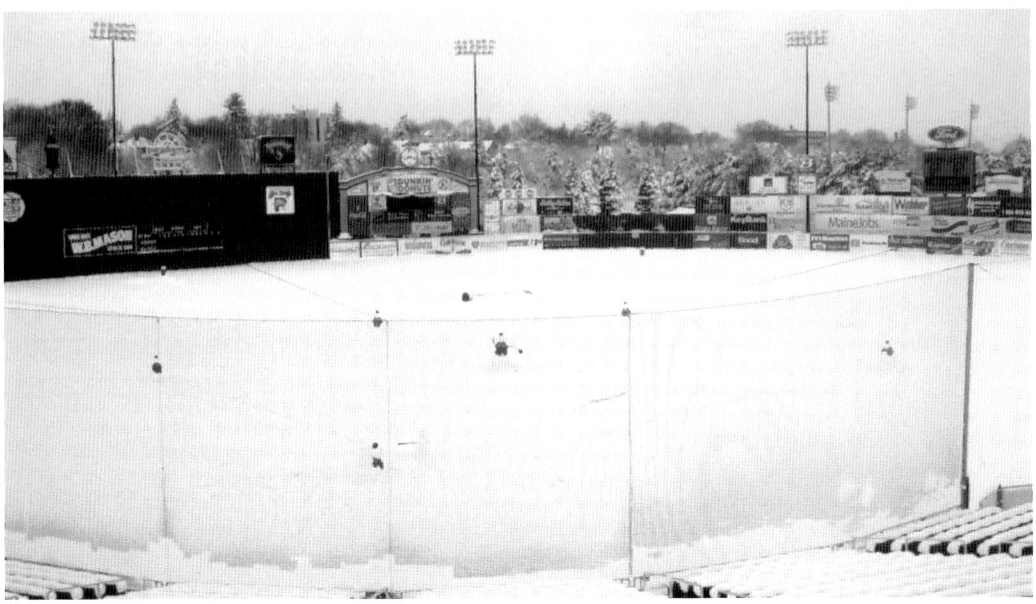

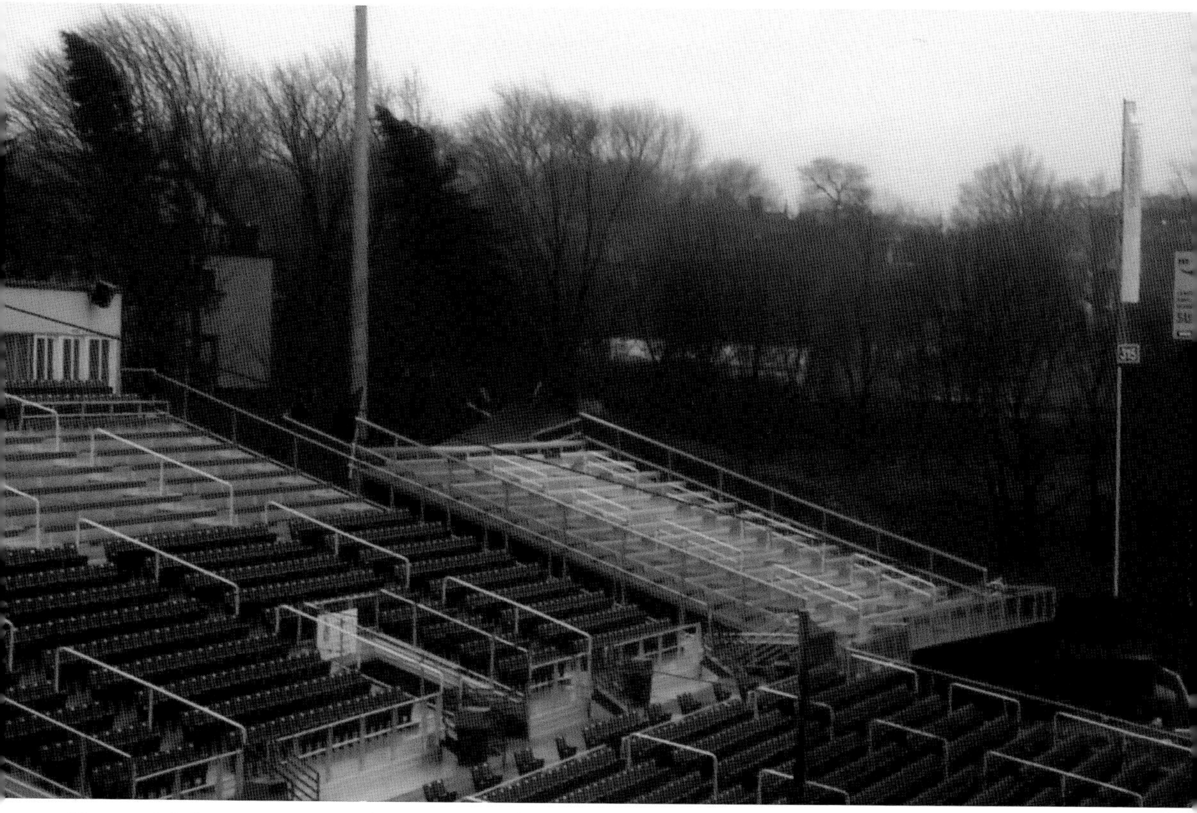

Torrential downpours, wind gusts more than 90 miles per hour—residents along the Atlantic coast, particularly in New England, are no strangers to the wrath of a nor'easter. Often called a "hurricane, junior class," a nor'easter, can, on rare occasions, take the circular shape of a hurricane. Characterized by several days of precipitation, these storms often strike in the winter and spring, doling out several feet of snow or several inches of rainfall before they are through. The storm that eventually became known as the spring 2007 nor'easter started in the southwestern United States as an upper-level disturbance. Moving east and before it reached the Atlantic, the storm dropped heavy snow and rains and produced severe thunderstorms. The storm stalled offshore in New York City, continuing to gain strength before moving north. At one point, the barometric pressure was equivalent to that of a category three (moderate) hurricane. (Courtesy of the Sea Dogs.)

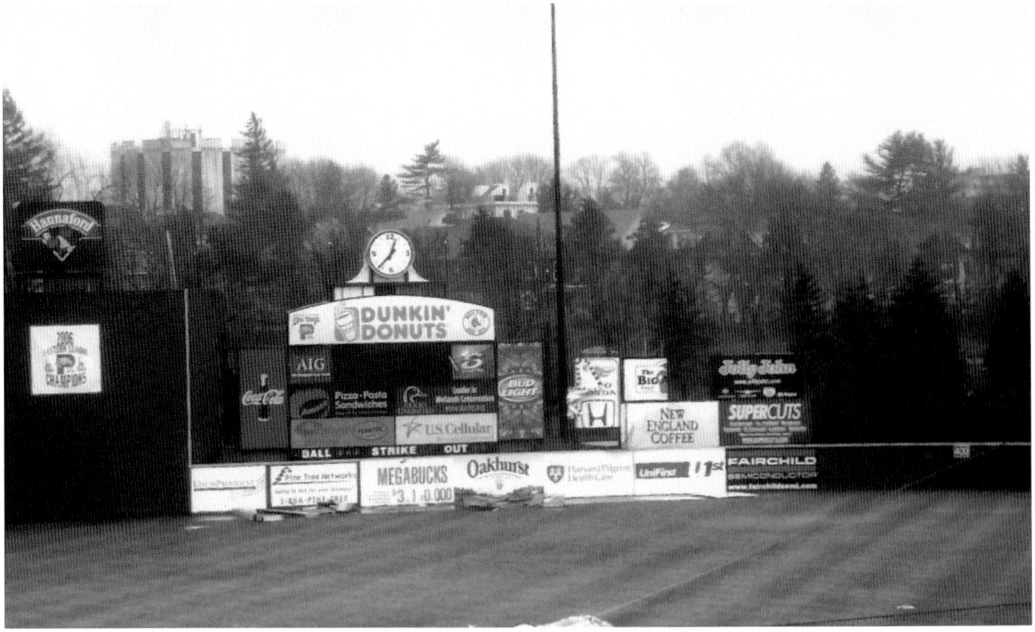

The term *nor'easter* derives naturally from historical spellings and pronunciations of the compass points and the direction of the winds these storms produce. For decades, Edgar Comee of Brunswick, Maine, waged a battle against the usage of the term *nor'easter* in the press. Comee argued that the term was "pretentious." His efforts, profiled just before his death at the age of 88, in the *New Yorker*, included the mailing of hundreds of postcards. The State of Maine estimated that it would cost at least $25 million to repair all the damage caused by the mid-April 2007 nor'easter. The nor'easter caused extensive damage to Hadlock Field and cancelled the Sea Dogs' second attempt at opening day. (Courtesy of the Sea Dogs.)

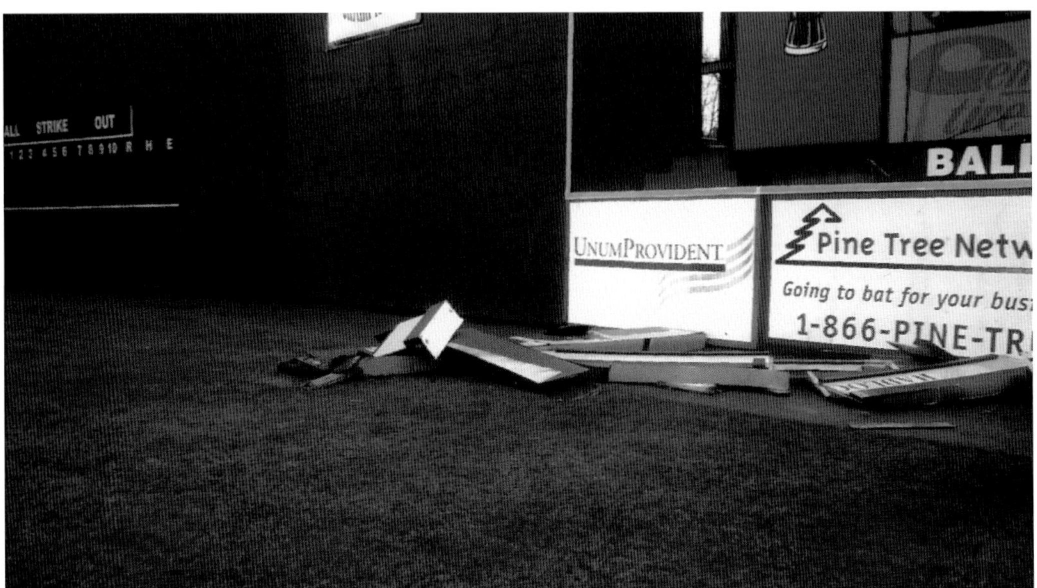

9

PEOPLE WILL COME

People will come. They'll come to Iowa for reasons they can't even fathom. They'll turn up your driveway not knowing for sure why they're doing it. They'll arrive at your door as innocent as children, longing for the past. Of course, we won't mind if you look around, you'll say. It's only $20 per person. They'll pass over the money without even thinking about it: for it is money they have and peace they lack. And they'll walk out to the bleachers; sit in shirtsleeves on a perfect afternoon. They'll find they have reserved seats somewhere along one of the baselines, where they sat when they were children and cheered their heroes. And they'll watch the game and it'll be as if they dipped themselves in magic waters. The memories will be so thick they'll have to brush them away from their faces. People will come. People will most definitely come.

—Terrence Mann, *Field of Dreams*

When the Eastern League announced in 1992 that it awarded Portland a minor-league franchise, it cited "city support" as one of the leading reasons.

In the stands, despite playing in a smaller market, the Sea Dogs have consistently been one of the attendance leaders in the Eastern League. In 2006, the Sea Dogs became one of the fastest franchises in Double-A history to welcome five million fans.

On the field, during a game, the fans have as much, if not more, fun as the players. Fans actively and wholeheartedly take part in the in-between-innings games and contests.

Off the field, the Sea Dogs family—Slugger, the players, and the front office—have all given back to the community that has embraced them. The organization has donated countless hours and dollars to the city.

And they keep coming in record numbers. The following attendance figures were recorded between 1994 and 2006: 375,197 (1994), 429,763 (1995), 408,503 (1996), 397,117 (1997), 398,800 (1998), 402,582 (1999), 370,702 (2000), 383,022 (2001), 382,738 (2002), 405,021 (2003), 434,684 (2004), 396,277 (2005), and 400,534 (2006), with 5,184,940 total.

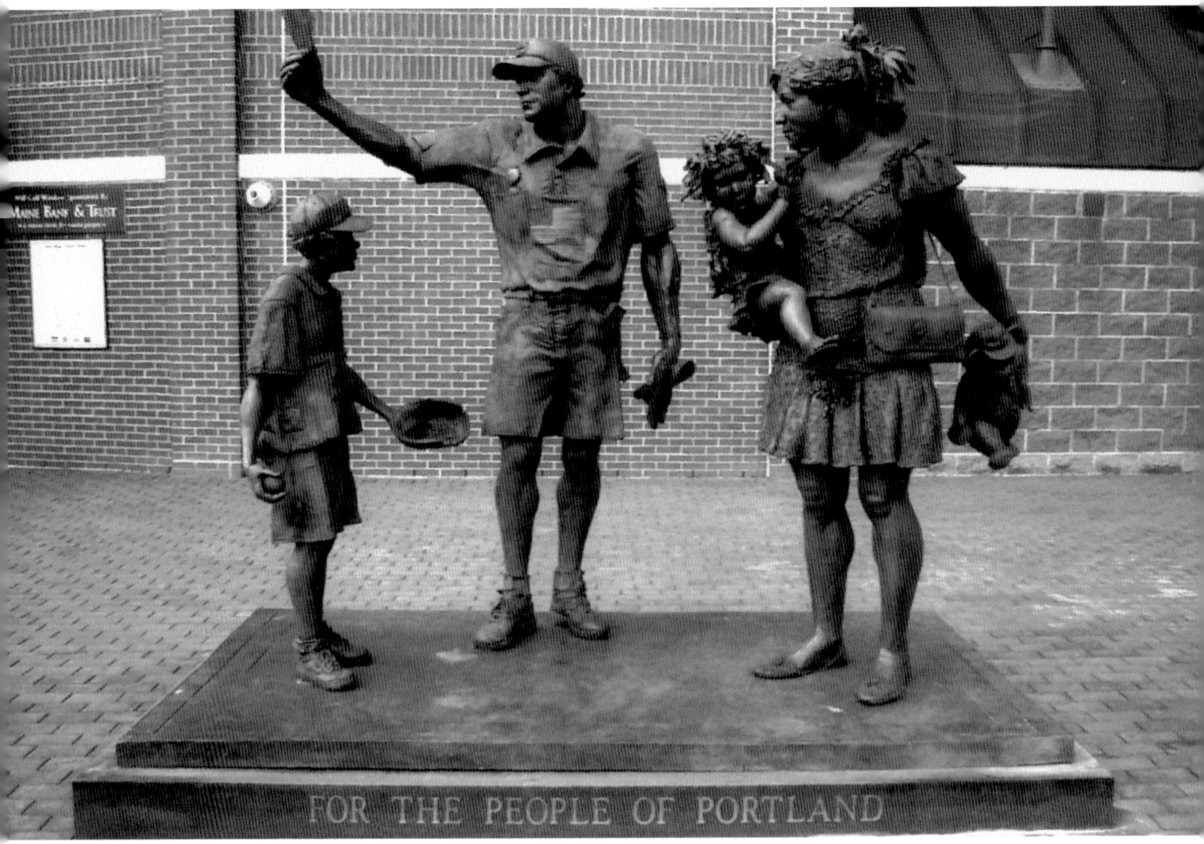

In April 2007, Portland Sea Dogs owner Dan Burke and his son Bill Burke presented the American Baseball Group monument to the City of Portland for its outstanding support. The bronze monument, designed and sculpted by nationally known artist Rhonda Sherbell, depicts a family attending a baseball game. The father holds up tickets to the game. A male child with glove-adorned hand is ready to snag a foul ball. The mother carries the baby daughter and her daughter's toy, a stuffed baseball bear. Measuring 9 feet tall and 11 feet long, the statue is on display in the front plaza at Hadlock Field just down from the Slugger statue by the ticket office. In 13 years of play in Portland and at Hadlock Field, more than five million fans have walked through the turnstiles. "When my father dreamed of this team, he never imagined the amount of support he would receive from the community," Bill Burke commented at the unveiling.

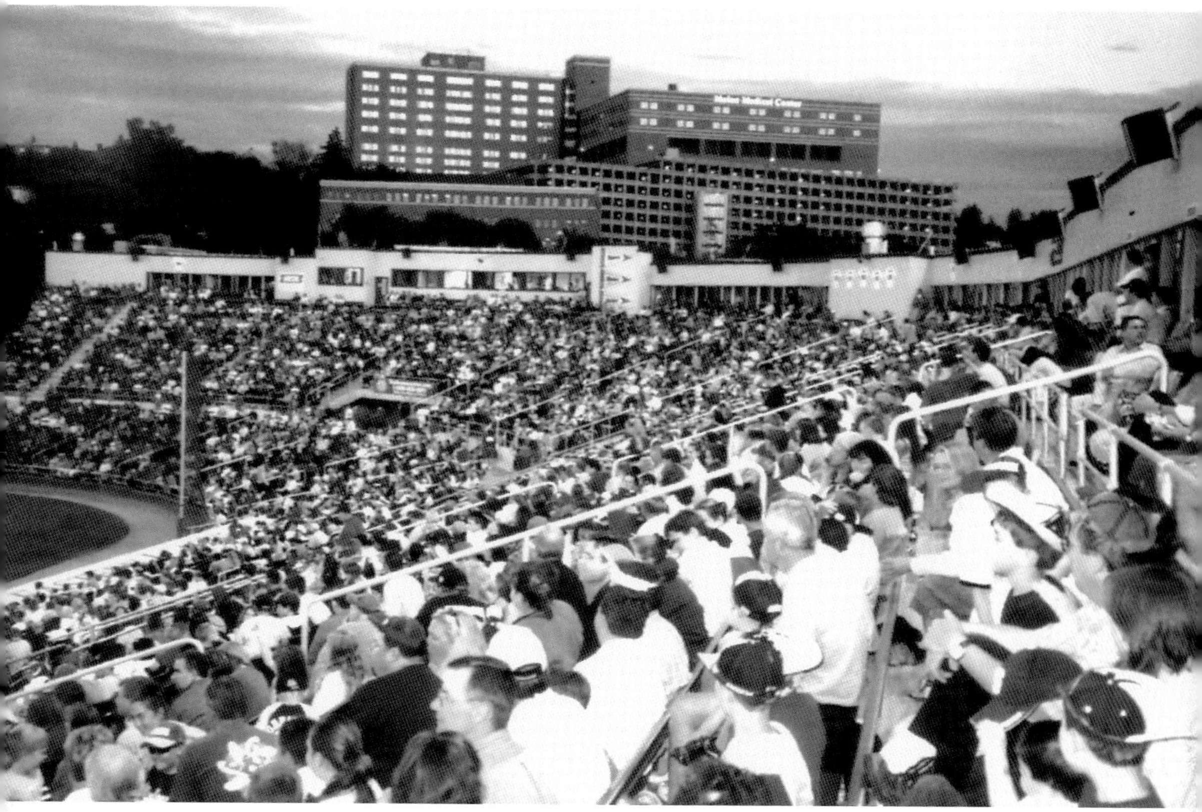

In 1915, Hugh Duffy, owner and manager of the Portland Duffs baseball club, called Portland and its fans "the finest minor league city I ever saw." In October 1992, the Eastern League expansion committee visited Portland. The committee left Portland, with heavy hitters Dan Burke and city manager Bob Ganley accentuating the positives, impressed. Three days later, the committee awarded the city a franchise. For the citizens of Portland, baseball's homecoming was a long time coming. As an indicator of things to come, on February 26, 1994, baseball-starved fans camped out overnight in 12-degree temperatures to be the first to purchase Sea Dogs tickets. The home opener sold out within hours. The Sea Dogs exceeded everyone's expectations when 375,197 came out to Hadlock Field in 1994, setting an Eastern League attendance record. (Courtesy of the Sea Dogs.)

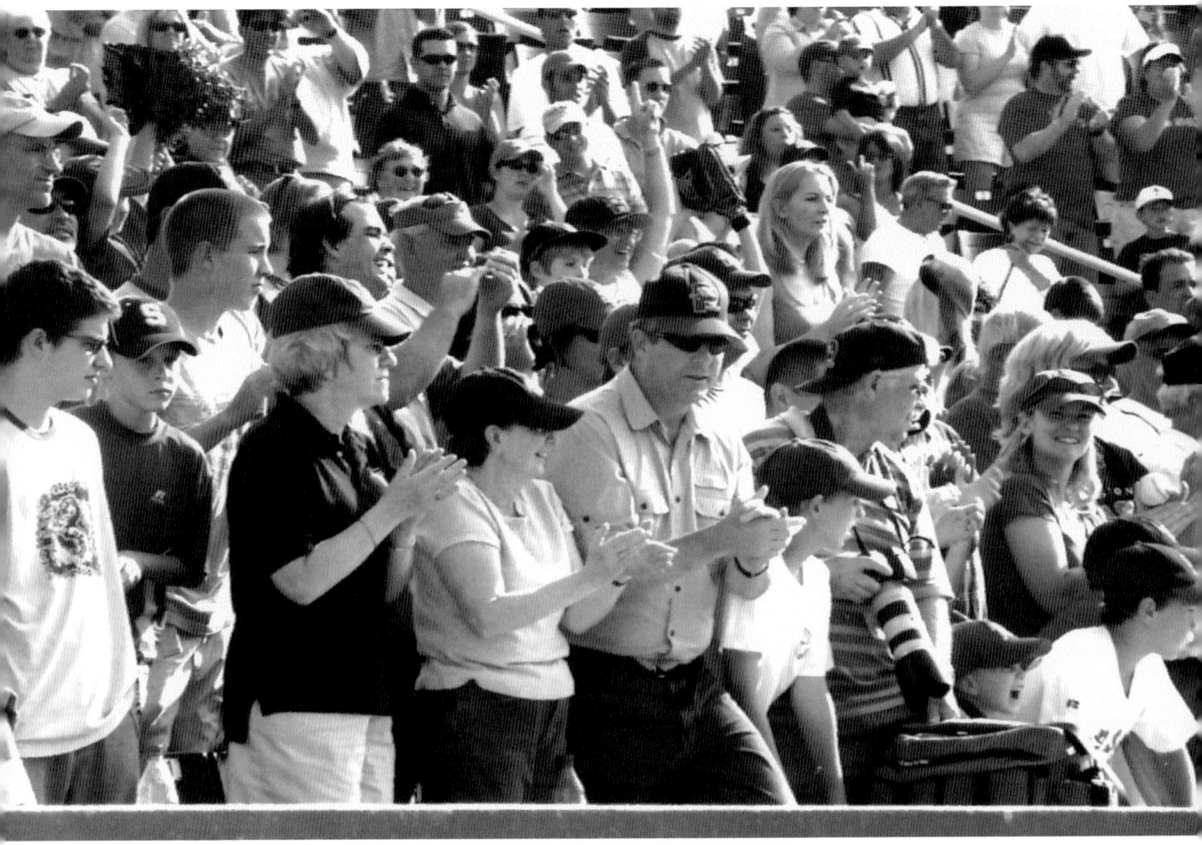

And they keep on coming, and in record numbers. The Sea Dogs average about 6,400 fans per game and attract more than 400,000 fans a season. The team consistently ranks among the top in attendance at the Double-A level. Upon announcing the Sea Dogs' new affiliation agreement with the Boston Red Sox in 2002, the Sea Dogs sold out 36 games in 2003. Season ticket sales swelled to more than 2,500. Because of the Sea Dogs' increasing popularity, Hadlock Field has undergone many expansion projects since its inaugural season in 1994. The expansions increased Hadlock Field's total capacity to 7,368. Sea Dogs devotees are a loyal and passionate group. Fans helped the Sea Dogs become one of the fastest franchises in Double-A history to welcome five million fans. During the past 13 seasons, the Sea Dogs welcomed fans number one million (1996), two million (1998), three million (2001), four million (2004), and five million (2006) in franchise history. (Courtesy of the Sea Dogs.)

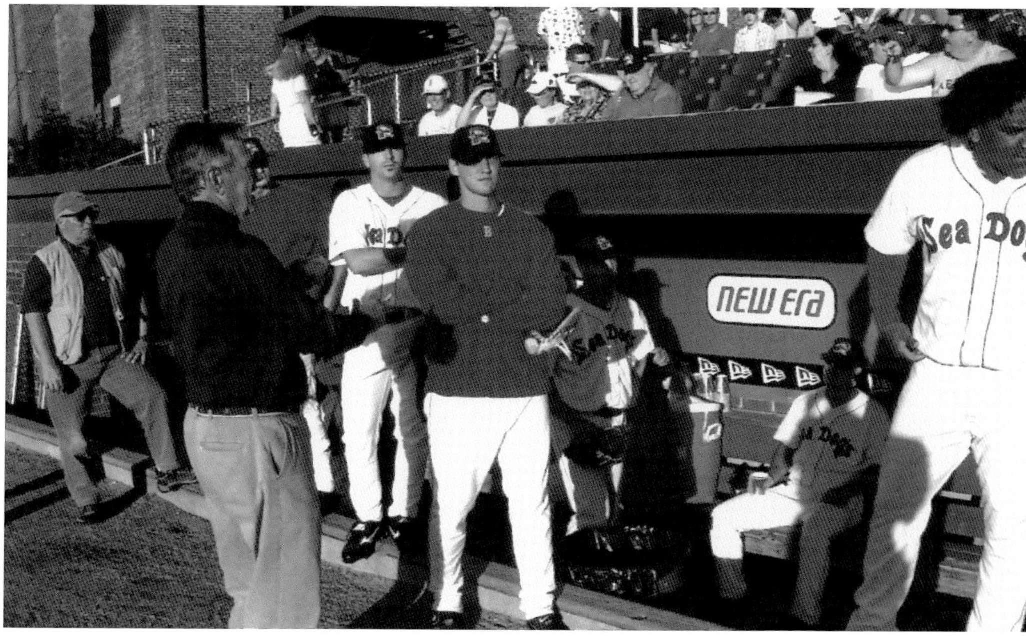

At Hadlock Field, not just on opening day but at any given game, an observant eye may catch a glimpse of a former president or rub elbows with a celebrity. Rubbed elbows include the likes of Frank and Kathie Lee Gifford and former NFL head coach Bill Parcells. Fans often spot Bangor native and horror writer Stephen King. The most famous Portland Sea Dogs fans, however, travel with an entourage. Attending a handful of games every season whenever they are vacationing in Kennebunkport are former president and first lady George H. W. and Barbara Bush. President Bush chats with Sea Dogs players and fans before tossing out the ceremonial first pitch before a game at Hadlock Field. (Courtesy of the Sea Dogs.)

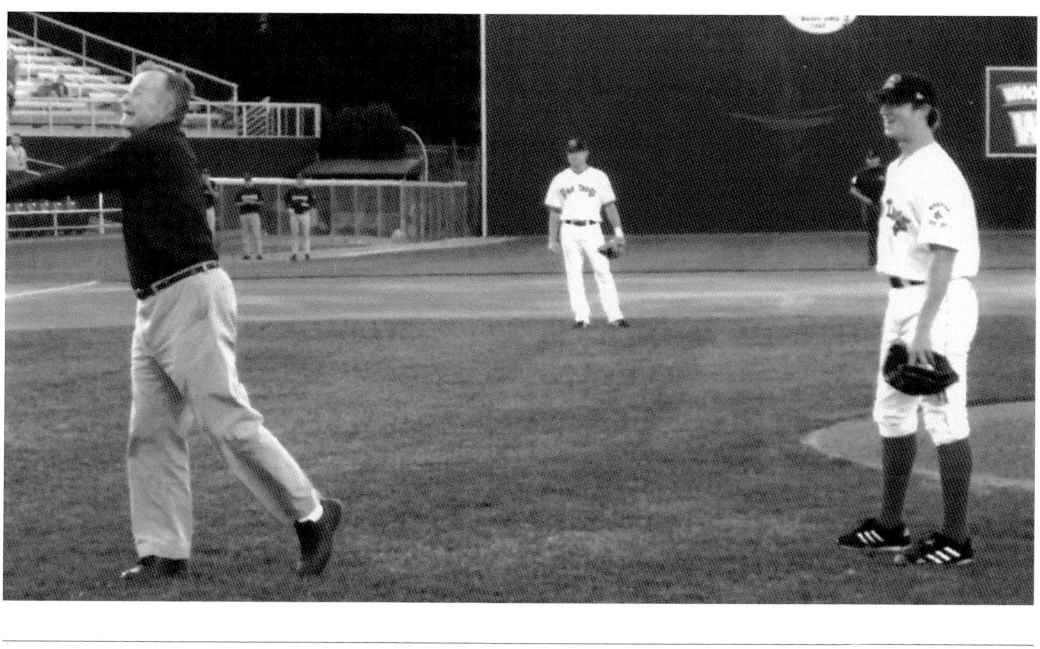

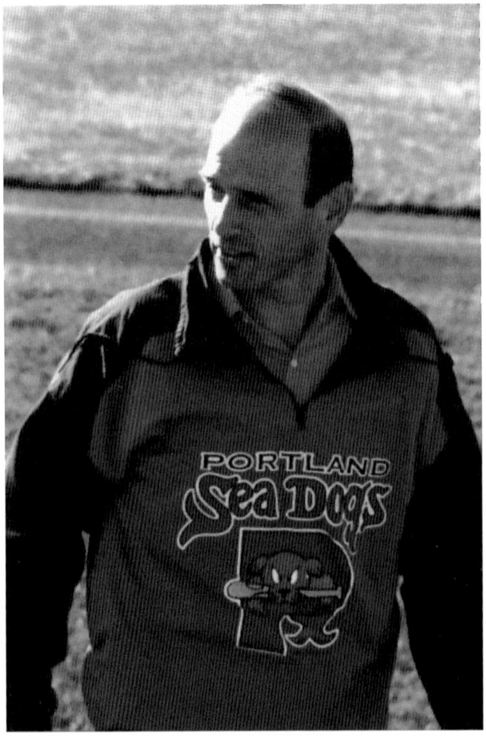

Reelected in November 2006 for a second term, and a frequent guest of the Sea Dogs, is Gov. John Elias Baldacci. Baldacci was first elected by the people to govern the state of Maine in 2002. He defeated Peter Cianchette and Jonathan Carter. Baldacci, born and raised in Bangor, is a cousin of former senator George Mitchell. (Courtesy of the Sea Dogs.)

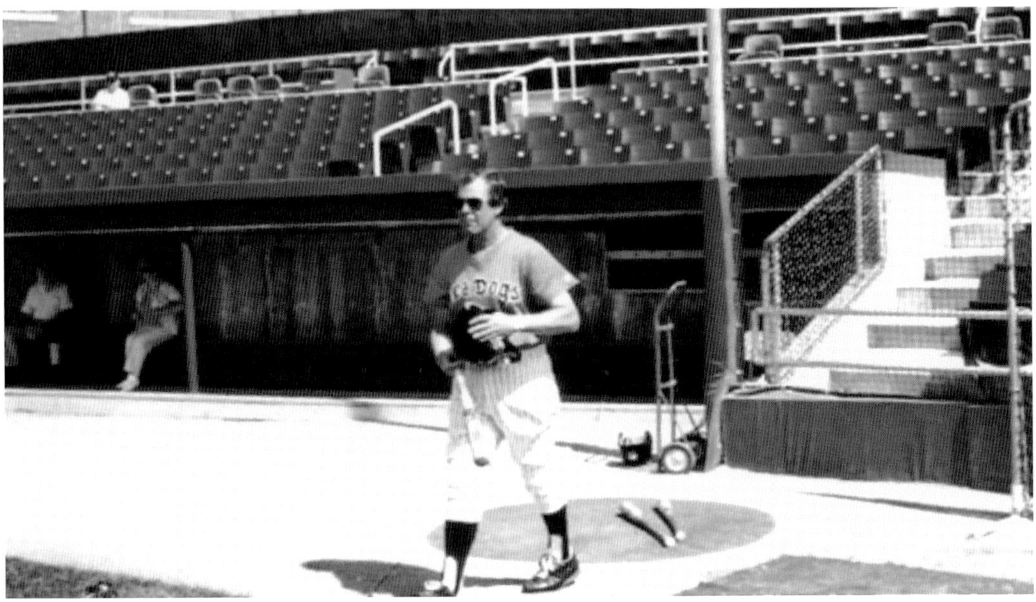

Another famous face in the Hadlock Field crowd until the time of his death was anchor and senior editor of ABC television's *World News Tonight* Peter Jennings. During his tenure with ABC News, Jennings established a reputation for excellence in broadcast journalism. One of the country's most distinguished journalists, Jennings passed away at age 67 from lung cancer on August 7, 2005. (Courtesy of the Sea Dogs.)

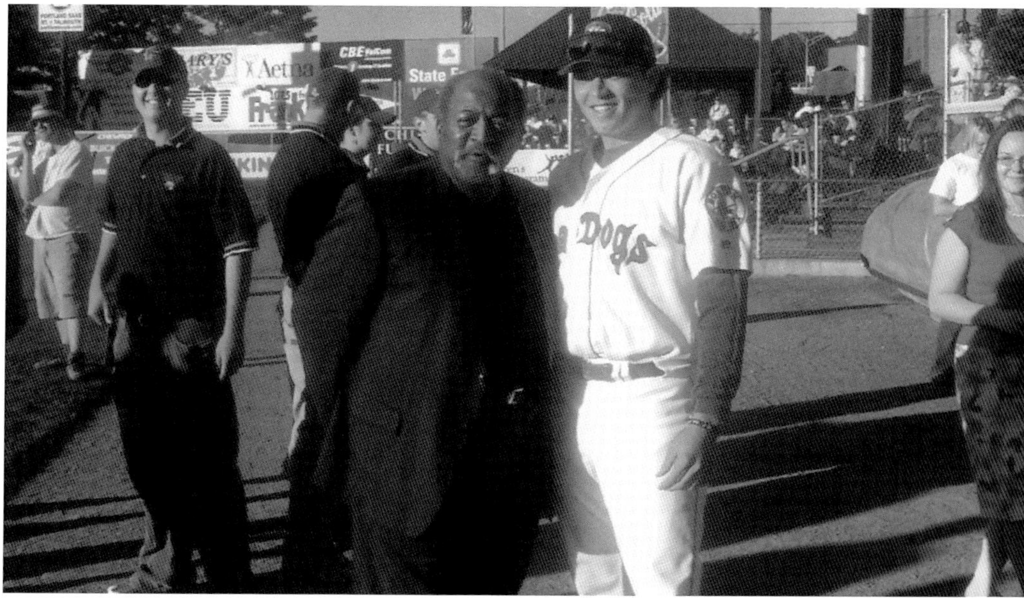

During the 2003 season, the Sea Dogs invited former Boston Red Sox greats to Hadlock Field. The former players threw out the ceremonial first pitch and signed autographs for the fans. Luis "El Tiante" Tiant (above) made his professional debut with the Cleveland Indians in 1964. In eight seasons with Boston, Tiant won 122 games with a 3.36 ERA. Tiant ranked in the Red Sox top five in five categories, including innings pitched, games started, and strikeouts (third) and wins and shutouts (fourth.) Eight-time all-star outfielder Jim Rice (below) was the only American League player since 1937 to have 400-plus bases in a single season. His lifetime totals include 2,452 hits, 382 homers, 1,451 RBIs, and 79 triples. (Courtesy of the Sea Dogs.)

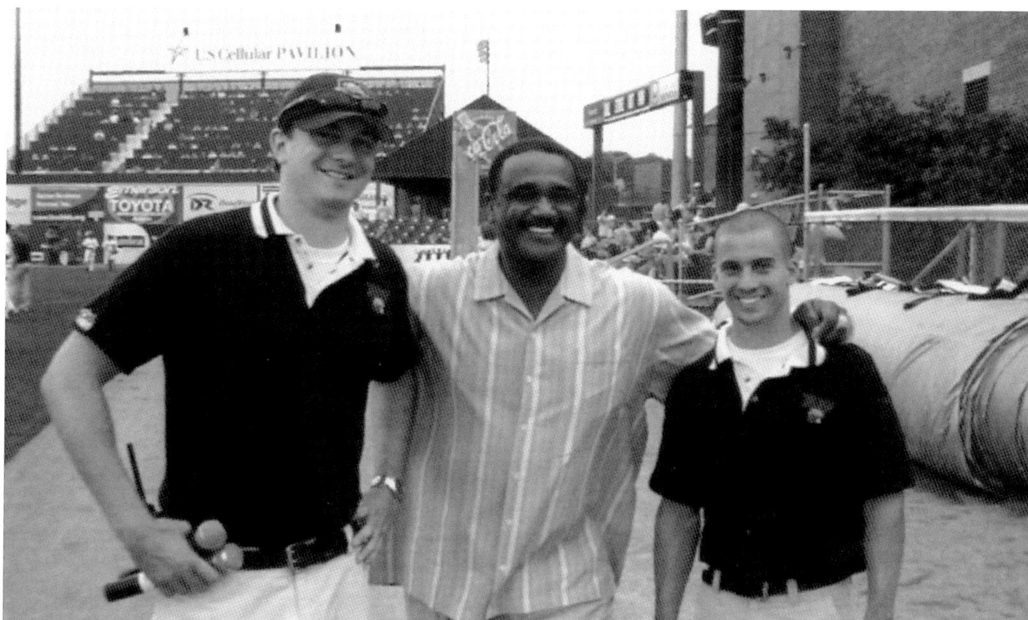

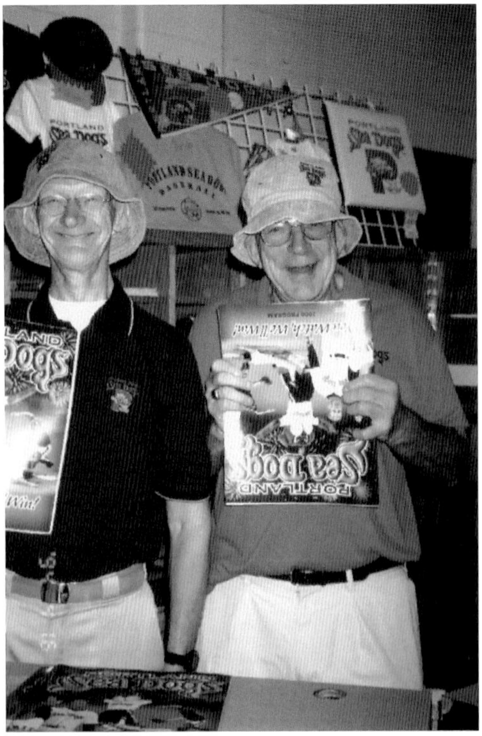

The first to greet fans walking through the turnstiles and entering Hadlock Field are program vendors Marty "Deputy Dog" Jensen (left) and Harold "Top Dog" Lucas (right). For Jensen and Lucas, selling programs is secondary to ensuring victory to a season ticket holder, providing directions to a new fan, or giving the youngest fans a Slugger sticker. Jensen and Lucas have become fan favorites and are just as popular as Slugger and just as well known as any player ever to wear a Portland Sea Dogs uniform. Jensen and Lucas (above) get silly stuffing programs before a game. Lucas and Jensen (below) "emerge" from the cornfield. (Below, courtesy of the Sea Dogs.)

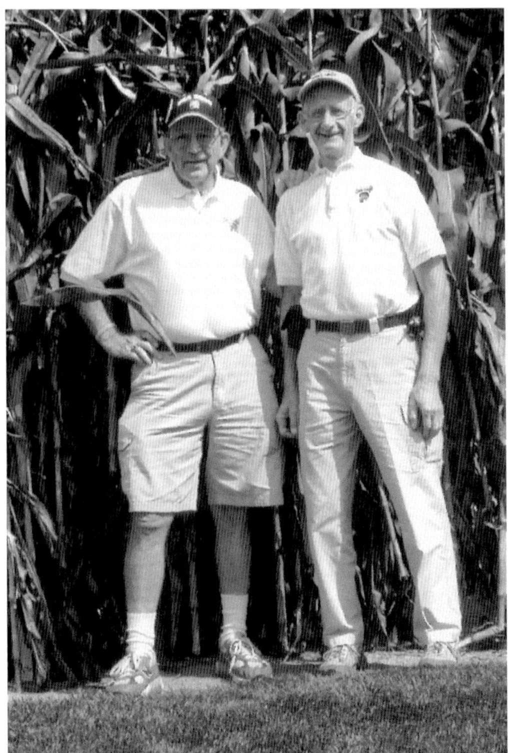

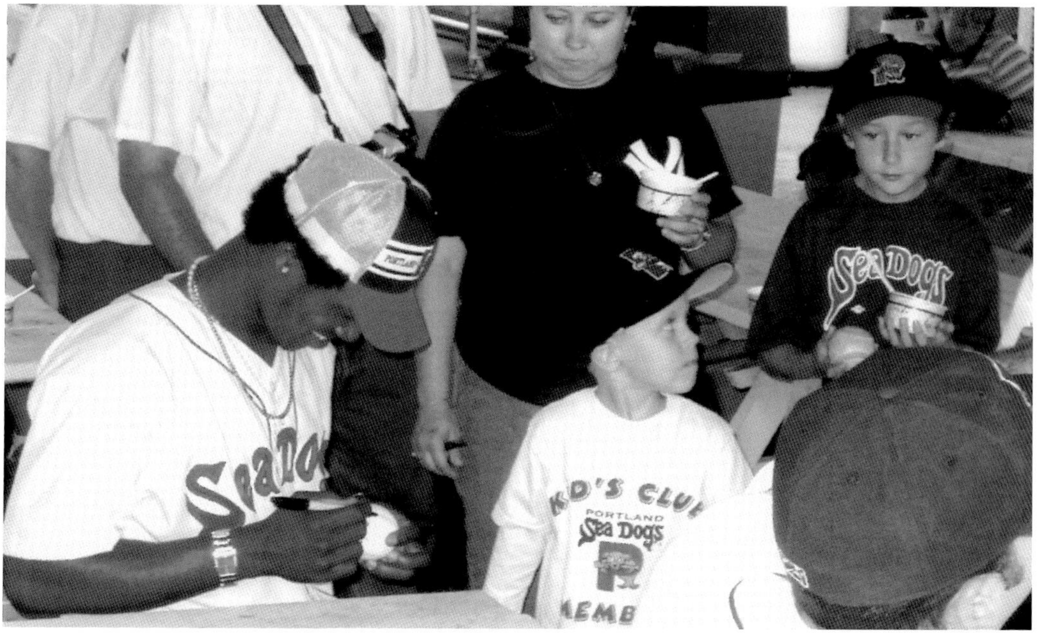

Making their players accessible to their fans, especially their youngest ones, is very important to the Sea Dogs organization. The opportunity to meet a potential major leaguer and to get his autograph is exciting for fans of any age. And being able to do that without any pushing and shoving is even better. To that end, 45 minutes before every home game a Sea Dogs player signs autographs in the main concourse. Fans, both young and old, have the opportunity to meet and get an autograph from future National League Rookie of the Year Hanley Ramirez. (Courtesy of the Sea Dogs.)

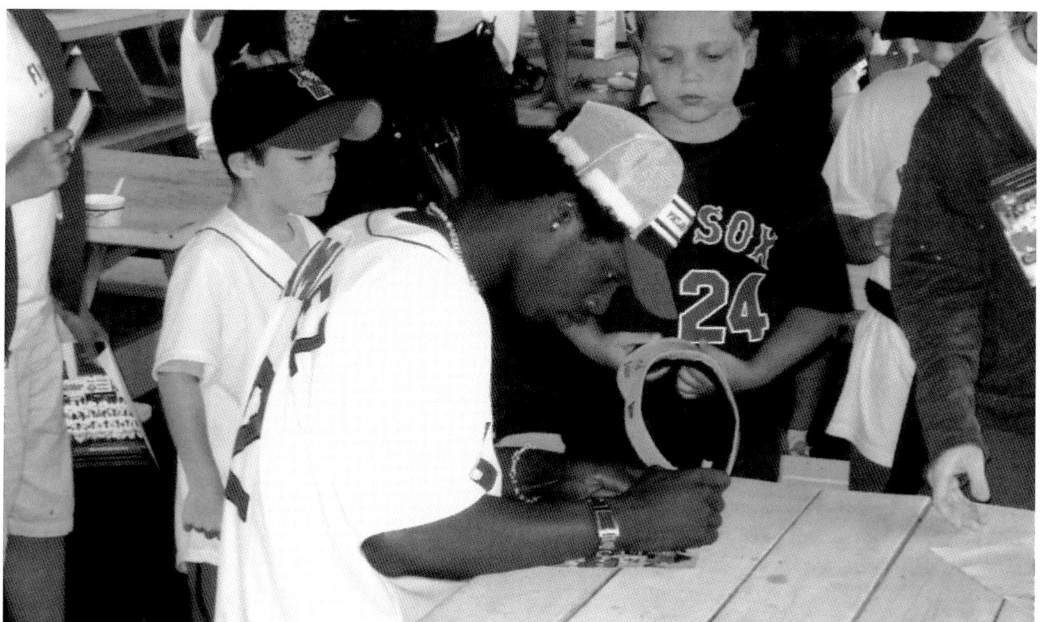

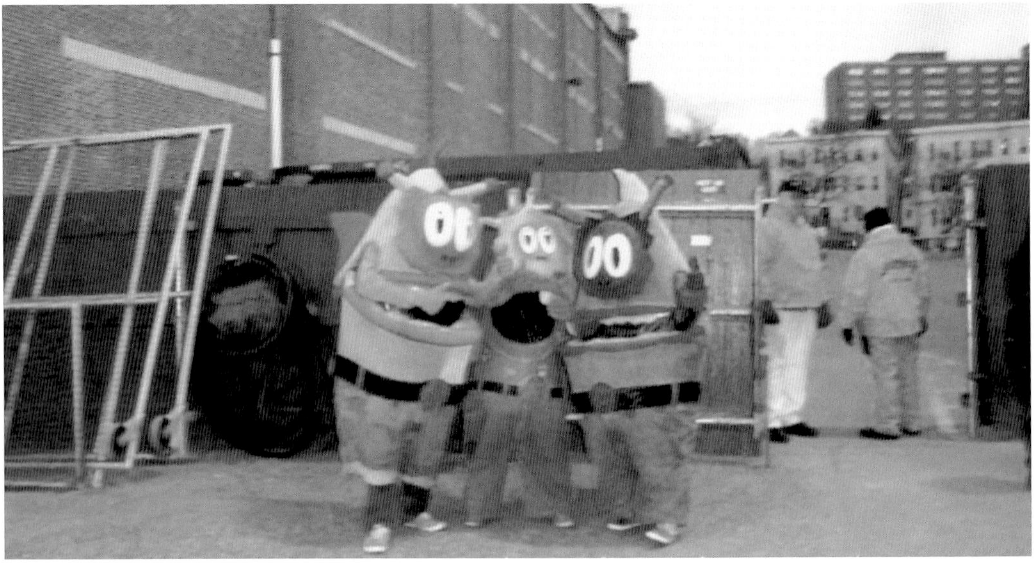

Throughout every game, the Trash Monster family stomps around the ballpark encouraging patrons to fill their "bellies" with trash. Resembling large fish with big mouths, the family encourages fans to keep the stadium clean and trash free. In 1998, in an on-field wedding ceremony, Green (male) and Orange (female) tied the knot. During the 2000 baseball season, Blue hatched from an egg. (Courtesy of the Sea Dogs.)

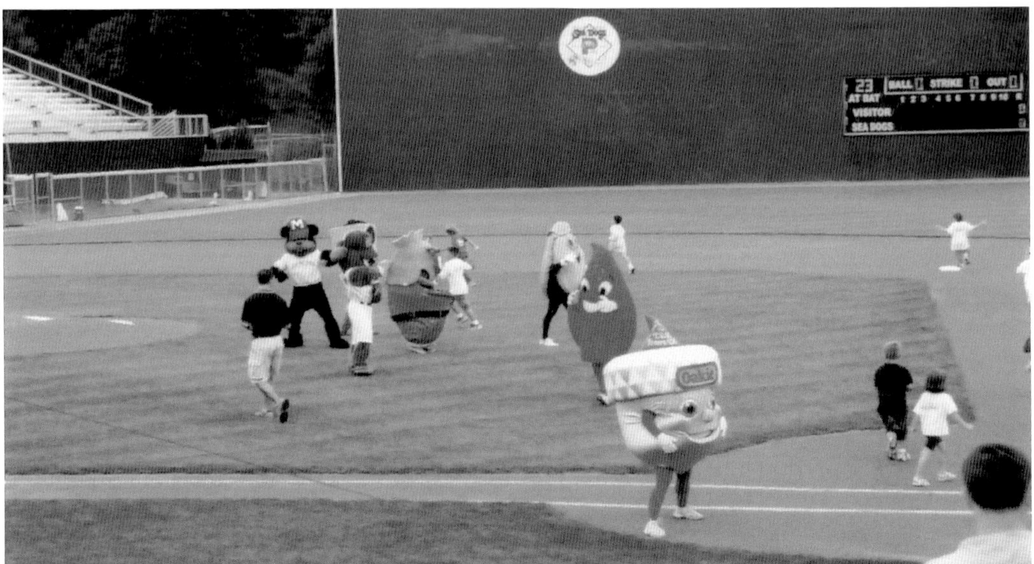

The Sea Dogs offer their young fans 16 and under the opportunity to join the Slugger's Kids Club. Two really cool perks include the annual baseball clinic, with an autograph session and ice-cream social with Sea Dogs players, and the annual Slugger's Buddies Kickball Game that takes place on the field before a game. Club members and Slugger's Buddies face off in the 2003 kickball game in this image. (Courtesy of Melanie Aber.)

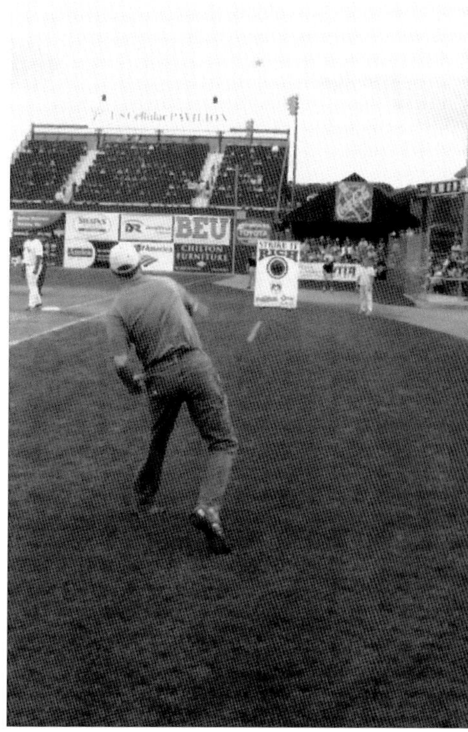

An entertaining staple in minor-league baseball is the between-innings games and contests. The games and contests are good, clean fun, and fans of all ages are eligible to win various prizes and cash. Chosen at random, the fan having the "lucky stamp" in his or her game day program is the contestant for that game's Strike It Rich contest. In the adult Strike It Rich, the contestant must throw three strikes through the hole in order to win a new car. In the children's version, the child must toss two strikes through the hole in order to win a savings bond and variety of other prizes. (Courtesy of the Sea Dogs.)

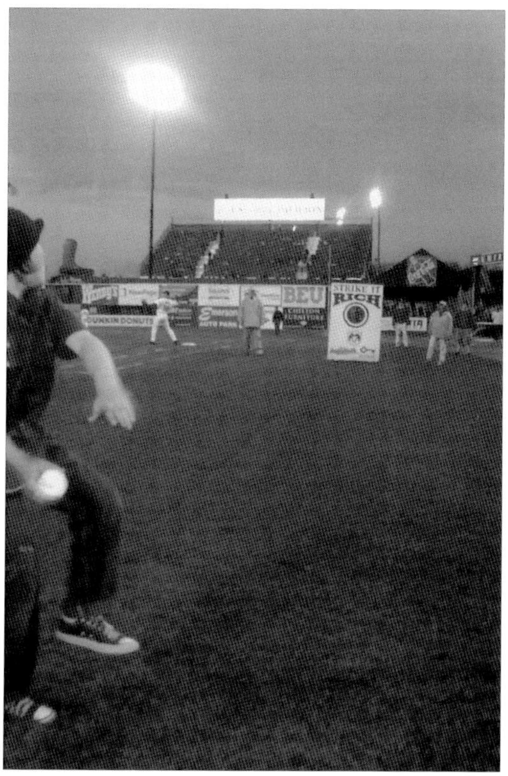

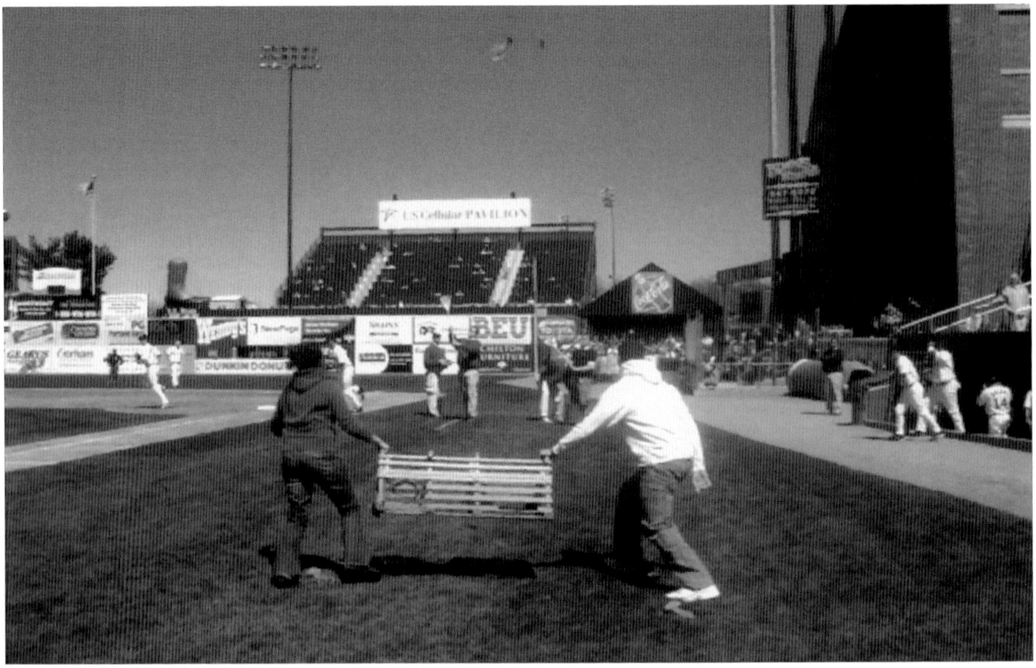

"Capturing" the true spirit of the state of Maine and its maritime history is the fan favorite Lobster Toss promotion. The crowd-pleasing promotion features the Sea Dogs staff at one end launching the state's most famous crustacean high into the air with a lacrosse stick. While at the other end, two fan contestants work together to snag the airborne rubber lobsters before they hit the ground. The contestants can only use the real lobster trap in their hands to catch the lobsters. (Courtesy of the Sea Dogs.)

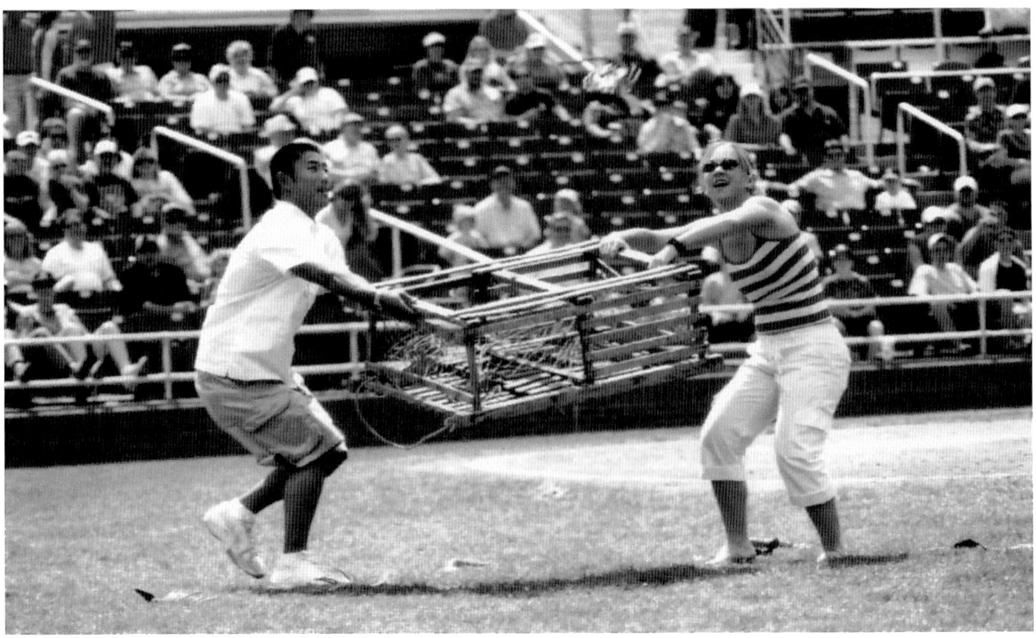

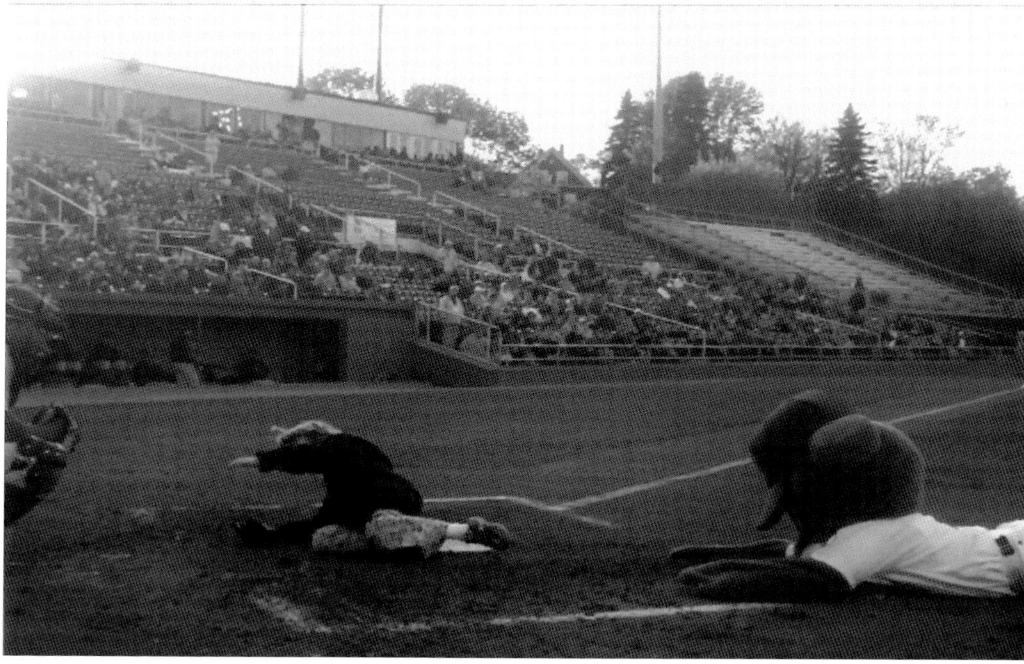

A crowd favorite in minor-league parks is the mascot race between a young fan and the team's mascot. In the mascot race at Hadlock Field, race time is in the middle of the fourth inning. A young contestant, usually between the ages of five and eight, is chosen at random before the baseball game begins. The contestant runs the bases, just like the players do (first, second, third, home), while Slugger runs the bases in the opposite direction (third, second, first, home). And they are off. The mascot race continues following this page turn. (Courtesy of the Sea Dogs.)

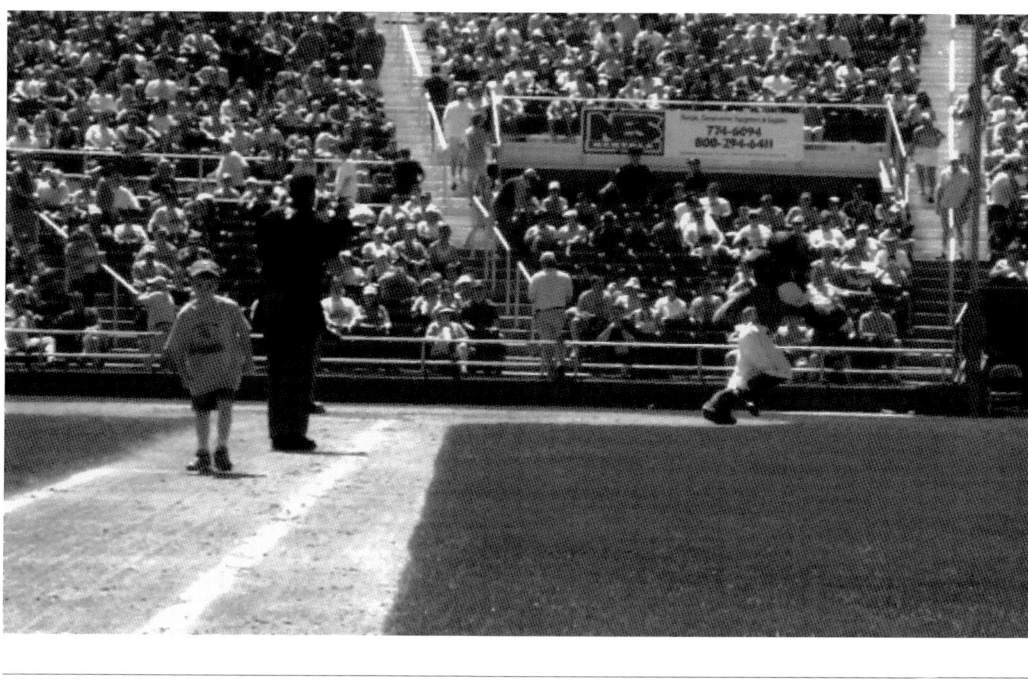

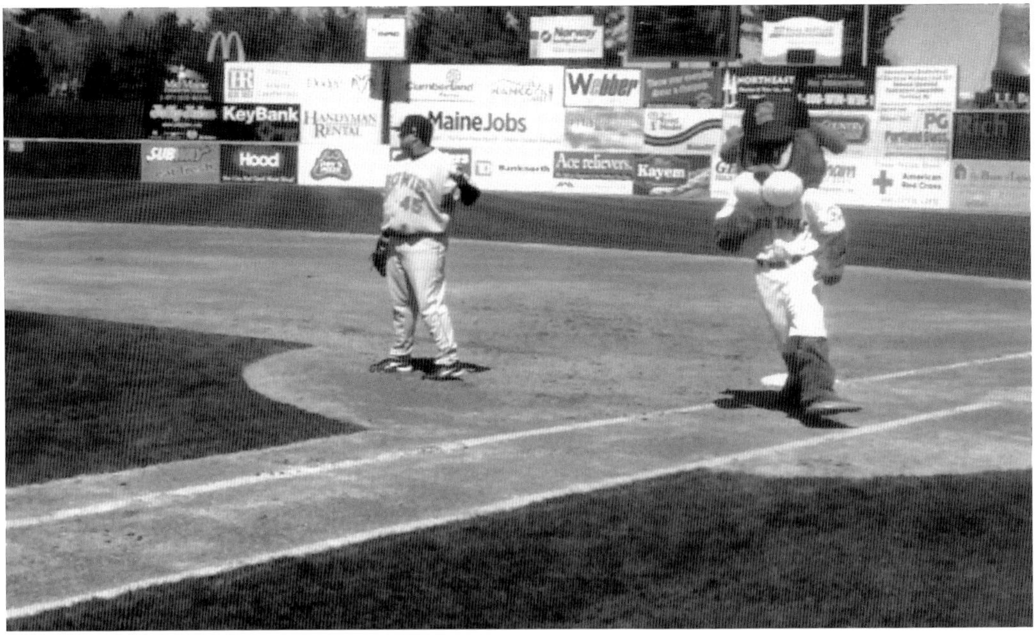

In this image, the mascot race from the previous page at Hadlock Field is already in progress. Slugger the Sea Dog rounds first base and starts heading for home. This looks as though it is going to be a close race. Slugger and his competitor, a young fan from the stands, both arrive at home plate simultaneously. It is too close to call. It looks like there will be a photo finish. The results will be in the next caption. (Courtesy of the Sea Dogs.)

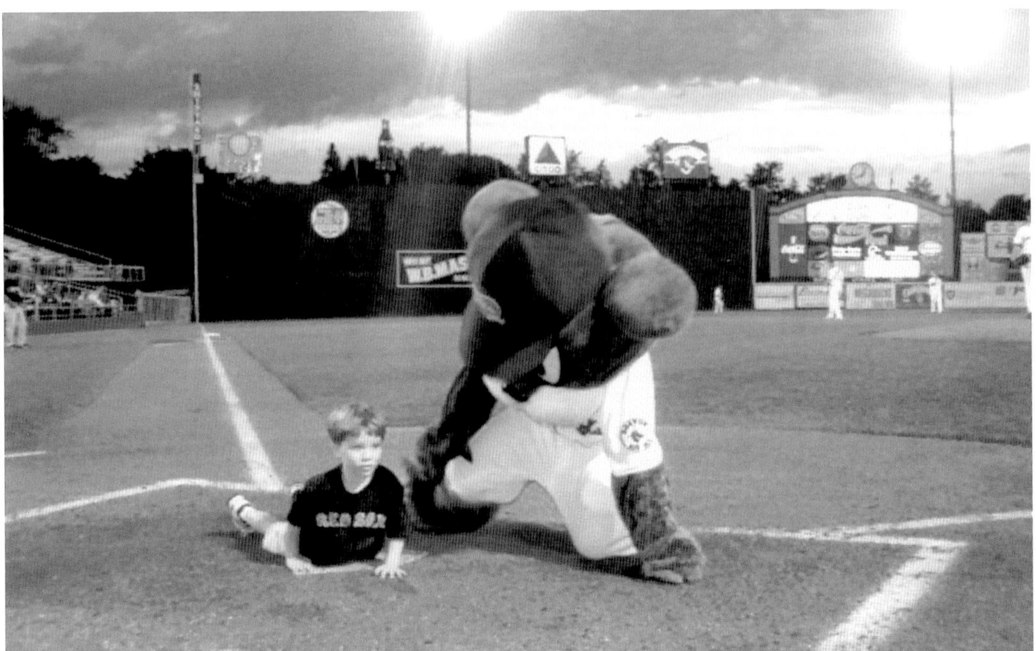

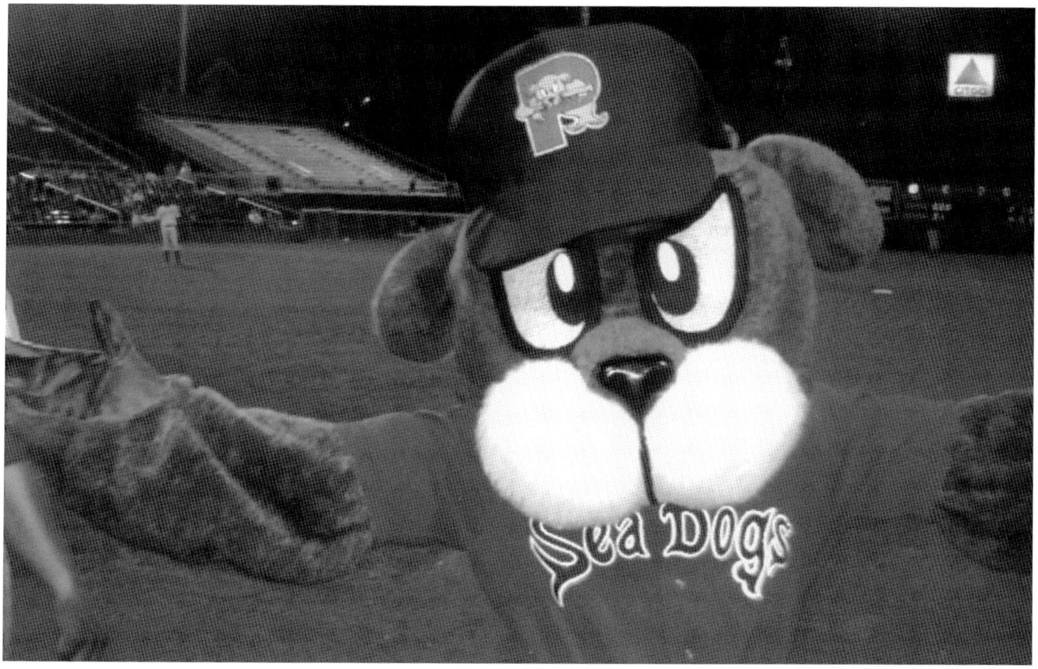

Despite a photo finish, the umpires call Slugger the Sea Dog (with the big cap and flippers) the loser. Slugger pleads his case to deaf ears, contending he beat his fellow competitor by "at least this much." Failing to prove his case, a frustrated Slugger shows his disappointment after losing yet another race to a young fan. After more than a dozen seasons, Slugger is still in search of his first win. Before leaving the field, Slugger goes over and asks his competitor for some tips on winning. (Courtesy of the Sea Dogs.)

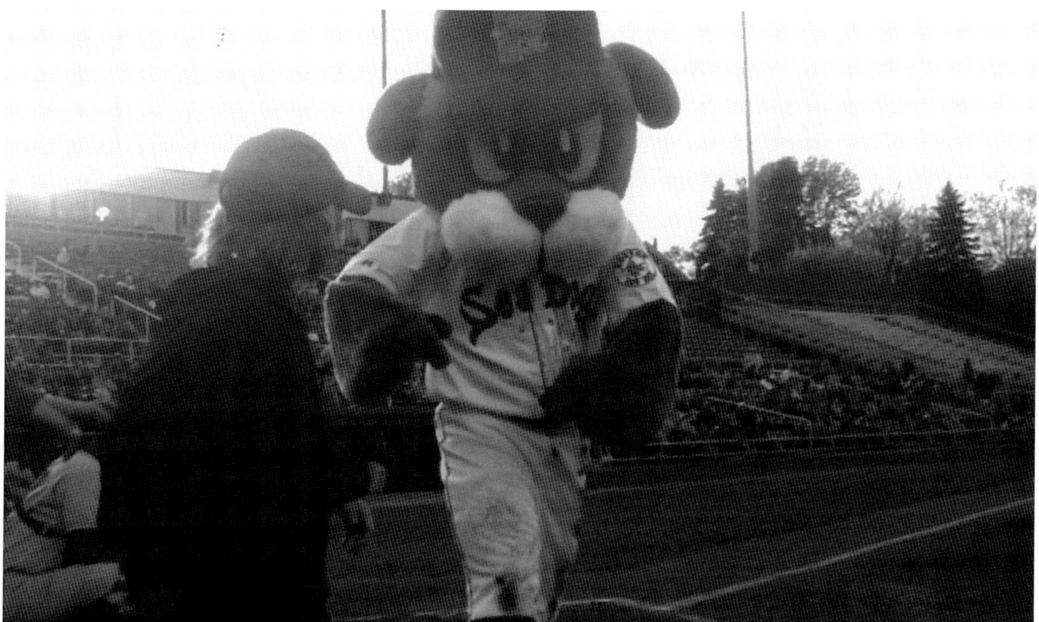

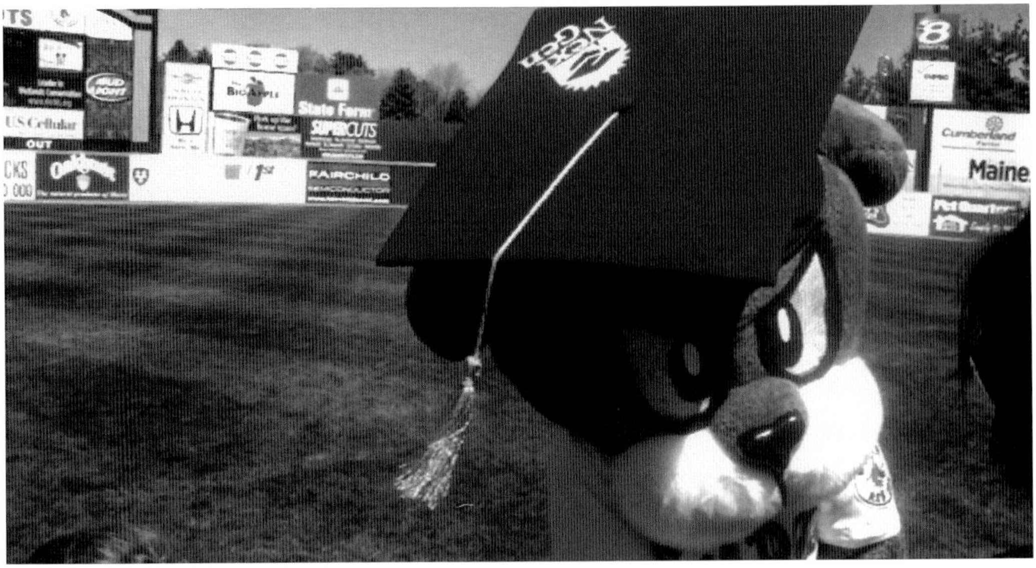

The Portland Sea Dogs have always taken great pride in being active in the Portland community, especially in the schools. In November 2005, the Finance Authority of Maine (FAME), recognized and honored the Sea Dogs for their contributions to the education of area students. Two of the organization's most successful and highly acclaimed educational programs are the Most Improved Student and Adopt-A-Sea-Dog. The Most Improved Student program recognizes area students, kindergarten through 12th grade, for being the most improved student in their classrooms. Teachers select students, and the students receive a complimentary ticket to a game and a certificate from the Sea Dogs recognizing their achievement. Several times during the spring, the Sea Dogs recognize the students in a pregame ceremony. Slugger greets and congratulates Most Improved Student recipients. (Courtesy of the Sea Dogs.)

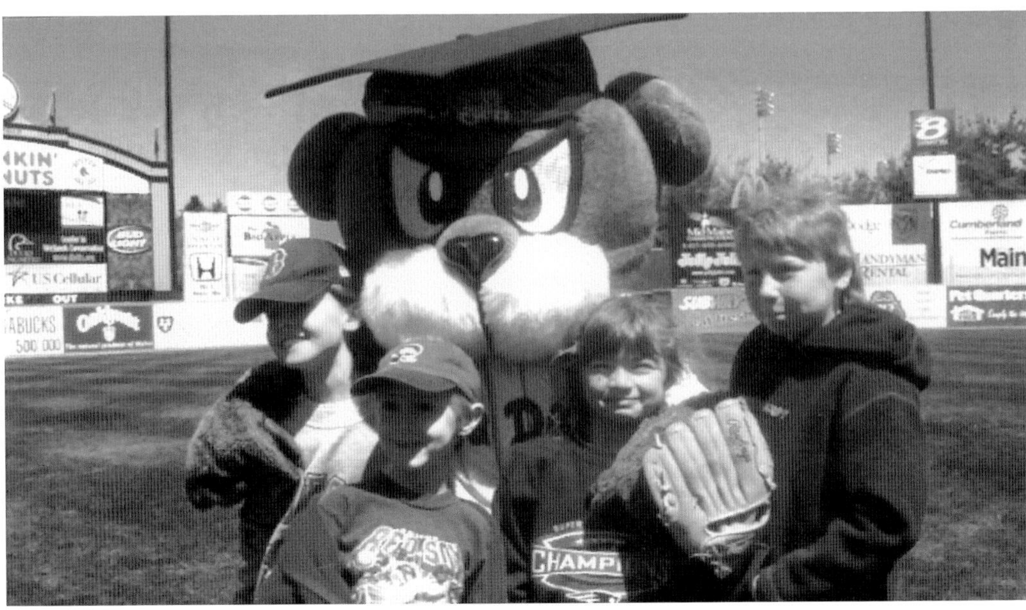

In the Adopt-A-Sea-Dog program, local schools adopt a Sea Dogs player, who then visits the school. At the school, the adopted player talks to the kids about the importance of staying in school, hard work, goal setting, and saying no to drugs and alcohol. The Sea Dogs then allow the school to purchase tickets to select dates at the lowest discount available. The school resells the tickets at face value and uses the event as a fund-raiser for the school. Once at the game, the school becomes very active in the game, from singing the national anthem to throwing out the first pitch and other activities. Former adopted Sea Dogs Adrian Gonzalez (right) and Nate Bump (below) are seen here. (Above, courtesy of the Sea Dogs; below, photograph by Stewart Smith.)

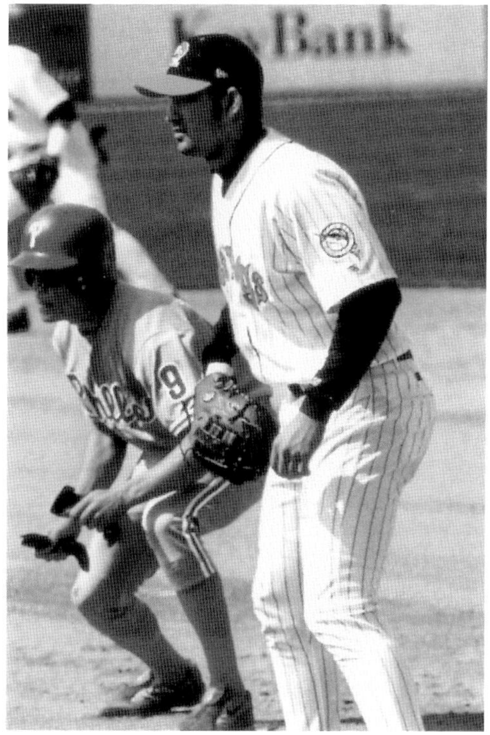

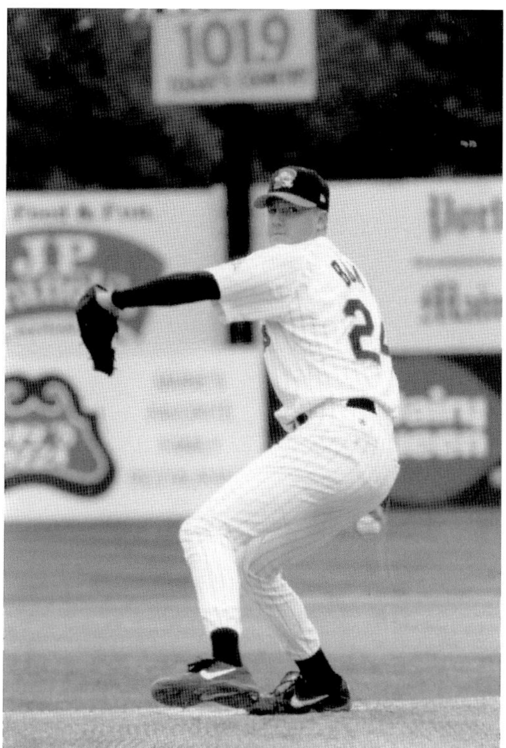

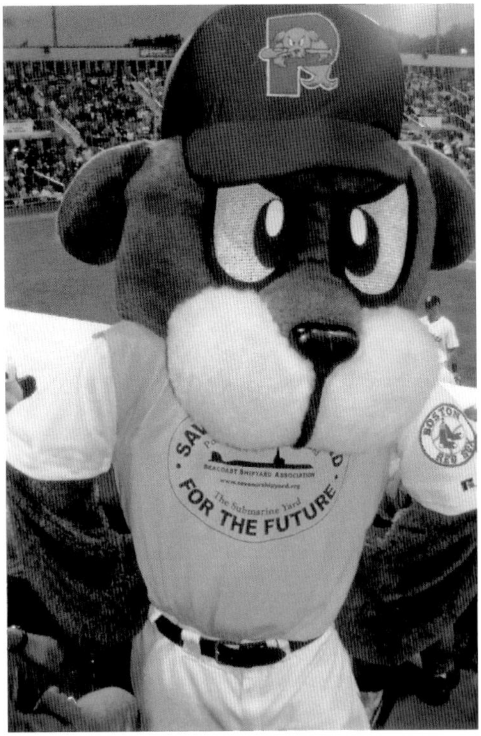

In 2005, Brunswick Naval Air Station and the Portsmouth Naval Shipyard were put on the closure and realignment list. Portland held a Save Our Bases promotion, donating 50 percent of all ticket sales to task forces committed to keeping the bases open. Supporters attended the game wearing yellow T-shirts and raised more than $8,000. Mainers were told that August that only one base would be closing. (Courtesy of the Sea Dogs.)

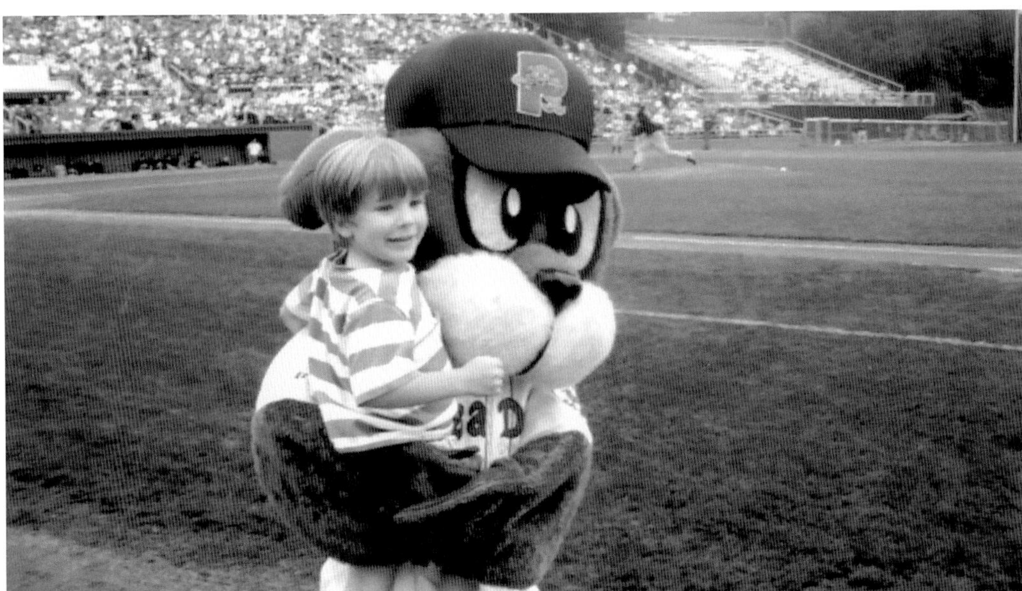

In 1994, Sea Dogs general manager Charlie Eshbach met John Menario, formerly of Peoples Heritage Bank. The men created the Strike Out Cancer in Kids Program, in which fans pledge money for each Sea Dogs strikeout thrown. Each season, a youngster is chosen to be the poster child for the program and gets his or her picture taken with Slugger. The program has raised more than $3 million since 1994. (Courtesy of the Sea Dogs.)

10

Field of Dreams

Once a place touches you like this, the wind never blows so cold again.
—Dr. Archibald "Moonlight" Graham, *Field of Dreams*

Before the conclusion of the 1997 season, general manager Charlie Eshbach half-jokingly presented his Fan Appreciation Day idea to Sea Dogs owner Dan Burke. Burke thought it was a great idea and said, "Let's do it."

In 1997, the first Portland Sea Dogs Field of Dreams promotion/Fan Appreciation Day took place on the last weekend of the season. Before the game, former radio announcer Andy Young told the tale of how the City of Portland built Hadlock Field. Young also told how the fans have supported the team in record numbers.

Afterward, the players, wearing old-time uniforms, emerged from a cornfield in center field. The players went into the stands and thanked the fans personally for their support throughout the season. The event was so well received that it became an annual fan favorite event.

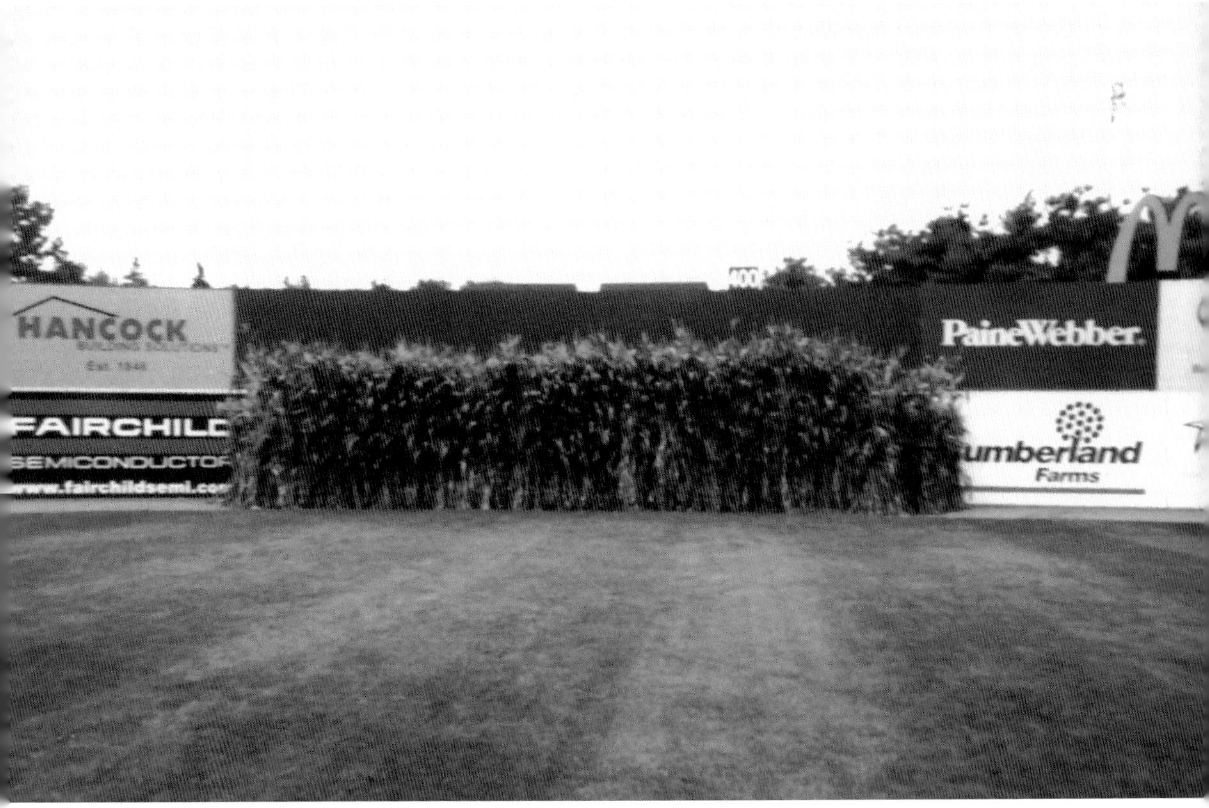

Since 1997, the Sea Dogs front office staff has constructed a cornfield in center field the evening (and into the night) before the final home game of the regular season. The first season the promotion took place, it took 8–10 hours to build it (the cornfield). Now, 10 seasons later, the science of cornfield building is a perfected art form, and the staff can construct it in two to three hours. The brainchild of Charlie Eshbach, the Portland Sea Dogs Field of Dreams Promotion/Fan Appreciation Day takes place on the last weekend of the season. Before the game, the Sea Dogs radio announcer reads a short story on how the City of Portland built Hadlock Field. He also tells how the fans have supported the team in record numbers since its first season in 1994. The players, wearing old-time uniforms, emerge from the cornfield and head into the stands to thank the fans personally for their support throughout the season.

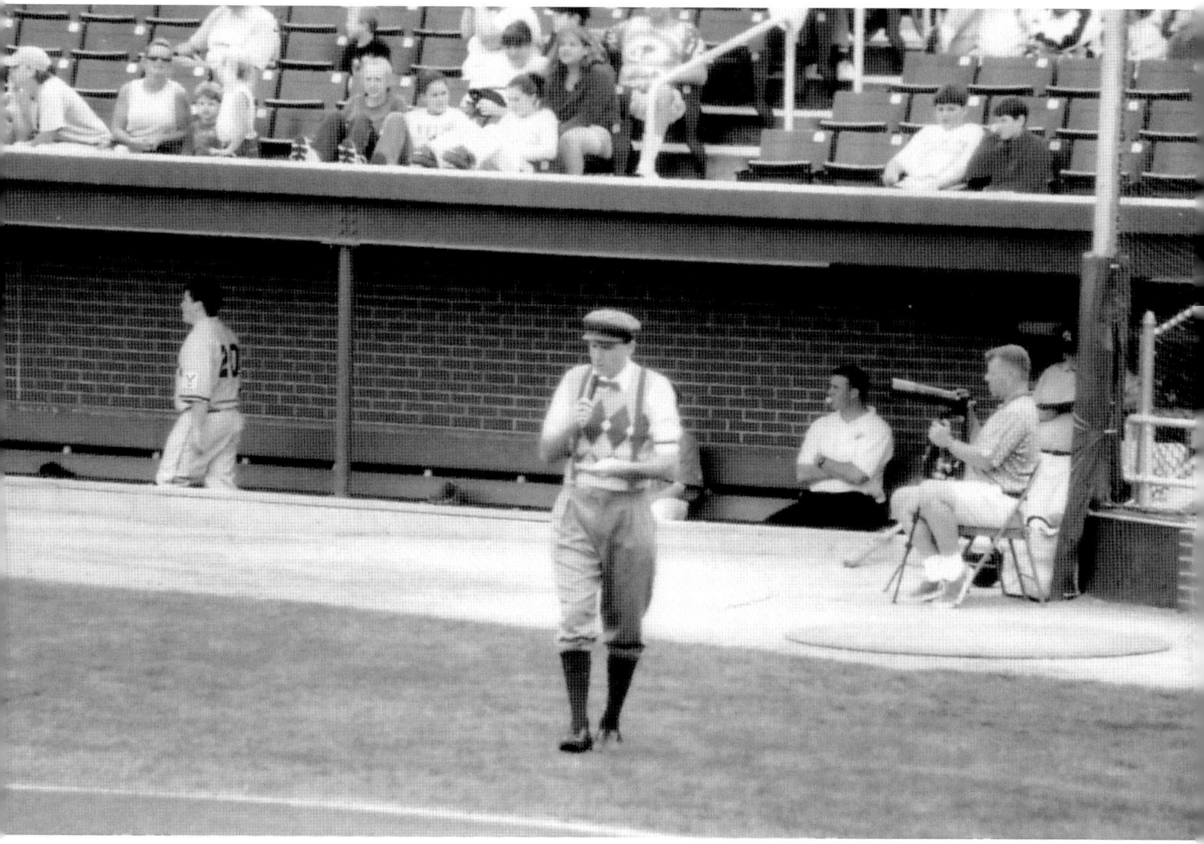

In his broadcasting career, Andy Young, a former radio play-by-play announcer, has called games from the Last Frontier to the (Sea) Doghouse. After graduation, the Alaska Goldpanners of Fairbanks hired the University of Connecticut graduate to be their announcer. The following season, Young moved to North Carolina, where he did the play-by-play for the Durham Bulls. Following a four-year hiatus from professional baseball, Young returned and announced games for the Burlington Indians in 1989–1990. Young then headed to Vero Beach with the Dodgers for two seasons, before returning to Burlington in 1993. Young stopped in Butte, Montana, in 1994 before heading to Maine. Young went "off the air" before the 2002 season and currently teaches English at a local high school. Young and his wife, Terry, have three children. A mysterious voice beckoned Young, dressed in old-time attire, to the field before a game in 1997. (Courtesy of the Sea Dogs.)

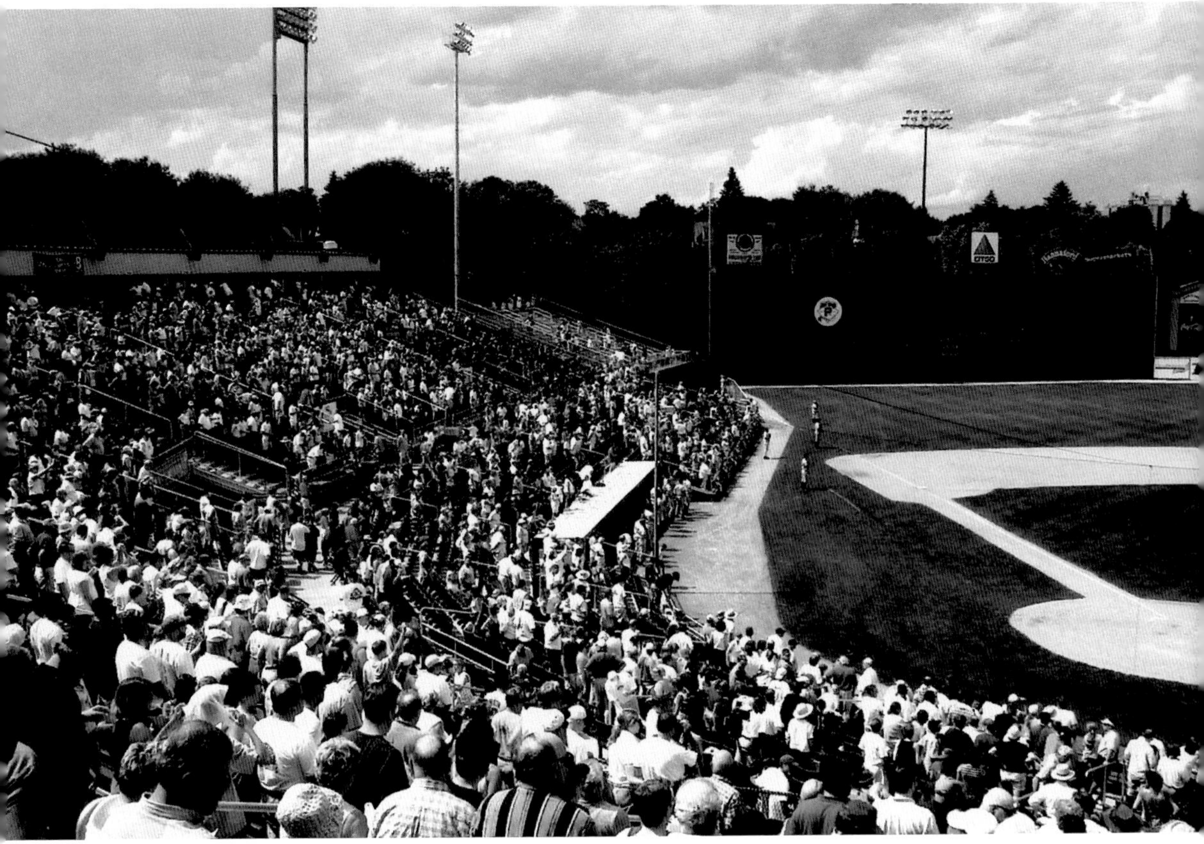

Before the Sea Dogs took the field in 1994, no one knew what to expect. Since their inaugural season in 1994, the fans of the Portland Sea Dogs have exceeded everyone's expectations. The unexpected became the expected. Since 1994, more than five million fans have come out to Hadlock Field and cheered the home team on to victory. It is this loyalty and steadfast allegiance shown by the fans that the Sea Dogs organization wanted to recognize and thank with this promotion. "If you build it, they will come. In 1994, the city of Portland did build it, and you the fans have come out [and] in record numbers ever since." In 2007, more than 400,000 fans attended a Sea Dogs home game. (Courtesy of the Sea Dogs.)

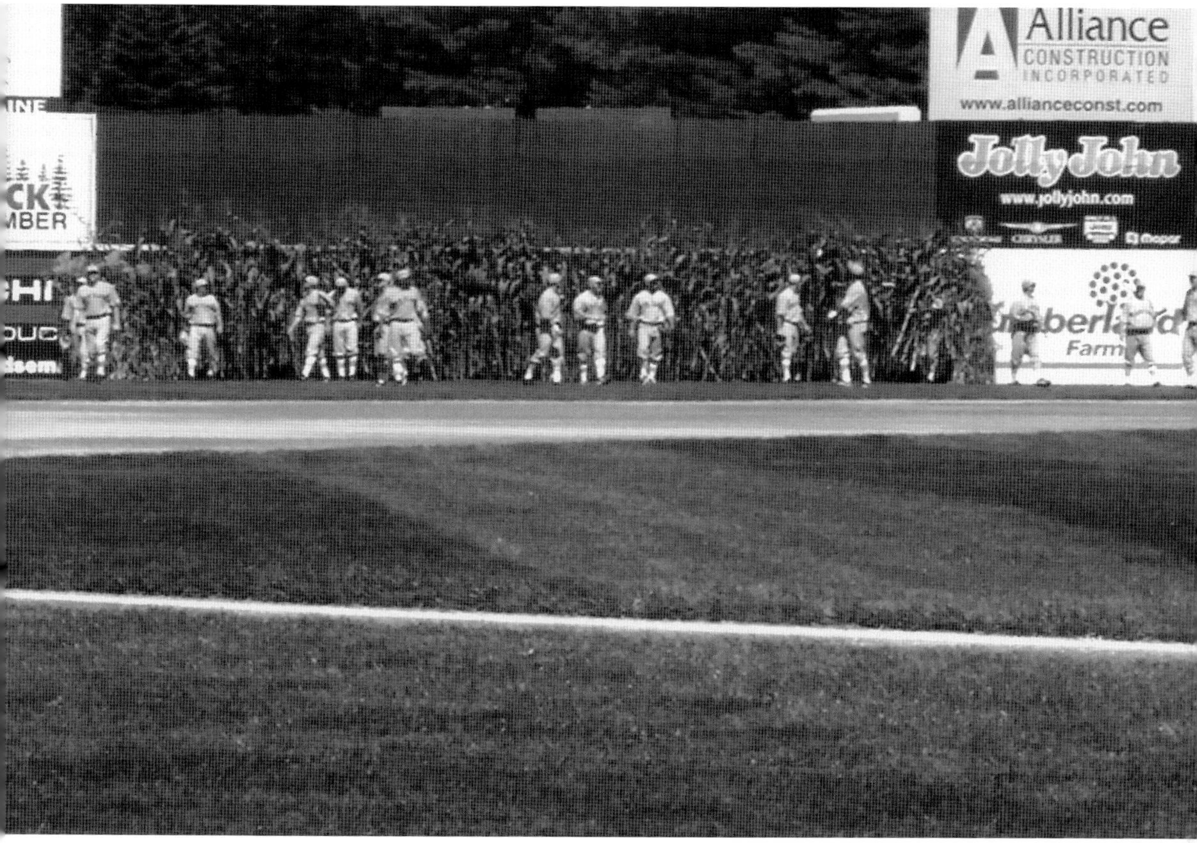

"Today the Sea Dogs will honor their past and will be donning replica 1926 Portland Eskimo uniforms." In 1926, after a five-year absence, baseball returned to the state of Maine with Portland reentering the struggling New England League. The name *Eskimos* are chosen in a name-the-team contest held by the *Portland Press Herald*. Contest winner Wendell Little claimed he came up with the nickname after a particularly bitterly cold March day. The Eskimos finished the season a dismal seventh. Only the Nashua Millionaires played worse, sparing the Eskimos a last-place finish. The only highlight in the forgettable season was the appearance of baseball commissioner Judge Kenesaw Mountain Landis at the home opener. Almost 70 years later, on August 15, 1997, the Sea Dogs, wearing their 1926 Portland Eskimo replica uniforms, emerge from the cornfield for the first time. (Courtesy of the Sea Dogs.)

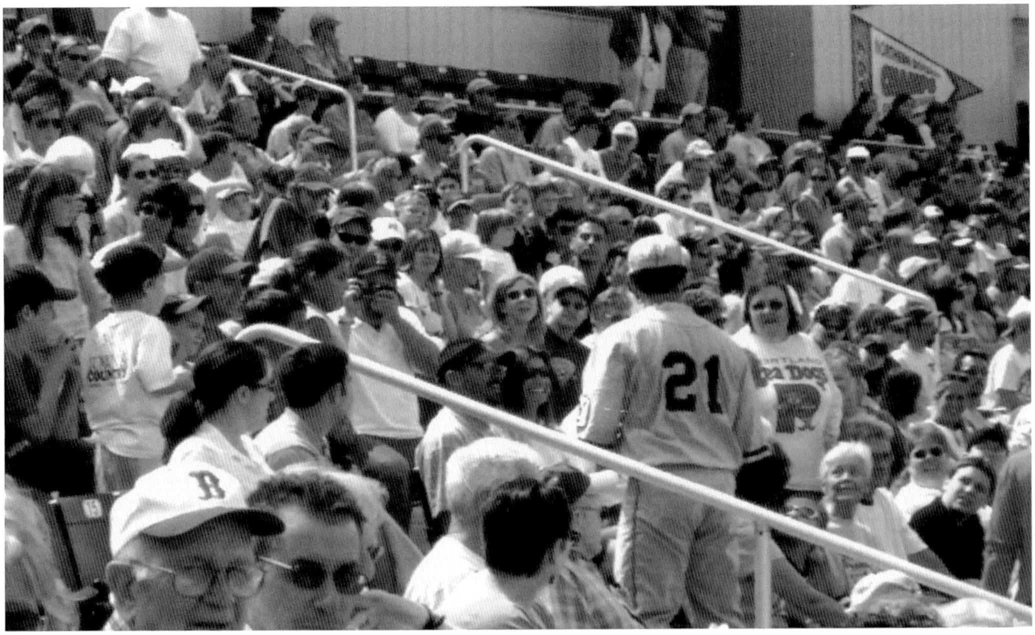

One hundred and thirty-seven major-league players have played games at Hadlock Field, which has provided the training grounds for future major-league talent for the Florida Marlins and currently the Boston Red Sox. Several of those players had pivotal roles in their teams' World Series championships. "Since 1923 the Eastern League has been a source of excitement. It has been filled with good times and dreams that will last forever. The Eastern League has been the breeding ground for 3,000 major leaguers. This field, Hadlock Field, is part of our present and part of our future." (Courtesy of the Sea Dogs.)

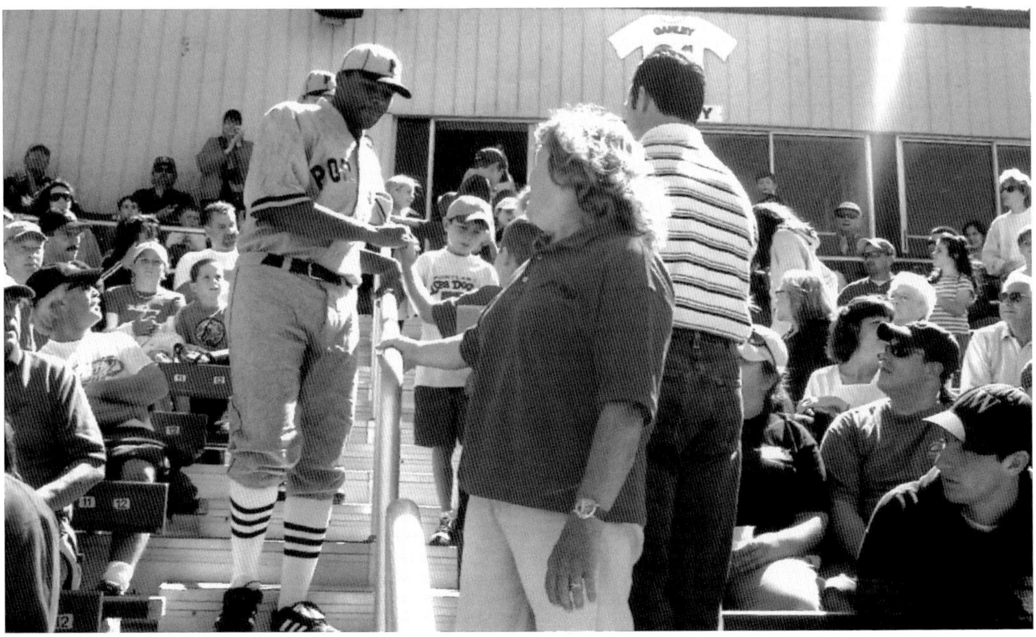

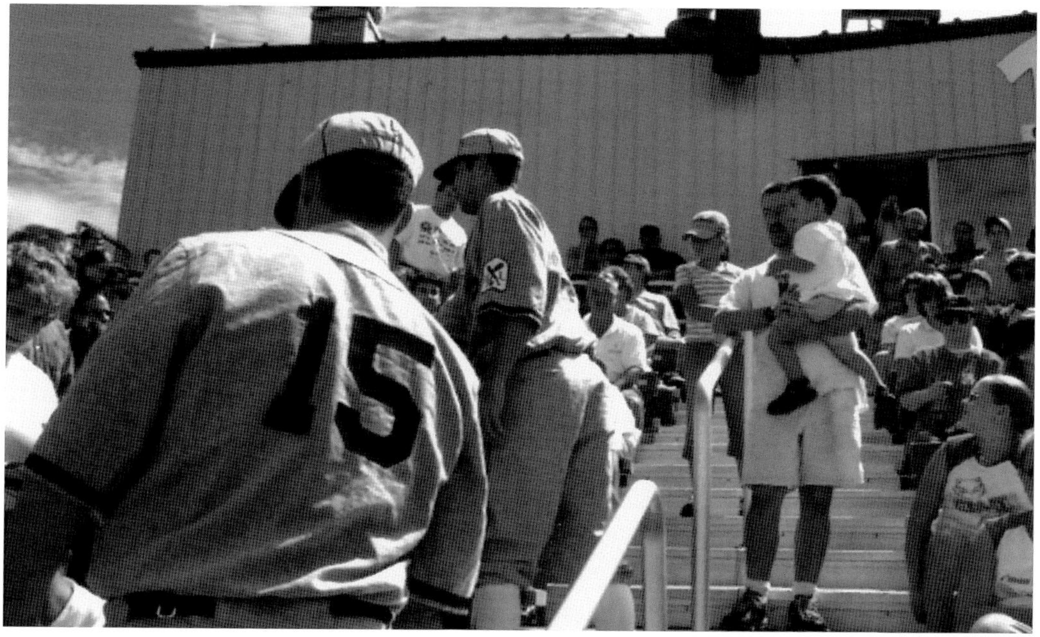

"On behalf of the players, management, and staff we thank you for your tremendous support. Ladies and gentlemen, your Portland Sea Dogs." One of the more memorable aspects to the annual Field of Dreams promotion occurs when the players meet and greet fans in the stands. To the soundtrack of the movie *Field of Dreams*, Portland Sea Dogs players, after emerging from the cornfield, walk toward the stands. The players continue into the stands, shaking hands and personally thanking the fans for their support during the season. (Courtesy of the Sea Dogs.)

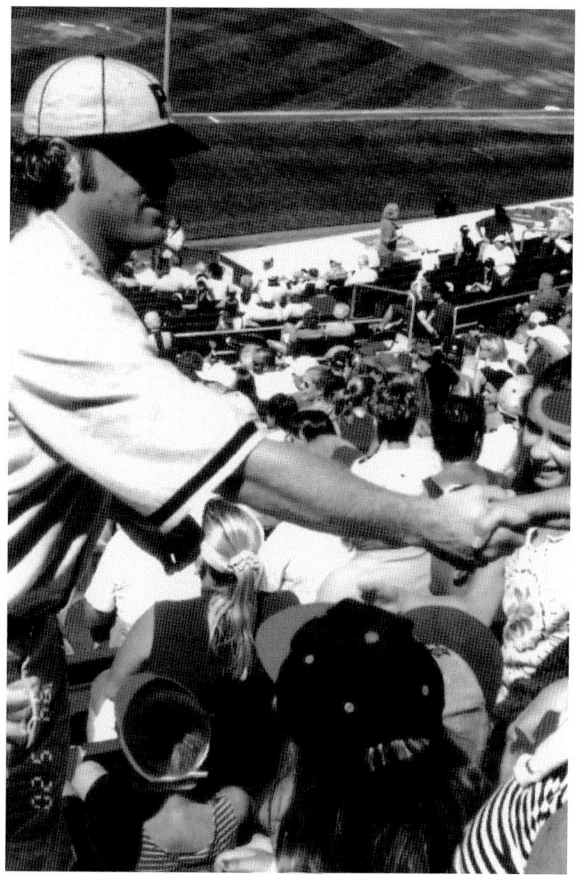

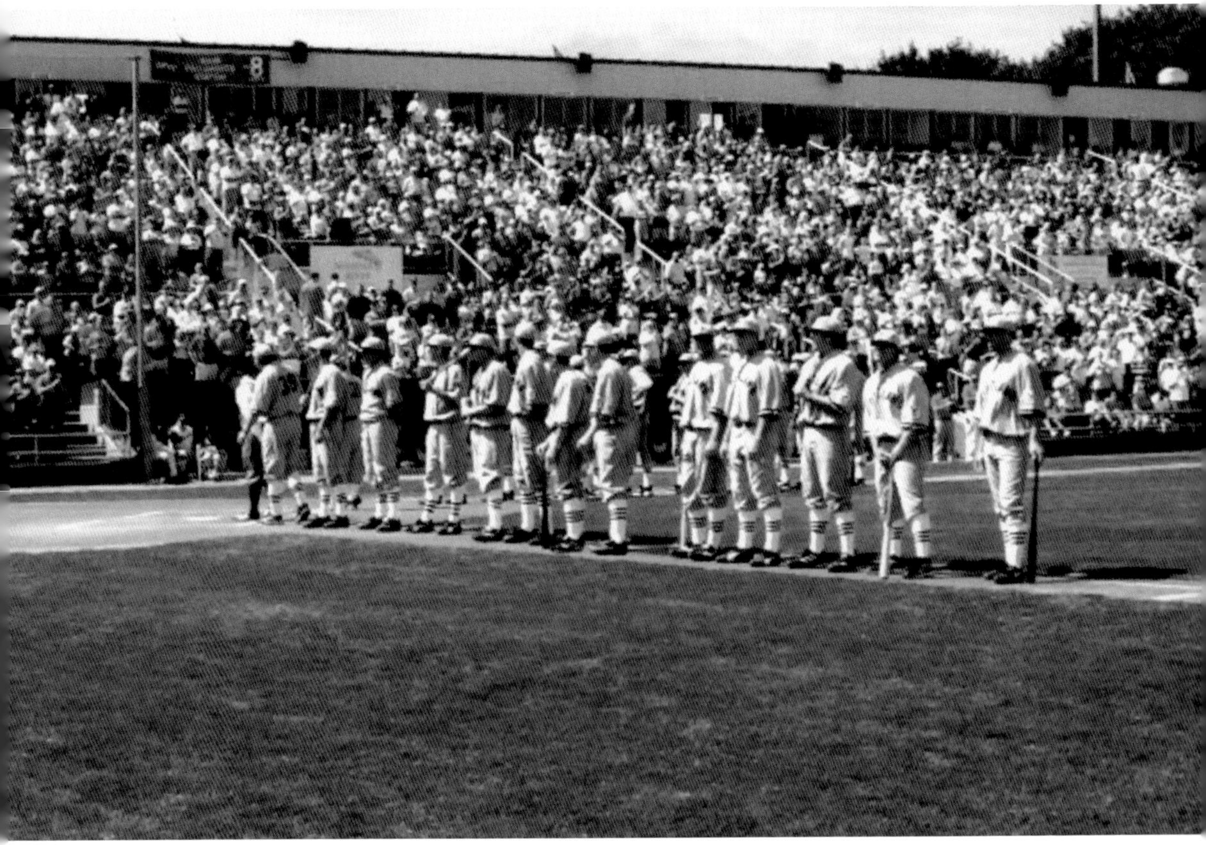

"The one constant through all the years has been baseball. America has rolled by like an army of steamrollers. It's been erased like a blackboard, rebuilt, and erased again. But baseball has marked the time. This field, this game, is a part of our past. It reminds us of all that once was good, and could be again," notes the speech given at the Field of Dreams promotion. The first promotion was a huge success. It quickly became a fan favorite and received much acclaim in minor-league baseball and has become a highly anticipated event. (Courtesy of the Sea Dogs.)

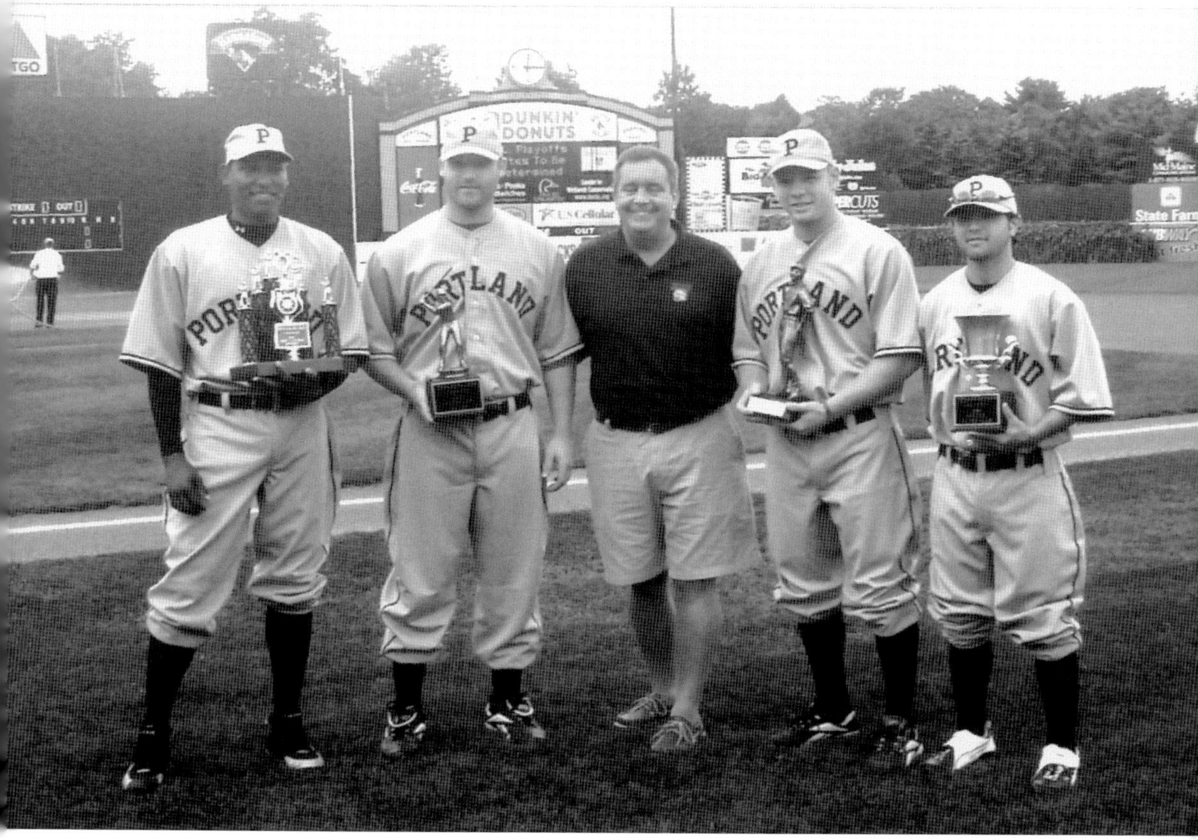

The winners of the annual Sea Dogs Team Awards for 2006 seen here are, from left to right, Devern Hansack (Pitcher of the Year), Barry Hertzler (Tenth Player), Brandon Moss (MVP), and Keoni De Renne (Citizen of the Year). Right-handed pitcher Barry Hertzler began the 2006 season in Portland's bullpen before a call-up to Pawtucket. Before his call-up, Hertzler recorded four saves with a 1.05 ERA. Hertzler returned to Portland in mid-August and picked up right where he left off. Hawaii native Keoni De Renne, only in his first season with Portland, quickly made a face for himself. A frequent volunteer at school and other Sea Dogs community functions, the infielder was always available to sign autographs, both before and after games. Quincy Foster (Tenth Player), Wynter Phoenix (Citizen of the Year), Brandon Leese (Pitcher of the Year), and Todd Betts (MVP) won the honors in 2000, the first season the awards were presented. (Courtesy of the Sea Dogs.)

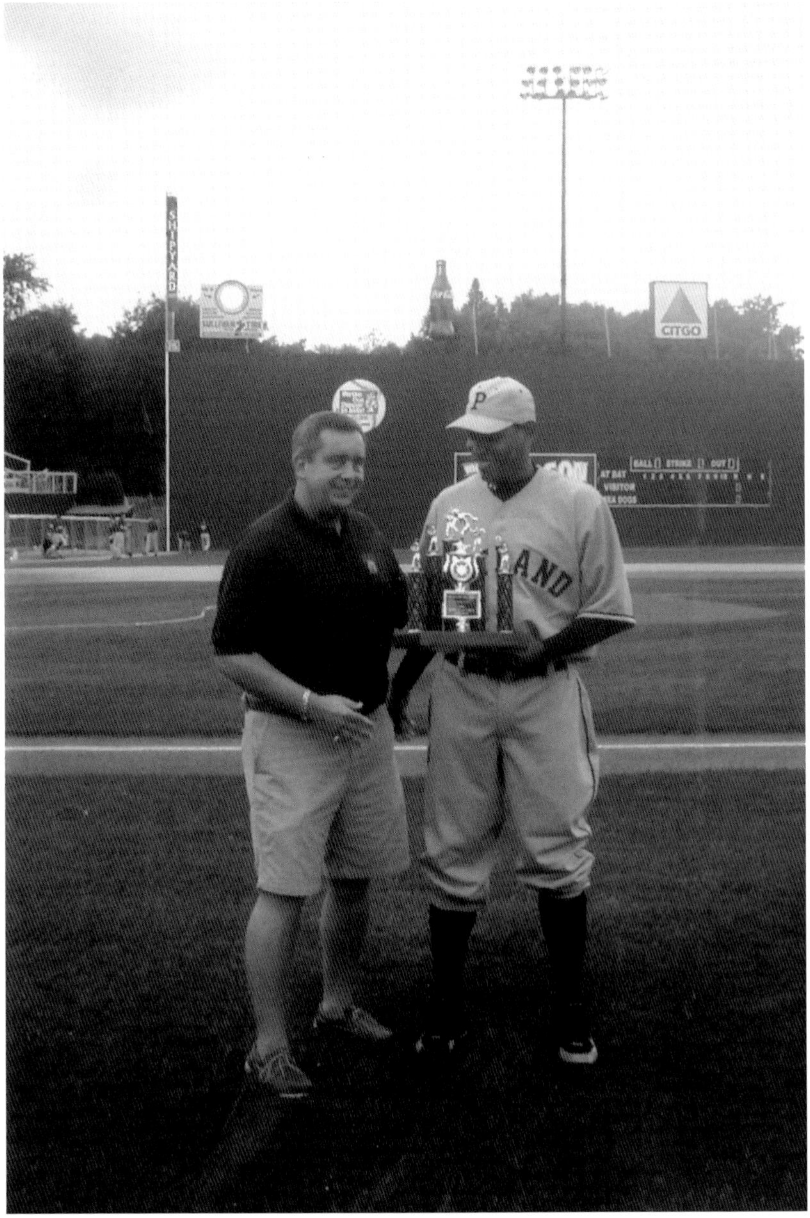

Devern Hansack returned to baseball in 2006 following a two-year absence from the game. The right-handed pitcher signed a minor-league free agent contract with the organization in December 2005, after playing winter ball for his native Nicaragua. Hansack led the league in strikeouts with 89. Hansack started and won the first game of the 2006 Eastern League Championship Series versus the Akron Aeros. Before Game 4, rumors started that the Red Sox were going to call up Hansack. However, Barry Hertzler's blown save in Game 4 pushed the best-of-five series to a fifth and deciding game. Hansack started the game and helped bring home Portland's first Eastern League title. During the locker room celebration, Hansack got the call—he would be heading for Boston. (Courtesy of the Sea Dogs.)

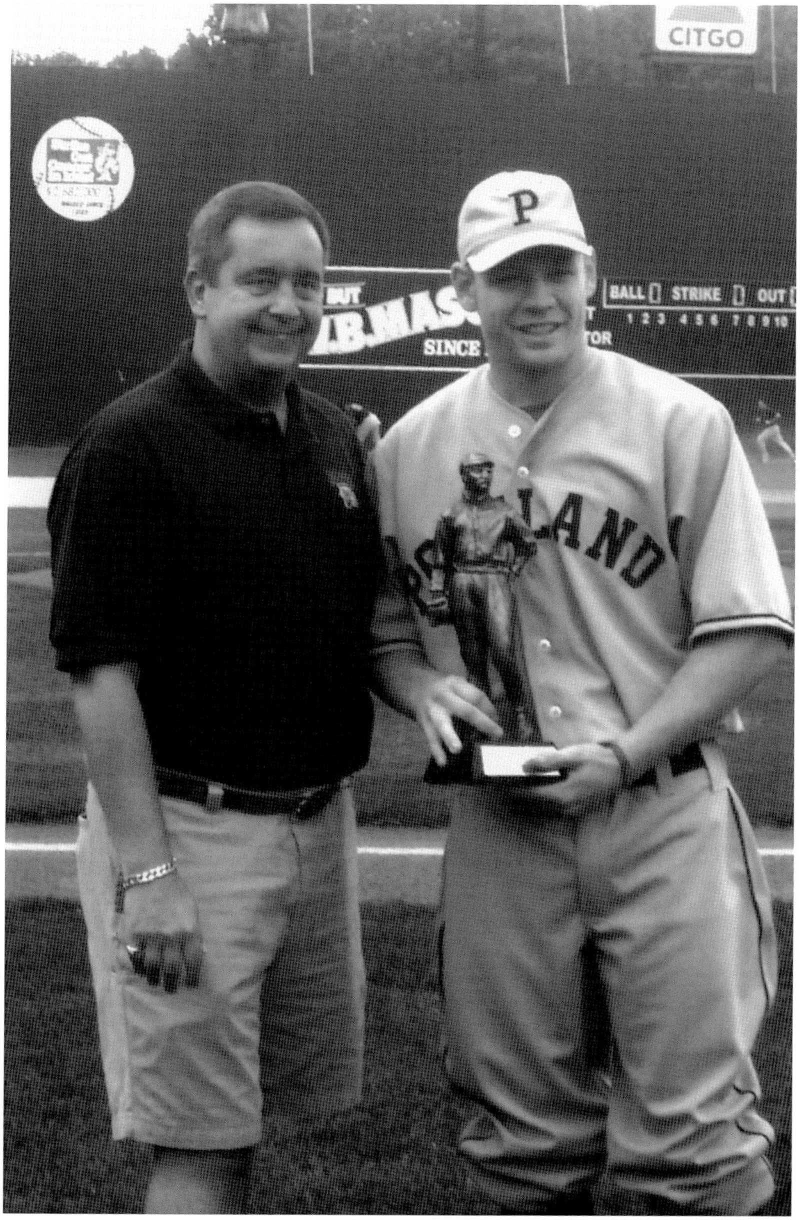

After two months and 48 games, Brandon Moss was only hitting a lowly .221. However, the slumping right fielder recovered, and by season's end, he won the Big Dog of the Year Award. The award honors the Portland Sea Dogs player who earns the most Player of the Game awards throughout the season. During the 2006 season, Moss took home the honor 14 times in 133 games. Moss's most memorable highlight during the 2006 season came during the postseason and the Sea Dogs' Game 4 victory in the Northern Division Championship Series. Moss hit a walk-off home run in the bottom of the 10th inning. The home run, Moss's second of the postseason, clinched the Northern Division Championship Series for the Sea Dogs over the Trenton Thunder. (Courtesy of the Sea Dogs.)

During the autumn of 2006, Pumpkin Valley Farm, with the Portland Sea Dogs, provided fans the opportunity to feel like Ray Kinsella, Kevin Costner's character in the movie *Field of Dreams*. An intricate corn maze allowed Sea Dogs fans to make their way through the team's name and a baseball diamond. However, the most impressive and most challenging section of the maze allowed visitors to navigate their path through the team's mascot and fan favorite, Slugger the Sea Dog. Only 30 minutes from Hadlock Field and charging a moderate admission fee, the Dayton farm challenged both directionally and nondirectionally impaired fans throughout October. However, fans could choose a "passport," consisting of 10 questions from different categories to help them navigate through the maze. (Courtesy of the Sea Dogs.)

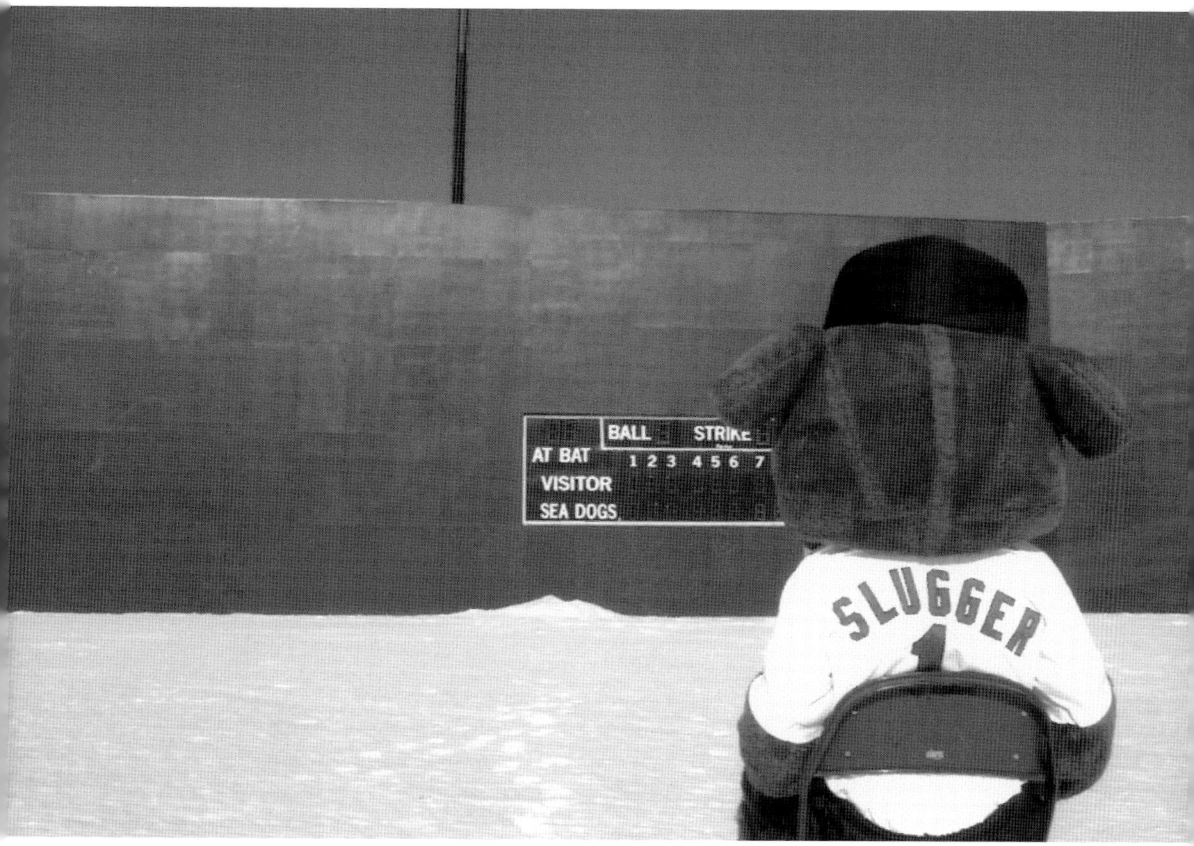

Slugger not only looks forward to the start of the next season but to the future of the Portland Sea Dogs. While he waits for spring to come, Slugger reflects on the past 14 seasons. In 2007, Portland and Boston extended their player development contract through 2012. In 2006, fan number five million came to Hadlock Field. In 2006, the Sea Dogs captured their first Eastern League championship in the team's 13-year history. Several Sea Dogs alumni played pivotal roles in helping their parent organizations, first the Marlins and then the Red Sox, win the World Series. Fans saw the return of a fan favorite when Kevin Millar signed with the Red Sox. Off the field, minor-league baseball recognized the front office in 1999 and 2000. The front office won the Bob Freitas and John H. Johnson Awards, the top awards in minor-league baseball. Like the blank score on the scoreboard, the future of the Sea Dogs waits to be recorded. (Courtesy of the Sea Dogs.)